Mastering Device Management: A Comprehensive Guide to Operating System Optimization

Table of Content

Chapter 1: Foundations of Device Management

- Define device management and its significance in operating systems.
- Explore the historical evolution of device management in computing.
- Discuss how devices are identified within an operating system.
- Introduce concepts like device drivers and their role in identification.
- Explain the process of configuring devices in an operating system.
- Provide examples of common configurations and their impact on system behavior.
- Explore communication protocols used in device management.
- Discuss the importance of standardized protocols for seamless device interaction.
- Detail the procedures involved in device startup and shutdown.
- Address the challenges and considerations in managing these processes.

Chapter 2: Understanding Operating System Architecture

- Define the concept of operating system architecture.
- Highlight the role of architecture in governing the behavior of an operating system.
- Break down the key components of operating system architecture.
- Explore the functions of the kernel, shell, and other essential elements.
- Discuss how operating systems manage memory resources.
- Explore memory allocation, virtual memory, and memory protection mechanisms.
- Explain how the operating system manages processes and schedules tasks.
- Introduce process scheduling algorithms and their impact on system performance.
- Explore the structure of file systems in operating systems.
- Discuss file organization, directory structures, and file access methods.

Chapter 3: The Role of Drivers in Device Management

- Define what device drivers are and their crucial role in device management.

- Explore how drivers act as intermediaries between hardware devices and the operating system.

- Identify and explain various types of device drivers, such as kernel-mode and user-mode drivers.

- Discuss the differences and specific use cases for each type.

- Detail the process of installing and configuring device drivers.

- Discuss best practices for ensuring compatibility and stability during installation.

- Explore the importance of keeping device drivers up to date.

- Discuss methods for updating drivers and potential challenges associated with maintenance.

- Introduce Plug-and-Play (PnP) technology and its impact on device driver management.

- Discuss how PnP simplifies the installation and configuration of new hardware.

Chapter 4: Optimizing Performance through Device Management

- Define performance optimization in the context of device management.
- Highlight the importance of optimizing device-related processes for overall system performance.
- Discuss strategies for efficient allocation of system resources to devices.
- Explore the impact of resource allocation on system responsiveness and stability.
- Introduce scheduling algorithms for managing device access and usage.
- Discuss how these algorithms contribute to fair and optimal device utilization.
- Explore the role of caching in optimizing device performance.
- Discuss how caching reduces latency and improves overall system responsiveness.
- Discuss the integration of parallel processing techniques for enhanced device handling.
- Explore how multi-core architectures impact device management strategies.

Chapter 5: Security Measures in Device Management

- Define the importance of security in device management within operating systems.
- Explore the potential risks and consequences of insecure device configurations.
- Discuss access control mechanisms for regulating device access.
- Explore how permissions are assigned and managed to ensure secure device interactions.
- Introduce authentication protocols for verifying the identity of devices.
- Discuss the role of secure authentication in preventing unauthorized access.
- Explore the use of encryption to secure communication between devices and the operating system.
- Discuss encryption algorithms and their application in device management.
- Explain the concept of secure boot and its role in preventing unauthorized code execution.
- Discuss trusted computing platforms and their impact on device security.

Chapter 6: Future Trends in Operating System Device Management

- Discuss the dynamic nature of technology and the continuous evolution of device management.
- Introduce the importance of staying abreast of emerging trends in operating systems.
- Explore how machine learning algorithms are being applied to optimize device management.
- Discuss predictive analytics for anticipating and addressing device-related issues.
- Discuss the impact of edge computing on device management strategies.
- Explore how edge devices are changing the landscape of operating system architectures.
- Explore the challenges and opportunities presented by the increasing number of IoT devices.
- Discuss strategies for managing diverse devices in an IoT-centric ecosystem.
- Introduce containerization and microservices as trends influencing device management.
- Discuss their role in enhancing scalability and flexibility in operating systems.

Chapter 7: Troubleshooting and Problem Resolution

- Define the importance of effective troubleshooting in device management.
- Explore the role of troubleshooting in maintaining system stability and performance.
- Discuss various diagnostic tools and utilities for identifying device-related issues.
- Explore the functionalities of tools such as system logs, diagnostic software, and built-in OS utilities.
- Identify and discuss common issues encountered in device management.
- Provide detailed solutions and troubleshooting steps for each identified problem.
- Explore strategies for troubleshooting devices remotely.
- Discuss the use of remote access tools and technologies for problem resolution.
- Highlight the importance of collaboration in complex troubleshooting scenarios.
- Discuss communication strategies among IT teams and support personnel.

Chapter 8: Case Studies - Successful Device Management Implementations

- Define the purpose of case studies in showcasing successful device management implementations.
- Highlight the practical application of concepts discussed throughout the book.
- Explore a case where a large enterprise successfully optimized device management for improved efficiency.
- Discuss the challenges faced and the strategies implemented for success.
- Examine a case study from the healthcare industry focusing on secure device management.
- Discuss how stringent security measures were implemented to safeguard patient data.
- Explore a case where a smart city successfully integrated and managed a diverse range of IoT devices.
- Discuss the scalability and interoperability challenges overcome in the implementation.
- Investigate a case study in the financial sector where real-time performance was crucial for success.
- Discuss how device management strategies contributed to high-speed data processing.

Introduction

Welcome to the immersive journey through "Mastering Device Management: A Comprehensive Guide to Operating System Optimization." In an era profoundly shaped by technology, the mastery of understanding and efficiently managing devices within an operating system is not merely advantageous but a pivotal skill. This comprehensive guide has been meticulously crafted to serve as your roadmap, guiding both novices and seasoned professionals toward becoming adept practitioners in the intricate realm of device management.

As we embark on this exploration, the significance of device management becomes evident in the very fabric of our technological existence. Devices, ranging from the humble keyboard to complex IoT sensors, intricately connect with operating systems, forming the backbone of our digital experiences. The seamless orchestration of these devices is a testament to the robustness of an operating system's device management.

The journey unfolds with "Foundations of Device Management," laying a solid groundwork by delving into fundamental concepts. From the identification of devices to basic configurations, readers will gain insights into the core principles that govern effective device management. The exploration continues with "Understanding Operating System Architecture," where the intricate components shaping the operating system's behavior are unraveled. Memory management, process scheduling, and file system structures are unveiled, providing a holistic understanding of operating system architecture.

In "The Role of Drivers in Device Management," the focus shifts to the unsung heroes—device drivers. These pieces of software act as intermediaries, facilitating communication between hardware devices and the operating system. The chapter explores driver types, installation processes, and the vital role they play in ensuring smooth device functionality. "Optimizing Performance through Device Management" takes center stage in the following chapter, offering strategies to enhance system performance. Resource allocation, caching mechanisms, and parallel processing techniques are unveiled to empower practitioners with tools for optimal device utilization.

Security takes precedence in "Security Measures in Device Management," emphasizing the critical importance of safeguarding devices within the operating system. Access control, encryption, and secure boot mechanisms are delved into, ensuring a comprehensive understanding of protective measures. As we peer into the future in "Future Trends in Operating System Device Management," emerging technologies such as machine learning, edge computing, and blockchain are explored. These trends provide a glimpse into the evolving landscape of device management, where innovation and adaptability are paramount.

The subsequent chapters further enrich the journey, addressing troubleshooting strategies in "Troubleshooting and Problem Resolution." From diagnostic tools to proactive troubleshooting, this chapter equips readers with the skills to navigate and resolve device-related issues effectively. The culminating chapter, "Case Studies: Successful Device Management Implementations," brings theory into practice. Real-world scenarios across diverse sectors, from healthcare to smart cities, showcase the tangible impact of adept device management.

In conclusion, "Mastering Device Management" transcends a conventional guide, becoming a companion in the dynamic landscape of operating systems. This compendium aims not only to impart knowledge but to instill a mindset of continuous learning and adaptability. Whether you are a system administrator, developer, or an enthusiastic learner, this guide endeavors to elevate your proficiency in optimizing operating systems by mastering the intricate dance of devices within. Let the journey begin, and may your mastery of device management reshape the future of digital experiences.

Chapter 1: Foundations of Device Management

Define device management and its significance in operating systems.

Device management refers to the set of activities and processes involved in controlling, configuring, and monitoring hardware devices within a computer system, particularly in the context of operating systems. This crucial aspect of computing is fundamental to the seamless functioning of hardware components, ensuring their coordination and interaction with the operating system. The significance of device management lies in its ability to facilitate efficient and reliable communication between software and hardware, enabling users to harness the full potential of their computing resources.

At its core, device management involves the initialization, configuration, and allocation of resources for various hardware devices such as processors, memory, input/output (I/O) devices, and storage devices. The operating system plays a pivotal role in orchestrating these activities, acting as an intermediary between the application software and the underlying hardware. One of the primary goals of device management is to provide a uniform and abstracted interface to application programs, shielding them from the intricate details of specific hardware implementations.

The initiation of device management begins during the boot process, where the operating system undertakes the task of recognizing and initializing hardware components. This process, known as system initialization, involves identifying the presence of hardware devices, loading necessary device drivers, and establishing communication channels between the operating system and the hardware. The successful completion of system initialization ensures that the operating system has a comprehensive understanding of the available hardware resources.

Configuration of hardware devices is a critical aspect of device management, as it involves setting parameters and options to tailor the behavior of each device according to the system's requirements. Device drivers, specialized software modules designed for specific hardware components, play a crucial role in this phase. These drivers act as intermediaries, translating generic operating system commands into device-specific instructions. By providing a standardized interface, device drivers enable the operating system to interact seamlessly with a wide array of hardware devices, promoting compatibility and ease of use.

Resource allocation is another key function of device management, ensuring that multiple applications can concurrently utilize hardware resources without conflicts. The operating system employs mechanisms such as scheduling algorithms to efficiently allocate processor time, memory management techniques to allocate and deallocate memory spaces, and I/O scheduling strategies to manage data transfer between peripheral devices and the CPU. Effective resource allocation contributes to optimal system performance, preventing bottlenecks and ensuring fair access to resources among competing applications.

In addition to configuration and resource allocation, device management encompasses the handling of interrupts and input/output operations. Interrupts are signals generated by hardware devices to gain the attention of the CPU, indicating the need for immediate processing. The operating system must efficiently manage and prioritize interrupts, ensuring that critical tasks are promptly addressed. Input/output operations involve the transfer of data between the

CPU and external devices, such as keyboards, mice, printers, and storage devices. Device management coordinates these operations, buffering data, and implementing strategies to enhance the efficiency of I/O processes.

The significance of device management becomes particularly evident in the context of system stability and reliability. Well-managed devices contribute to a stable and robust computing environment by preventing conflicts, minimizing errors, and ensuring the proper functioning of hardware components. Without effective device management, the system may encounter issues such as resource contention, device conflicts, and unreliable communication between software and hardware, leading to system crashes, data corruption, and overall degradation of performance.

Moreover, device management plays a crucial role in supporting plug-and-play functionality, allowing users to seamlessly connect and disconnect peripheral devices without requiring manual intervention. The operating system, through its device management capabilities, can dynamically detect and configure newly connected devices, providing a user-friendly experience and enhancing the system's flexibility.

Security considerations are also intertwined with device management, as unauthorized access to hardware resources can pose significant risks. Device drivers and firmware must be secure to prevent potential vulnerabilities that could be exploited by malicious entities. The operating system's role in managing access control to devices and enforcing security policies contributes to the overall security posture of the system.

As computing environments evolve, the complexity and diversity of hardware devices continue to grow. Device management becomes even more critical in modern computing scenarios where heterogeneous systems, multi-core processors, and a myriad of interconnected devices are prevalent. Virtualization technologies further complicate device management by introducing abstraction layers between the physical hardware and virtualized instances. In such environments, effective device management becomes essential for optimizing resource utilization, ensuring compatibility, and maintaining the integrity of virtualized systems.

In conclusion, device management is a foundational aspect of operating systems, serving as the linchpin that connects software and hardware in a cohesive and efficient manner. Its significance extends across various dimensions, including system initialization, configuration, resource allocation, interrupt handling, input/output operations, system stability, plug-and-play functionality, and security enforcement. As computing landscapes continue to advance, the role of device management becomes increasingly crucial, enabling the seamless integration of diverse hardware components and fostering a reliable and secure computing environment.

Explore the historical evolution of device management in computing.

The historical evolution of device management in computing traces a fascinating journey that parallels the advancements in hardware and the growing complexity of computing systems. The early days of computing, marked by the emergence of mainframe computers in the 1950s, laid the foundation for the rudimentary aspects of device management. During this era, computing systems were relatively simple, with a limited set of hardware components such as central processing units (CPUs), memory, and punched card readers. The primary focus of device management was on coordinating the flow of data between these components, often through manual intervention and control panel settings.

As computing technology progressed into the 1960s, the advent of operating systems like the IBM OS/360 marked a significant leap in device management capabilities. These early operating systems introduced basic functionalities for managing I/O devices and interrupt handling. However, the concept of device drivers as specialized software modules was not prevalent during this period. Instead, users often had to manually configure devices and write specific code to interact with hardware components, making the process cumbersome and error-prone.

The 1970s witnessed a transformative phase with the emergence of mini-computers and the birth of the microprocessor. Operating systems such as Unix, developed at Bell Labs, began to incorporate more sophisticated device management features. The introduction of device drivers became crucial during this era, as they provided a standardized interface between the operating system and hardware devices. Device drivers abstracted the hardware details, enabling software developers to write applications without delving into the intricacies of individual devices. This abstraction layer laid the groundwork for greater compatibility and ease of use, fostering a more user-friendly computing environment.

The 1980s marked the era of personal computers, with IBM PCs and the rise of MS-DOS becoming prominent. MS-DOS, while lacking the multitasking capabilities of contemporary operating systems, introduced a basic form of device management through its use of interrupt-driven I/O and simple device drivers. However, device management in these early personal computer systems was still relatively primitive compared to the sophisticated functionalities we take for granted today.

The late 1980s and early 1990s saw the advent of graphical user interfaces (GUIs) and the proliferation of desktop operating systems like Microsoft Windows and Apple Macintosh. These systems introduced more advanced device management capabilities, with plug-and-play functionalities that enabled users to connect and disconnect devices without manual intervention. The development of the Universal Serial Bus (USB) standard in the mid-1990s further streamlined device connectivity, contributing to the user-friendly nature of modern computing.

The 1990s also witnessed the emergence of networking technologies, leading to the widespread adoption of local area networks (LANs) and the birth of the internet. Device management evolved to encompass not only local hardware components but also networked devices. The management of network interfaces, routers, and other communication devices became integral to ensure seamless connectivity and data transfer. Operating systems incorporated networking stacks and protocols, adding a layer of complexity to device management.

The turn of the century brought about significant changes with the rise of mobile computing and the proliferation of portable devices. Smartphones and tablets became ubiquitous, introducing new challenges for device management. Operating systems for mobile devices, such as Android and iOS, had to adapt to the constraints of limited resources, diverse hardware architectures, and the need for efficient power management. Device management in this context evolved to prioritize mobility, battery life, and seamless integration with a multitude of sensors and communication interfaces.

Virtualization technologies, which gained prominence in the mid-2000s, introduced a new dimension to device management. Hypervisors and virtual machine monitors abstracted physical hardware, enabling the creation of virtualized instances with their own virtual devices. Device management in virtualized environments became crucial for optimizing resource allocation, ensuring isolation between virtual machines, and facilitating the dynamic provisioning of virtual devices.

In recent years, the proliferation of cloud computing has further transformed device management. Cloud services often abstract the underlying hardware from users, relying on virtualization and remote management of devices. Device management in the cloud context involves orchestrating resources across distributed data centers, ensuring scalability, and facilitating the seamless integration of diverse hardware configurations.

The evolution of device management has been marked by a continuous quest for abstraction, automation, and standardization. Modern operating systems incorporate sophisticated device management frameworks that dynamically detect and configure hardware, support a wide array of devices through standardized interfaces, and ensure security through robust access control mechanisms. As we look to the future, the integration of artificial intelligence and machine learning into device management holds the potential to further enhance automation, predictive analysis, and adaptive resource allocation, ushering in a new era of intelligent computing environments. The historical journey of device management reflects not only the evolution of technology but also the relentless pursuit of making computing more accessible, efficient, and user-friendly.

Discuss how devices are identified within an operating system.

Device identification within an operating system is a critical aspect of ensuring seamless communication between software and hardware components. The process involves a systematic approach to recognizing and managing the diverse array of devices connected to a computer system. At its core, device identification is about establishing a unique and standardized means of referencing each hardware component, enabling the operating system to interact with them in a consistent manner. Historically, in the early days of computing, identification was often manual, with users required to configure devices using physical switches or jumpers on the hardware. However, as computing systems evolved, the need for a more automated and user-friendly approach became evident.

One fundamental method of device identification is through the use of unique hardware addresses assigned to each device. This is particularly prevalent in network interfaces where Media Access Control (MAC) addresses are employed. The MAC address is a globally unique identifier assigned to a network interface card, allowing the operating system to identify and differentiate between different network devices. The address is embedded in the hardware and is usually assigned by the manufacturer, ensuring uniqueness across the entire spectrum of devices. Operating systems use these addresses to manage network traffic, implement access control, and facilitate communication between devices on a network.

Another crucial aspect of device identification is the concept of device drivers. Device drivers serve as software intermediaries between the operating system and the hardware, translating generic operating system commands into instructions that are specific to each device. During the initialization process, the operating system identifies and loads the necessary device drivers to establish communication with connected hardware components. These drivers often contain information about the devices they support, including device identifiers and characteristics. The use of device drivers allows the operating system to abstract the complexities of various hardware implementations, providing a standardized interface for application software.

Device identification also involves the use of unique identifiers or codes embedded within the hardware itself. For example, in the context of storage devices like hard drives and solid-state drives, each device is assigned a universally unique identifier (UUID) or serial number. The operating system can retrieve and utilize these identifiers to differentiate between storage devices, manage file systems, and implement storage-related functionalities. UUIDs are particularly valuable in scenarios where devices may be added or replaced, ensuring that the operating system can consistently identify and address each storage device.

In modern computing environments, the concept of Plug and Play (PnP) has significantly influenced device identification. PnP allows devices to be automatically detected and configured by the operating system without requiring user intervention. When a new device is connected, the operating system initiates a process of device enumeration, where it systematically identifies and assigns resources to the newly detected device. This process involves querying the device for its characteristics, cross-referencing these characteristics with a database of known devices, and dynamically configuring the operating system to support the newly added hardware.

The use of standardized protocols and interfaces also plays a pivotal role in device identification. For example, the Universal Serial Bus (USB) standard specifies a protocol that allows devices to communicate with the operating system in a standardized manner. Each USB device is assigned a unique vendor identifier (VID) and product identifier (PID), which the operating system uses to recognize and differentiate between connected USB devices. This standardized approach simplifies the process of identifying and managing a wide range of USB peripherals, from keyboards and mice to printers and external storage devices.

Moreover, the Advanced Configuration and Power Interface (ACPI) has become integral to device identification and power management in modern computing. ACPI provides a standardized framework for operating systems to discover and configure hardware components, including devices such as processors, input devices, and power sources. By defining a set of tables that contain information about the system's configuration, ACPI enables the operating system to identify and communicate with devices in a uniform manner, facilitating features like power management and system configuration.

Device identification is not limited to traditional computing devices; it extends to a diverse range of hardware components, including graphics cards, audio devices, and sensors. Graphics Processing

Units (GPUs), for example, often have unique identifiers and features that the operating system uses to allocate resources and facilitate graphics rendering. Audio devices may have identifiers that allow the operating system to route audio signals appropriately and configure audio settings. Sensors, prevalent in mobile devices and modern laptops, provide data on various environmental factors and are identified by the operating system to enable applications to utilize this information.

In the context of networked environments, the Domain Name System (DNS) plays a crucial role in device identification. DNS translates human-readable domain names into IP addresses, facilitating the identification and communication of devices over the internet. This hierarchical naming system ensures that devices can be identified globally, enabling seamless communication across diverse networks.

Security considerations are paramount in device identification. Unauthorized access to hardware devices can pose significant risks, and robust identification mechanisms are essential to mitigate these risks. Secure Boot, for example, is a security feature that ensures only authenticated and signed device drivers are loaded during the boot process. This prevents the loading of malicious or unsigned drivers, enhancing the security of the device identification and initialization process.

As computing environments continue to evolve, device identification remains a dynamic and evolving field. The Internet of Things (IoT) introduces a myriad of interconnected devices, from smart thermostats to industrial sensors, each requiring unique identification within the broader ecosystem. Blockchain technology is being explored as a means to enhance the security and traceability of device identification, ensuring that devices can be trusted within a network.

In conclusion, device identification within an operating system is a multifaceted process that has evolved significantly over the histo-

ry of computing. From manual configuration and hardware addresses to the use of device drivers, standardized protocols, and automated Plug and Play mechanisms, the methods employed for identifying
devices have adapted to meet the growing complexity and diversity of computing systems. The seamless interaction between software
and hardware, facilitated by effective device identification, is fundamental to the user experience and the reliability of modern computing environments.

**Introduce concepts like device drivers and their role in iden-
tification.**

Device drivers are essential software components that serve as
intermediaries between the operating system and hardware devices,
playing a pivotal role in facilitating communication and ensuring the
seamless integration of diverse hardware into a computing system. In
the realm of computing, where an extensive array of hardware components exists, each with its unique specifications and functionalities, device drivers act as crucial translators, enabling the operating
system to interact with these devices in a standardized manner. Their
role is especially significant in abstracting the complexity of hardware implementations, providing a uniform interface that application software can utilize without delving into the intricate details of
specific devices.

The primary purpose of device drivers lies in bridging the gap between the high-level commands issued by the operating system and
the low-level instructions required by hardware devices. When the
operating system initializes, it identifies and loads the appropriate
device drivers to establish communication with connected hardware
components. This initialization process involves recognizing the various devices present in the system, a task that might be performed
through methods such as Plug and Play (PnP) enumeration or manual configuration, depending on the system's architecture and design.

One of the fundamental aspects of device drivers is their ability to provide a standardized interface for applications. By encapsulating the unique characteristics and communication protocols of specific devices, device drivers shield application developers from the complexities associated with individual hardware implementations. This abstraction layer simplifies the programming process, allowing developers to write code that can seamlessly interact with a broad range of devices, from printers and storage devices to graphics cards and network interfaces.

Device drivers typically consist of routines and functions that enable the operating system to send commands and receive data from hardware devices. These routines are designed to handle various tasks, such as initializing the device, managing data transfer, handling interrupts, and implementing error recovery mechanisms. The driver acts as a translator, converting generic commands from the operating system into device-specific instructions that the hardware can understand and execute.

Moreover, device drivers contain information about the characteristics and capabilities of the associated hardware. This information, often in the form of data structures or configuration settings, allows the operating system to understand the capabilities of the device and configure it accordingly. For example, a graphics card driver might provide information about supported display resolutions and color depths, enabling the operating system to configure the graphics card to match the user's preferences.

The evolution of device drivers parallels the advancements in computing technology. In the early days of computing, drivers were often tightly coupled with the operating system, and users had to obtain specific drivers for each hardware component. As computing systems became more complex and diverse, the need for a more modular and flexible approach to device drivers became apparent. Modern operating systems adopt a modular driver architecture, where drivers can be dynamically loaded and unloaded based on the presence or absence of specific hardware. This modular design enhances the system's flexibility, allowing it to support a wide range of devices without requiring a monolithic kernel that includes all possible drivers.

One notable shift in device driver development is the move towards open-source drivers and standardized interfaces. Open-source drivers, developed collaboratively by the community, provide transparency, and allow users to inspect and modify the code. Standardized interfaces, such as those conforming to industry standards like USB and PCI, promote interoperability and simplify the development of drivers for a diverse range of hardware. This approach encourages collaboration and accelerates the adoption of new hardware technologies.

In addition to supporting a diverse range of devices, device drivers contribute significantly to the stability and reliability of the operating system. A poorly designed or malfunctioning driver can lead to system crashes, data corruption, and degraded performance. Operating systems incorporate mechanisms for driver verification and signing to ensure that only trusted and properly validated drivers are loaded. Features like driver isolation and fault tolerance contribute to the overall robustness of the system, preventing a misbehaving driver from compromising the stability of the entire operating environment.

Security considerations are paramount in the realm of device drivers. Malicious or poorly designed drivers can pose significant security risks, potentially leading to system vulnerabilities and unauthorized access. Secure Boot, a security feature implemented in many modern operating systems, ensures that only signed and authenticated drivers are loaded during the boot process, preventing the execution of unsigned or malicious code. The isolation of drivers from the kernel through mechanisms like User-Mode Driver Framework

(UMDF) and Kernel-Mode Driver Framework (KMDF) further enhances security by minimizing the potential impact of a compromised driver.

The deployment and management of device drivers have also evolved with technological advancements. Automatic driver updates, often facilitated through Windows Update or similar mechanisms, ensure that users have access to the latest drivers with bug fixes, performance improvements, and support for new devices. Driver repositories and online databases simplify the process of obtaining and updating drivers, reducing the manual effort required by users to ensure their systems are equipped with the most compatible and secure drivers.

As computing ecosystems expand to include emerging technologies such as virtualization and containerization, device drivers adapt to these new paradigms. Virtualization technologies introduce the concept of virtual devices, which are emulated or virtualized instances of physical hardware. Hypervisors and virtual machine monitors leverage virtual device drivers to manage the communication between virtual machines and the underlying physical hardware. These virtual drivers mimic the behavior of physical drivers but operate within the context of virtualized environments.

In conclusion, device drivers stand as integral components in the intricate tapestry of computing systems, facilitating the interaction between operating systems and an expansive array of hardware devices. Their role in abstraction, standardization, and mediation between software and hardware has evolved to meet the challenges posed by diverse and ever-advancing technologies. From ensuring compatibility and interoperability to enhancing security and stability, device drivers continue to be a cornerstone in the dynamic landscape of computing, adapting to the demands of modern computing environments while remaining crucial for the seamless functioning of hardware and software integration.

Explain the process of configuring devices in an operating system.

The process of configuring devices in an operating system is a multifaceted and integral aspect of ensuring that hardware components seamlessly integrate with the software environment. Configuration encompasses a range of activities, including device recognition, initialization, assignment of resources, and establishment of communication channels. This intricate process begins during the system boot-up phase, where the operating system undertakes the crucial task of identifying the various hardware devices connected to the computer. This identification process can be achieved through mechanisms such as Plug and Play (PnP) enumeration, where the operating system dynamically detects and recognizes newly connected devices, or through manual configuration in cases where devices need explicit setup.

Once devices are identified, the operating system proceeds to initialize them. Initialization involves preparing the hardware for interaction with the software by loading the necessary device drivers. These drivers serve as the bridge between the operating system and the specific hardware components, translating high-level commands into instructions that the hardware understands. During the initialization phase, the operating system may also query the devices for essential information, such as their capabilities, configuration settings, and unique identifiers. This information becomes crucial for the subsequent steps in the configuration process.

Resource allocation is a critical step in configuring devices, ensuring that each hardware component receives the necessary resources to function effectively within the system. Resources may include memory addresses, interrupt request (IRQ) lines, direct memory access (DMA) channels, and input/output (I/O) ports. The operating system, often in collaboration with the system's firmware or Basic Input/Output System (BIOS), assigns these resources based on the information gathered during device initialization. Proper resource allocation prevents conflicts between devices, promoting stable and efficient operation.

The assignment of device drivers plays a significant role in the configuration process. Device drivers, as specialized software modules, facilitate communication between the operating system and hardware devices. The operating system loads the appropriate drivers based on the identified hardware, ensuring that each device has the necessary software support to function optimally. In modern computing environments, this process is often automated through mechanisms like Windows Update or Linux package management systems, which can fetch and install the latest drivers from online repositories.

Configuration settings for devices are managed through the operating system, allowing users to customize and tailor the behavior of connected hardware components. User preferences, such as display resolutions for monitors, audio settings for sound cards, or network settings for network interfaces, are configured through user interfaces provided by the operating system. These settings, stored in configuration files or registry entries, ensure that the devices operate according to the user's preferences.

Plug and Play functionality has greatly influenced the configuration process, especially in modern computing environments. With Plug and Play, the operating system automatically configures and recognizes newly connected devices without requiring manual intervention. This capability streamlines the user experience, making it more intuitive and user-friendly. When a user connects a new device, the operating system dynamically identifies, initializes, and configures the device, enabling seamless integration without the need for explicit user actions.

Network configuration is a specific subset of device configuration that involves setting up and managing network-related parameters. This includes configuring network interfaces, assigning IP addresses, specifying DNS servers, and managing routing tables. Network configuration is vital for establishing connectivity, whether in local area networks (LANs), wide area networks (WANs), or the broader internet. Operating systems provide interfaces and utilities for users to configure network settings, and the configuration process ensures proper communication between the computer and other devices on the network.

In the context of storage devices, configuration involves initializing and formatting the storage media to prepare it for data storage. During this process, the operating system may create file systems, partition the storage, and assign drive letters or mount points. Configuration settings for storage devices may include parameters such as file system type, cluster size, and encryption options. Proper storage configuration ensures that the operating system can effectively manage and utilize the available storage space.

Security considerations are embedded throughout the device configuration process. Secure Boot, a security feature implemented in modern operating systems, ensures that only signed and authenticated drivers and firmware are loaded during the boot process. This mitigates the risk of loading malicious or unauthorized code that could compromise the system's security. Additionally, access control mechanisms and user permissions are integral to device configuration, preventing unauthorized users or applications from making changes to critical system settings.

As technology evolves, the configuration process adapts to accommodate new paradigms such as virtualization. In virtualized environments, the configuration of virtual devices and their interaction with underlying physical hardware becomes a key aspect. Hypervisors and virtual machine monitors play a role in managing the configuration of virtual devices, ensuring proper resource allocation and communication between virtual machines and the host system.

Cloud computing introduces another layer of complexity to device configuration, particularly in environments where resources are dynamically provisioned and managed. Configuration in the cloud involves setting up virtual instances, configuring network settings, and defining security policies. Cloud orchestration tools and Infrastructure as Code (IaC) frameworks automate the configuration process, allowing users to define and deploy complex configurations through code.

In conclusion, the process of configuring devices in an operating system is a dynamic and intricate series of steps that ensure the harmonious integration of hardware and software components. From device recognition and initialization to resource allocation, driver assignment, and user-specific customization, the configuration process is foundational to the functionality and user experience of modern computing systems. As computing environments continue to evolve with emerging technologies, the configuration process remains adaptable, accommodating new challenges and paradigms to meet the ever-changing demands of users and applications.

Provide examples of common configurations and their impact on system behavior.

Common configurations in a computing system encompass a diverse array of settings and parameters that govern the behavior of both hardware and software components. These configurations play a crucial role in tailoring the system to meet specific requirements, optimize performance, and ensure compatibility with various applications. One prominent example lies in the configuration of network settings, where parameters such as IP addresses, subnet masks, gateway addresses, and DNS servers determine how a computer interacts with other devices on a network. The impact of network configurations is profound, influencing communication, data transfer, and connectivity. For instance, a misconfigured IP address may result in the inability to communicate with other devices on the same network, leading to connectivity issues and hindering access to network resources.

Similarly, the configuration of storage devices involves critical settings that influence system behavior. File system configuration, specifying parameters such as cluster size and file allocation unit size, directly impacts how data is stored and retrieved from storage media. The choice of file system, whether it be FAT32, NTFS, ext4, or others, affects compatibility, security features, and file size limitations. Incorrect storage configurations can lead to inefficiencies, data corruption, or incompatibility with certain file types. For instance, choosing a file system with limited file size support may pose challenges when working with large multimedia files.

Display configurations, encompassing settings such as screen resolution, refresh rate, and color depth, significantly impact the visual experience of users. Adjusting these settings appropriately ensures that the display meets user preferences and accommodates the capabilities of the connected monitor or screen. Incorrect display configurations may result in distorted images, flickering screens, or even damage to the hardware in extreme cases. Display configurations are especially crucial for tasks such as graphic design, gaming, and multimedia content creation, where precise and optimized visuals are essential for a satisfactory user experience.

Power management configurations are integral for optimizing energy consumption and extending the battery life of mobile devices. Users can configure settings such as screen brightness, sleep timeouts, and power plan profiles to balance performance and energy efficiency. Proper power management configurations are crucial for laptops, tablets, and other portable devices, ensuring that they operate efficiently while maximizing battery longevity. Misconfigurations in power management settings can lead to premature battery depletion, reduced system responsiveness, and compromised user mobility.

Security configurations represent a paramount concern in computing, influencing the overall resilience of the system against potential threats. Secure Boot is an example of a security configuration that ensures only signed and authenticated firmware and drivers are loaded during the boot process, mitigating the risk of malware infiltration. Access control configurations, including user permissions and role-based access, dictate who can access certain files, directories, or system resources. Firewall configurations control network traffic, safeguarding the system from unauthorized access and potential cyber threats. Misconfigurations in security settings can result in vulnerabilities, unauthorized access, data breaches, and compromise the integrity of the entire system.

Device driver configurations are essential for the proper functioning of hardware components. Device drivers provide a standardized interface between the operating system and specific hardware, allowing seamless communication. Users can configure driver settings to optimize performance, enable specific features, or troubleshoot compatibility issues. For example, configuring printer drivers involves selecting print quality, paper size, and other settings that impact the appearance of printed documents. Misconfigurations in device drivers can lead to hardware malfunctions, system crashes, or reduced performance.

Software configurations, encompassing settings within applications and the operating system, profoundly influence user experience and system behavior. Application-specific configurations allow users to customize preferences, define default behaviors, and tailor the software to their workflow. For instance, configuring email client settings includes specifying server details, email synchronization preferences, and security protocols. Operating system configurations, such as those related to system updates, automatic backups, and notification settings, impact the overall system management and user interaction. Inconsistent or incompatible software configurations may lead to application crashes, data loss, or conflicts between different software components.

Virtualization configurations, prevalent in modern computing environments, involve settings related to the creation and management of virtual machines. Virtualization platforms allow users to configure parameters such as virtual CPU allocation, memory size, and network configurations for each virtual machine. These configurations impact resource utilization, isolation between virtual machines, and overall system performance. Proper virtualization configurations are essential for achieving optimal resource allocation and ensuring the effective operation of virtualized environments. Misconfigurations can lead to resource contention, reduced performance, and potential security vulnerabilities.

In the context of web servers and network services, configurations play a pivotal role in defining how these services operate. Web server configurations include settings related to server directories, file permissions, and security protocols. Network service configurations, such as those for Domain Name System (DNS) or Dynamic Host Configuration Protocol (DHCP) servers, determine how network resources are allocated and accessed. Misconfigurations in server settings can result in service disruptions, security vulnerabilities, and compromise the availability of critical network services.

Database configurations, found in database management systems (DBMS), influence how data is stored, accessed, and managed. Configuration settings for database servers may include parameters such as cache size, indexing options, and security policies. Optimizing database configurations is crucial for achieving efficient query performance, ensuring data integrity, and preventing unauthorized access. Inadequate or misconfigured database settings can lead to suboptimal performance, data corruption, or security breaches.

The impact of configurations on system behavior extends to cloud computing environments. Cloud configurations involve settings related to virtual machine instances, storage configurations, security groups, and networking parameters. Cloud users configure these settings to define the characteristics and behavior of their virtual infrastructure. Proper cloud configurations are vital for achieving scalability, optimizing costs, and ensuring the security of cloud-based applications. Misconfigurations in cloud settings can lead to resource inefficiencies, security vulnerabilities, and potential data breaches.

In conclusion, configurations in a computing system are pervasive and influential, shaping the behavior of both hardware and software components. Examples of common configurations, ranging from network and storage settings to display and security configurations, demonstrate the diverse impact that these settings have on the functionality, performance, and security of a computing environment. Understanding and appropriately configuring these parameters are essential for optimizing system behavior, ensuring compatibility, and providing a satisfactory user experience. As technology continues to advance, the significance of proper configurations remains paramount in adapting systems to new challenges and emerging paradigms in computing.

Explore communication protocols used in device management.

Communication protocols in device management serve as the foundation for establishing seamless and efficient interaction between hardware devices and the operating system. These protocols define the rules and conventions that govern the exchange of information, commands, and data between the software and hardware components of a computing system. One of the fundamental communication protocols is the Universal Serial Bus (USB) standard. USB provides a standardized interface for connecting and communicating with a wide array of peripherals, including printers, storage devices, and input devices. The USB protocol encompasses specifications for data transfer rates, power delivery, and device enumeration, allowing the operating system to dynamically detect and configure connected USB devices.

Another vital communication protocol is the Peripheral Component Interconnect (PCI) bus. PCI is a standardized local bus architecture that facilitates communication between the central processing unit (CPU) and various peripheral devices, such as graphics cards, network adapters, and storage controllers. The PCI protocol defines the electrical and physical characteristics of the bus, along with data transfer protocols. PCI Express (PCIe), an evolution of the PCI protocol, provides higher data transfer rates and improved efficiency, supporting the demanding communication needs of modern computing systems.

In the realm of networking, the Transmission Control Protocol (TCP) and Internet Protocol (IP) form the backbone of communication between devices on a network. TCP/IP is a suite of protocols that governs data transmission over networks, ensuring reliable and ordered delivery of data between devices. IP addresses uniquely identify devices on a network, allowing for seamless communication across different hardware platforms. Dynamic Host Configuration Protocol (DHCP) is another communication protocol within the TCP/IP suite, responsible for dynamically assigning IP addresses to devices on a network, simplifying the configuration process and promoting efficient network management.

Ethernet is a widely used communication protocol in local area networks (LANs). It defines the physical and data link layer specifications for wired network communication. Ethernet enables devices to communicate by framing data into packets and facilitating their transmission over the network medium. The Ethernet protocol supports a variety of data transfer speeds, from the traditional 10/100 Mbps to gigabit and beyond, catering to the increasing demands of modern networking.

Wireless communication protocols, such as Wi-Fi, play a pivotal role in connecting devices without the need for physical cables. The Wi-Fi protocol, based on the IEEE 802.11 standards, allows devices to communicate over radio frequencies. Wi-Fi protocols define aspects such as data rates, encryption methods, and channel usage, ensuring secure and reliable wireless communication. Bluetooth is another wireless protocol, designed for short-range communication between devices. Bluetooth facilitates connections for peripherals like keyboards, mice, and audio devices, enhancing the flexibility and convenience of device interactions.

For storage devices, communication protocols like Serial ATA (SATA) and Peripheral Component Interconnect Express (PCIe) govern the transfer of data between storage media and the rest of the system. SATA is a widely used protocol for connecting hard disk drives (HDDs) and solid-state drives (SSDs). It specifies the electrical and physical characteristics of the connection, as well as data transfer rates. PCIe, as mentioned earlier in the context of buses, is also employed as a communication protocol for storage devices, offering high-speed data transfer capabilities and low latency.

In the context of multimedia and audio devices, protocols such as High Definition Multimedia Interface (HDMI) and Audio/Video Bridging (AVB) are prominent. HDMI is widely used for transmitting high-definition video and audio signals between devices, such as computers, monitors, and televisions. AVB, on the other hand, is a set of standards for delivering synchronized, high-quality audio and video streams over Ethernet networks, making it suitable for professional audio and multimedia applications.

The Simple Network Management Protocol (SNMP) is crucial for the management and monitoring of networked devices. SNMP allows for the exchange of management information between network devices and management systems. It enables administrators to monitor device performance, configure settings, and detect and address issues proactively. SNMP is extensively used in network management systems to ensure the efficient operation of interconnected devices.

In the realm of printers and imaging devices, communication protocols such as Printer Command Language (PCL) and PostScript are instrumental. PCL and PostScript are page description languages that define the layout and appearance of printed pages. Printers receive data formatted in these languages, interpret the instructions, and produce the desired output. These protocols contribute to standardizing communication between computers and printers, ensuring compatibility and consistent print quality.

The Advanced Configuration and Power Interface (ACPI) is a communication protocol that facilitates the configuration and power management of devices, particularly in the context of laptops and other mobile devices. ACPI defines a set of tables containing information about a device's configuration, capabilities, and power requirements. The operating system utilizes this information to manage device power states, optimize power consumption, and ensure proper device initialization.

In the context of device connectivity and communication over the internet, protocols such as Hypertext Transfer Protocol (HTTP) and Hypertext Transfer Protocol Secure (HTTPS) are fundamental. HTTP is the foundation for communication on the World Wide Web, allowing the retrieval and transfer of hypertext. HTTPS, an extension of HTTP, adds a layer of security through encryption, ensuring that data exchanged between devices and servers is protected from eavesdropping and tampering.

Universal Plug and Play (UPnP) is a set of protocols that enable devices to discover and interact with each other on a network. UPnP facilitates automatic configuration and communication between devices, allowing them to seamlessly connect and share resources without manual intervention. This protocol is particularly relevant in scenarios where devices, such as printers, media players, and cameras, need to establish connections and collaborate without user intervention.

As computing environments evolve, Internet of Things (IoT) devices rely on communication protocols designed for efficient and lightweight interactions. MQTT (Message Queuing Telemetry Transport) is one such protocol used in IoT for communication between devices with low bandwidth and high latency constraints. CoAP (Constrained Application Protocol) is another lightweight protocol designed for constrained devices, enabling them to communicate over the web efficiently.

In conclusion, communication protocols in device management are the linchpin of modern computing, providing standardized rules for the interaction between diverse hardware and software components. From USB and PCI for local communication to TCP/IP for networked environments, these protocols ensure seamless connectivity, data transfer, and collaboration. As computing ecosystems continue to expand and diversify, the development and adoption of new communication protocols, particularly in emerging technologies like IoT and 5G, remain pivotal in shaping the future of device management and interconnected systems.

Discuss the importance of standardized protocols for seamless device interaction.

Standardized protocols play a pivotal role in ensuring the seamless interaction of devices within computing environments, providing a common language and set of rules that enable interoperability, compatibility, and efficient communication. The importance of standardized protocols becomes particularly pronounced in the increasingly complex and interconnected landscape of modern computing, where a diverse array of devices, from computers and smartphones to IoT sensors and networked appliances, coexist and collaborate. At its core, the adoption of standardized protocols fosters a level of consistency that is fundamental for achieving a cohesive and functional ecosystem of interconnected devices.

One of the primary benefits of standardized protocols lies in the facilitation of interoperability. Devices manufactured by different vendors and developers, running various operating systems and software applications, need to communicate effectively to provide a seamless user experience. Standardized protocols ensure that devices adhere to a common set of rules and specifications, allowing them to understand and interpret the data and commands exchanged. For example, in networking, the Transmission Control Protocol (TCP) and Internet Protocol (IP) form the backbone of internet communication, enabling devices from different manufacturers and running different operating systems to communicate over a standardized and universally accepted framework. This interoperability is essential for the internet's functionality, as it enables devices to seamlessly exchange information across diverse networks.

Compatibility is another critical aspect influenced by standardized protocols. Devices may have different functionalities, capabilities, and communication requirements. Standardized protocols define a uniform set of rules for various functionalities, such as data transfer, power management, and device discovery. USB (Universal Serial Bus), for instance, provides a standardized interface for connecting peripherals to computers. Whether it's a printer, keyboard, or external storage device, the use of the USB protocol ensures that these devices are compatible with a wide range of computers, regardless of the manufacturer or operating system. This compatibility simplifies the user experience, as users can confidently connect devices without worrying about intricate compatibility issues.

Efficient communication is enhanced through standardized protocols, contributing to streamlined processes, reduced errors, and optimized performance. When devices communicate using a common protocol, they can exchange information more seamlessly, leading to faster and more reliable interactions. In the context of data transfer, standardized protocols such as USB, Ethernet, and Wi-Fi define the rules for encoding, transmission, and decoding of data. These protocols ensure that data is transferred efficiently, minimizing the risk of errors and ensuring a reliable and high-performance communication channel. Efficient communication is particularly crucial in scenarios where real-time interactions, such as video streaming or online gaming, demand low latency and high throughput.

Moreover, standardized protocols simplify the development and maintenance of software applications that interact with devices. Application developers can leverage standardized protocols to communicate with a wide variety of devices without needing to implement device-specific communication mechanisms for each device. For instance, in the context of web development, HTTP (Hypertext Transfer Protocol) serves as a standardized protocol for communication between web browsers and servers. This standardization allows developers to create web applications that can interact with servers across different platforms and devices, fostering a more straightforward and scalable development process.

The use of standardized protocols is especially crucial in the domain of cybersecurity and data integrity. Standardized protocols often come with built-in security mechanisms, such as encryption and authentication, which contribute to the protection of sensitive data during transmission. In the context of secure communication over the internet, HTTPS (Hypertext Transfer Protocol Secure) ensures that data exchanged between devices and servers is encrypted, safeguarding it from eavesdropping and tampering. By adhering to standardized security protocols, devices can establish secure communication channels, reducing the risk of unauthorized access, data breaches, and other cybersecurity threats.

Scalability is a key consideration in the design and deployment of computing systems, and standardized protocols play a crucial role in achieving scalable solutions. As the number and diversity of connected devices increase, the need for scalable communication becomes more pronounced. Standardized protocols provide a foundation for scalable architectures by ensuring that new devices can seamlessly integrate into existing ecosystems. The scalability of protocols like MQTT (Message Queuing Telemetry Transport) in IoT environments allows for the efficient exchange of information between a vast number of devices, contributing to the growth and expansion of IoT ecosystems without sacrificing performance or reliability.

Standardized protocols also contribute to the development of open and inclusive ecosystems. In an open ecosystem, diverse devices from different manufacturers and developers can coexist and collaborate without being constrained by proprietary communication mechanisms. Open ecosystems foster innovation, competition, and the development of a vibrant marketplace where users have the freedom to choose devices based on their preferences and needs. The adoption of standards such as Bluetooth for wireless communication or USB for wired connections contributes to the creation of open ecosystems, where devices from various vendors can seamlessly interact, promoting healthy competition and innovation.

The concept of Plug and Play (PnP), enabled by standardized protocols, simplifies the user experience by automating the process of device discovery and configuration. When a user connects a new device, the operating system, through standardized protocols, can dynamically recognize and configure the device without requiring manual intervention. PnP relies on protocols such as USB, PCI, and UPnP to identify devices, load necessary drivers, and allocate resources, ensuring that users can easily add or remove devices from their systems with minimal effort. This user-friendly approach enhances accessibility and encourages the widespread adoption of new devices without imposing a steep learning curve on users.

Furthermore, standardized protocols contribute to the longevity and sustainability of technology ecosystems. As devices evolve and new technologies emerge, the adherence to established standards ensures backward compatibility and the continued functionality of existing devices within evolving environments. For example, the compatibility of modern USB-C connectors with older USB-A ports demonstrates how standardized protocols enable the coexistence of new and legacy devices. This compatibility extends the lifespan of existing devices and reduces electronic waste, contributing to a more sustainable and environmentally friendly approach to technology.

In conclusion, the importance of standardized protocols for seamless device interaction is paramount in the contemporary landscape of computing. These protocols underpin interoperability, compatibility, efficient communication, and security, shaping the foundation of interconnected systems. Whether in networking, storage, communication over the internet, or the development of applications, standardized protocols provide a common ground for diverse devices to collaborate and communicate effectively. As technology continues to advance, the role of standardized protocols remains critical in fostering innovation, scalability, and the creation of open ecosystems that benefit users, developers, and the broader computing industry.

Detail the procedures involved in device startup and shutdown.

The procedures involved in device startup and shutdown are fundamental aspects of the overall lifecycle management of computing devices. These processes encompass a series of well-defined steps that govern the initialization, operation, and termination of a device. During the startup phase, a device undergoes a sequence of operations to transition from a powered-off state to an operational state, while the shutdown phase involves the orderly cessation of processes and the powering down of the device. Understanding these procedures is crucial for efficient device management, ensuring the stability, integrity, and reliability of the device throughout its lifecycle.

The startup process begins with the application of power to the device, triggering the power-on self-test (POST). POST is a diagnostic routine that the device's firmware, such as the Basic Input/Output System (BIOS) in the case of computers, executes to verify the integrity of essential hardware components. This includes checking the processor, memory modules, storage devices, and other critical components for proper functionality. The results of the POST determine whether the device can proceed with the startup process or if there are issues that require attention.

Following a successful POST, the device's firmware proceeds to initialize essential hardware components. This involves configuring the system's hardware settings, detecting and initializing connected peripheral devices, and establishing the necessary communication channels between the hardware and firmware. The firmware loads the operating system into memory, allowing the device to transition to a state where it can execute higher-level software instructions.

The next phase in the startup process involves the loading and initialization of the operating system (OS). The OS is a fundamental software component that manages the device's resources, facilitates communication between software applications and hardware components, and provides a user interface. During startup, the OS undergoes initialization routines, configuring device drivers, establishing communication with connected peripherals, and preparing the device for user interaction. For example, in the case of personal computers running Windows, the OS may display the familiar Windows logo and initiate background processes to prepare the user environment.

As the operating system initializes, user-specific configurations and settings come into play. User authentication processes, such as entering a password or using biometric methods, verify the identity of the user and determine the level of access they have to the device. Once authenticated, the operating system proceeds to load user-specific preferences, application settings, and other personalized configurations that define the user's computing environment. This customization ensures a tailored user experience and the availability of specific applications and resources based on individual preferences.

The graphical user interface (GUI) or command-line interface (CLI) is presented to the user once the startup process is complete. The GUI provides a visual representation of the device's user interface, typically involving icons, windows, and menus, while the CLI relies on text-based commands for interaction. The presentation of the user interface marks the transition from the startup phase to the operational state, where users can initiate applications, perform tasks, and engage with the device based on their requirements.

Throughout the operational state, the device performs a myriad of tasks based on user interactions and background processes. Users can launch applications, access files, connect to networks, and perform various computing tasks depending on the device's functionality and the user's intentions. Background processes, managed by the operating system, handle essential functions such as memory management, file system operations, and device driver communication. The operational state represents the period during which the device fulfills its intended functions, serving the needs and requirements of the user or application.

When it comes to the shutdown process, the goal is to bring the device to a state where it can be safely powered off without risking data loss or corruption. The user initiates the shutdown process through the operating system's user interface or specific commands. The operating system, in response to the shutdown request, begins a series of procedures to gracefully terminate ongoing processes, close applications, and ensure the integrity of data stored in memory and on storage devices.

One crucial aspect of the shutdown process is the initiation of an orderly shutdown sequence for running applications and processes. The operating system sends signals to applications, notifying them of the impending shutdown and allowing them to save any unsaved data or perform necessary cleanup tasks. This graceful termination prevents data loss, corruption, and ensures that applications exit their operational state without causing issues to the overall system.

As applications and processes conclude their operations, the operating system proceeds to close open files and release allocated resources. This involves finalizing write operations to storage devices, ensuring that all changes to files and system configurations are safely committed. The operating system may also perform additional cleanup tasks, such as closing network connections, releasing memory, and updating system logs to record the events leading up to the shutdown.

Once applications have been closed, and resources have been released, the operating system instructs the device's firmware to initiate the power-off sequence. The firmware communicates with the device's hardware, signaling each component to cease operation and enter a low-power or powered-off state. For example, in the case of computers, the Advanced Configuration and Power Interface (ACPI) plays a crucial role in managing power states and coordinating the shutdown process.

Prior to the final power-off state, the operating system may prompt the user with notifications or messages to ensure that they are aware of the impending shutdown. This serves as a user-friendly approach, allowing users to save any unsaved work, close open applications, or take any necessary actions before the device powers off.

The device enters the powered-off state when all hardware components have completed their shutdown procedures. In this state, the device no longer consumes active power, and it is safe to disconnect power sources or perform maintenance tasks. The powered-off state represents the end of the device's operational cycle until the next startup sequence is initiated.

In some scenarios, devices may enter sleep or hibernate modes rather than a complete shutdown. These power-saving states allow devices to conserve energy while retaining the current state in memory. Sleep mode maintains a low-power state, allowing for quick resumption of operation, while hibernate mode saves the device's current state to storage and powers off completely. Both sleep and hibernate modes aim to balance user convenience with power efficiency, providing quicker access to the operational state while minimizing power consumption during periods of inactivity.

In conclusion, the procedures involved in device startup and shutdown are intricately designed sequences that govern the transition between powered-off and operational states. From the initiation of power-on self-tests and firmware initialization during startup to the graceful termination of processes, application closures, and eventual power-off during shutdown, these processes ensure the reliable, secure, and user-friendly operation of computing devices. Understanding the intricacies of startup and shutdown procedures is essential for effective device management, user experience optimization, and the overall lifecycle management of computing devices.

Address the challenges and considerations in managing these processes.

Managing the processes of device startup and shutdown involves navigating a complex landscape of technical challenges and user-oriented considerations. These challenges span various aspects of device management, from ensuring the security and integrity of data during shutdown to optimizing the startup time for a seamless user experience. Addressing these challenges requires a holistic approach that considers hardware, software, user expectations, and the broader context of the computing environment.

One significant challenge in managing device startup and shutdown is the need for efficient and rapid transitions between power states. Users expect their devices to start up quickly, providing near-instant access to the operational state. Conversely, during shutdown, users prefer a swift and predictable process that ensures the secure closure of applications and the safe storage of data. Achieving these quick transitions requires a careful balance between hardware capabilities, firmware efficiency, and the optimization of operating system processes.

Optimizing startup time involves streamlining the power-on self-test (POST) and firmware initialization processes. While these routines are essential for ensuring the integrity of hardware components, they can contribute to extended startup times. Manufacturers and developers strive to minimize the duration of these procedures without compromising the reliability of hardware checks. Efficient firmware design and hardware advancements, such as fast-boot technologies, contribute to reducing the time it takes for devices to transition from a powered-off state to an operational one.

However, the quest for faster startup times must be balanced with the need for thorough hardware checks and initialization. Skipping essential tests could lead to undetected hardware issues, potentially compromising the device's stability and reliability. Striking the right balance requires continuous advancements in firmware design, hardware diagnostics, and testing methodologies to ensure that startup times are optimized without sacrificing the robustness of the initialization process.

Security considerations during both startup and shutdown are paramount in device management. During the startup process, the device must ensure the integrity of the firmware, operating system, and critical system files. Secure Boot, a security feature implemented in modern computing systems, helps mitigate the risk of loading malicious or unauthorized code during the startup phase. This ensures that the device boots into a trustworthy and verified state, protecting against unauthorized modifications and potential security threats.

Similarly, during shutdown, security measures must be in place to safeguard user data. The graceful termination of applications and processes is crucial for preventing data loss or corruption. Applications need to be notified of the impending shutdown and given the opportunity to save any unsaved work or perform necessary cleanup tasks. File systems must ensure that all write operations are completed before the device powers off, preventing the loss of critical data and maintaining the consistency of stored information.

The challenge arises when certain applications or processes resist termination, leading to delays in the shutdown process. Unresponsive applications or background processes may hinder the orderly closure of the device, potentially resulting in data loss or the need for manual intervention by the user. Addressing this challenge involves implementing mechanisms within the operating system to identify and handle unresponsive processes effectively, allowing for a smoother and more secure shutdown experience.

User expectations and experience are crucial factors in managing device startup and shutdown processes. Users demand a seamless and intuitive experience, expecting devices to respond promptly to their commands. Slow startup times or erratic shutdown behaviors can lead to frustration and dissatisfaction. Striking a balance between rapid transitions and reliable operations is essential for meeting user expectations.

User customization and personalization further complicate device management considerations. Users configure their devices with specific settings, preferences, and startup applications, influencing the time it takes for a device to become fully operational. Managing user-specific configurations during startup and ensuring a consistent and reliable experience across different user profiles require careful attention to the design of the startup process and the handling of user-specific data.

Considerations for managing user expectations extend to the shutdown process as well. Users should be informed of the impending shutdown, allowing them to save their work and prepare for the device to power off. Transparent communication during the shutdown process helps build trust and ensures that users are aware of the device's state. Balancing user autonomy with the need for orderly shutdown procedures involves implementing user-friendly interfaces, notifications, and prompts that guide users through the process without causing disruption.

Compatibility with various hardware configurations and peripherals poses another challenge in device management. As computing ecosystems encompass a wide array of devices from different manufacturers, ensuring seamless startup and shutdown processes across diverse hardware configurations becomes a complex task. Device drivers and firmware must be designed to accommodate various peripherals, storage devices, and network interfaces. Compatibility challenges often arise when new hardware components are introduced, requiring updates to device drivers and firmware to ensure proper recognition and initialization.

Moreover, managing the startup and shutdown processes in heterogeneous computing environments, where devices with different operating systems and architectures coexist, requires standardized protocols and communication mechanisms. Interoperability challenges may emerge, especially in networked environments where devices need to communicate during startup or shutdown. Implementing standardized communication protocols and ensuring adherence to industry standards become critical for addressing these compatibility challenges and fostering a cohesive computing ecosystem.

In virtualized and cloud computing environments, additional considerations come into play. Virtual machines and cloud instances require efficient startup procedures to minimize resource allocation time and enhance scalability. The orchestration of virtualized environments, where multiple instances may start or shut down simultaneously, necessitates sophisticated management tools and frameworks. Balancing the dynamic nature of virtualized resources with the need for efficient startup and shutdown procedures requires ongoing advancements in virtualization technologies and cloud management platforms.

Environmental considerations, especially in the context of mobile devices and battery-powered systems, add complexity to the management of startup and shutdown processes. Power consumption during startup and shutdown needs to be optimized to extend battery life and ensure energy efficiency. Balancing the need for quick access to operational states with power-saving measures becomes crucial, particularly in scenarios where devices operate on limited power sources.

In conclusion, managing the processes of device startup and shutdown involves addressing a multitude of challenges that span technical, user-oriented, and environmental considerations. Striking the right balance between rapid transitions, security measures, user experience, and compatibility requires continuous innovation, advancements in firmware and hardware design, and a user-centric approach to device management. As technology evolves and computing environments become more diverse, the ongoing refinement of startup and shutdown processes remains a critical aspect of providing reliable, secure, and user-friendly computing experiences.

Chapter 2: Understanding Operating System Architecture

Define the concept of operating system architecture. Operating system architecture is the structural framework that defines the organization and interaction of the various components within an operating system (OS). It serves as the blueprint for how the operating system functions, providing a hierarchical and modular design that orchestrates the management of hardware resources and facilitates user interactions with the computer system. The architecture of an operating system is a critical aspect of its design, influencing its performance, scalability, flexibility, and overall functionality.

At its core, operating system architecture establishes a layering of abstraction that allows for the efficient management of hardware resources while shielding users and applications from the complexities of underlying hardware details. This abstraction enables the operating system to provide a consistent and standardized interface to applications, hiding the intricacies of hardware variations and allowing software developers to write programs that are independent of specific hardware configurations. The layered structure of operating system architecture typically includes components such as the kernel, device drivers, system libraries, and user interfaces.

The kernel is the nucleus of the operating system, responsible for managing core functions such as process scheduling, memory management, file system operations, and input/output operations. It serves as the intermediary between the hardware and the higher-level components of the operating system. The design and efficiency of the kernel have a profound impact on the overall performance and responsiveness of the operating system. Monolithic, microkernel, and hybrid kernel architectures represent different approaches to organizing the kernel and its interactions with the rest of the operating system components.

In a monolithic kernel architecture, all essential operating system functions reside within a single, large kernel module. This design simplifies communication between kernel components but may lead to a lack of modularity and flexibility. In contrast, microkernel architecture advocates for a minimalistic kernel that delegates most operating system functions to user-space processes, enhancing modularity and fault isolation. Hybrid kernels combine elements of both monolithic and microkernel architectures, seeking a balance between performance and modularity.

Device drivers are integral components of operating system architecture, responsible for facilitating communication between the operating system and peripheral devices. They provide an abstraction layer that allows the operating system to interact with a wide range of hardware devices without requiring detailed knowledge of their specific implementations. The modular nature of device drivers enables the operating system to support new hardware additions or updates seamlessly. Device drivers can be dynamically loaded and unloaded, allowing the operating system to adapt to changing hardware configurations.

System libraries form another layer in the operating system architecture, offering a set of standardized functions and routines that applications can utilize. These libraries provide an abstraction layer above the kernel, simplifying complex tasks for application developers. Common system libraries include those for file management, networking, and graphical user interfaces. Application Programming Interfaces (APIs) define the interfaces through which applications interact with system libraries, ensuring compatibility and standardization.

The user interface (UI) components, including command-line interfaces (CLI) and graphical user interfaces (GUI), represent the outermost layer of operating system architecture, serving as the point of interaction between users and the computer system. CLI allows users to interact with the operating system through text commands, while GUI provides a visual representation of the system, offering icons, windows, and menus for user interactions. The design and usability of the user interface significantly impact the overall user experience and play a crucial role in making the operating system accessible to a wide range of users.

The concept of operating system architecture extends beyond the internal organization of components to encompass various design principles and characteristics. One such principle is modularity, emphasizing the division of the operating system into separate, interchangeable components. Modular design enhances maintainability, as updates or modifications to one module do not necessarily affect others. This allows for easier debugging, testing, and scalability as the operating system evolves.

Scalability is a critical consideration in operating system architecture, especially in modern computing environments with diverse hardware configurations and varying workloads. A scalable architecture accommodates the growth of system resources and adapts to increased demands without compromising performance. The ability to efficiently manage multi-core processors, large memory capacities, and diverse storage configurations is essential for ensuring scalability in contemporary operating systems.

Concurrency and synchronization mechanisms are fundamental aspects of operating system architecture, particularly in systems that support multitasking and parallel processing. The architecture must provide mechanisms to manage concurrent execution of multiple processes, preventing conflicts and ensuring the correct sharing of resources. Techniques such as locks, semaphores, and inter-process communication mechanisms are crucial for maintaining consistency and preventing data corruption in concurrent environments.

Security is a paramount concern in operating system architecture, necessitating the implementation of robust mechanisms to protect against unauthorized access, malware, and other security threats. Access control mechanisms, encryption, and secure boot processes are integral components of a secure operating system architecture. The architecture must also facilitate the isolation of processes and prevent one application from compromising the integrity of others or the underlying system.

Reliability and fault tolerance are additional considerations in operating system architecture. A reliable architecture ensures that the operating system functions predictably and consistently under various conditions. Fault tolerance mechanisms, such as redundancy and error recovery, contribute to the stability of the system, minimizing the impact of hardware failures or unexpected events.

Real-time capabilities are essential for operating systems deployed in time-sensitive environments, such as embedded systems or mission-critical applications. Real-time operating system architectures prioritize deterministic behavior, ensuring that tasks are executed within predefined time constraints. This is crucial in scenarios where timely responses and predictability are paramount, such as in industrial control systems or aerospace applications.

The evolution of operating system architecture is influenced by advancements in hardware technologies, changing computing paradigms, and emerging application requirements. Cloud computing, edge computing, and the Internet of Things (IoT) present new challenges and opportunities for operating system design. Operating systems designed for these environments must exhibit characteristics such as flexibility, adaptability, and efficient resource utilization to meet the unique demands of distributed and interconnected computing infrastructures.

In conclusion, operating system architecture is a foundational concept that defines the structure and organization of operating systems. It encompasses the internal components such as the kernel, device drivers, system libraries, and user interfaces, as well as overarching design principles and characteristics. The architecture plays a pivotal role in shaping the performance, scalability, security, and reliability of operating systems, adapting to the evolving landscape of computing technologies and user requirements. A well-designed operating system architecture is essential for providing a stable, efficient, and user-friendly computing experience across a diverse range of hardware and application scenarios.

Highlight the role of architecture in governing the behavior of an operating system.

The role of architecture in governing the behavior of an operating system is foundational, influencing every aspect of its design, functionality, and interaction with both hardware and software components. Operating system architecture serves as the guiding framework that shapes how the system manages resources, processes user requests, and maintains overall stability and reliability. This architectural blueprint not only defines the internal structure of the operating system but also plays a crucial role in determining its performance, scalability, security, and adaptability to evolving technological landscapes.

At its core, architecture establishes the hierarchical organization of the operating system, delineating the relationships and interactions among its various components. The kernel, positioned at the heart of the architecture, forms the nucleus responsible for core functions such as process scheduling, memory management, and input/output operations. The architecture dictates whether the kernel follows a monolithic, microkernel, or hybrid design, each with its own implications for system performance and modularity. This kernel-centric architectural decision governs how efficiently the operating system can mediate between user applications and underlying hardware.

The layered structure inherent in operating system architecture is pivotal in managing complexity and abstraction. By dividing the operating system into distinct layers, such as the kernel, device drivers, system libraries, and user interfaces, architecture enables a clear separation of concerns. Each layer abstracts and encapsulates specific functionalities, allowing for modularity, ease of maintenance, and the implementation of standardized interfaces. This layering not only simplifies the development and maintenance of the operating system but also contributes to its extensibility and adaptability to new technologies.

Furthermore, architecture profoundly influences the user experience through the design and implementation of the user interface (UI). Whether through command-line interfaces (CLI) or graphical user interfaces (GUI), the architecture defines how users interact with the operating system. The UI acts as the outermost layer of the architecture, providing a point of entry for users to issue commands, navigate files, and launch applications. Architectural decisions regarding UI design impact the accessibility, intuitiveness, and overall usability of the operating system, directly affecting how users perceive and interact with their computing environment.

Concurrency and synchronization mechanisms embedded in the architecture govern how the operating system manages the execution of multiple processes simultaneously. The architecture must facilitate concurrent execution while ensuring the correct sharing of resources and preventing conflicts. Concepts like process scheduling, locks, semaphores, and inter-process communication mechanisms are integral components of the architecture that dictate how the operating system maintains consistency and prevents data corruption in scenarios of concurrent access.

Security considerations are paramount in operating system architecture, influencing the implementation of access control mechanisms, encryption, and secure boot processes. The architecture defines how the operating system protects against unauthorized access, malware, and other security threats. Architectural decisions directly impact the system's ability to isolate processes, prevent unauthorized modifications, and maintain the integrity of sensitive data. Security features such as user authentication, file permissions, and secure communication protocols are intricately woven into the fabric of the architecture to establish a robust security posture.

Reliability and fault tolerance are inherent aspects of operating system architecture, ensuring that the system functions predictably and consistently under various conditions. The architecture must incorporate mechanisms for error detection, recovery, and redundancy to enhance the reliability of the system. Architectural decisions influence how the operating system responds to hardware failures, unexpected events, and attempts to recover from errors, ultimately contributing to the stability of the system in mission-critical scenarios.

Scalability, a key consideration in modern computing environments, is intricately tied to architectural decisions. The architecture must be designed to accommodate the growth of system resources and adapt to increased demands without compromising performance. The ability to efficiently manage multi-core processors, large memory capacities, and diverse storage configurations is essential for ensuring scalability. Architectural choices determine how well the operating system can leverage advancements in hardware technologies and efficiently utilize available resources.

Real-time capabilities are embedded in the architecture to address time-sensitive requirements in specific applications or embedded systems. Real-time operating system architectures prioritize deterministic behavior, ensuring that tasks are executed within predefined time constraints. Architectural decisions influence how the operating system handles time-critical processes, providing a foundation for applications in industrial control systems, telecommunications, and other domains where timely responses are crucial.

The concept of architecture extends beyond the internal organization of components to encompass design principles that guide the overall behavior of the operating system. A well-designed architecture adheres to principles such as modularity, encapsulation, abstraction, and separation of concerns. Modularity, for instance, promotes the division of the operating system into interchangeable components, enhancing maintainability and facilitating updates. Encapsulation ensures that the internal details of components are hidden, promoting information hiding and preventing unintended interactions. Abstraction allows for the creation of simplified interfaces that shield users and applications from underlying complexities. Separation of concerns supports the isolation of functionalities, preventing unintended dependencies between components.

Environmental considerations, including mobile devices and battery-powered systems, introduce additional challenges that architecture must address. Power consumption during startup, operation, and shutdown needs to be optimized to extend battery life and ensure energy efficiency. Architectural decisions impact how the operating system manages power states, handles transitions between active and low-power modes, and optimizes resource usage in environments with limited power sources.

Moreover, the architecture of an operating system is subject to evolution as computing paradigms shift and new technologies emerge. Cloud computing, edge computing, and the Internet of Things (IoT) present new challenges and opportunities that require architectural adaptations. Operating systems designed for these environments must exhibit characteristics such as flexibility, adaptability, and efficient resource utilization to meet the unique demands of distributed and interconnected computing infrastructures.

In conclusion, the role of architecture in governing the behavior of an operating system is all-encompassing, influencing its design, functionality, and interactions at every level. Operating system architecture acts as the guiding framework that shapes how the system manages resources, processes user requests, and maintains overall stability and reliability. The decisions made in architectural design have profound implications for performance, scalability, security, and adaptability, determining the operating system's ability to meet the diverse needs of users and applications in the ever-evolving landscape of computing.

Break down the key components of operating system architecture.

The key components of operating system architecture encompass a multifaceted structure that governs the organization, interaction, and functionality of the entire operating system. At the core of this architecture lies the kernel, serving as the nucleus that manages essential functions such as process scheduling, memory management, file system operations, and input/output operations. The kernel acts as the intermediary between user applications and the hardware, translating high-level commands into instructions that the hardware can execute. The design of the kernel plays a pivotal role in determining the efficiency, responsiveness, and overall performance of the operating system.

Within the kernel, various architectural approaches define its internal structure. Monolithic kernel architecture consolidates all essential operating system functions into a single, large kernel module. While this design simplifies communication between kernel components, it may lack modularity and flexibility. In contrast, microkernel architecture advocates for a minimalistic kernel that delegates most operating system functions to user-space processes. This enhances modularity, fault isolation, and adaptability to changing requirements. Hybrid kernels amalgamate elements of both monolithic and microkernel designs, aiming to strike a balance between performance and modularity.

Device drivers represent another crucial component in operating system architecture, facilitating communication between the operating system and peripheral devices. These drivers provide an abstraction layer, enabling the operating system to interact with a diverse range of hardware devices without requiring intricate knowledge of specific implementations. The modularity of device drivers allows for dynamic loading and unloading, accommodating changes in hardware configurations seamlessly. The efficiency and compatibility of device drivers significantly contribute to the operating system's ability to support new hardware additions or updates.

System libraries form an additional layer in the operating system architecture, offering a set of standardized functions and routines that applications can utilize. These libraries abstract complex tasks, providing a simplified interface for application developers. Common system libraries include those for file management, networking, and graphical user interfaces. Application Programming Interfaces (APIs) define the interfaces through which applications interact with system libraries, ensuring compatibility and standardization across diverse software applications.

The user interface (UI) components represent the outermost layer of operating system architecture, acting as the point of interaction between users and the computer system. Command-line interfaces (CLI) allow users to interact with the operating system through text commands, while graphical user interfaces (GUI) provide visual representations with icons, windows, and menus. The design and usability of the user interface are critical aspects of architecture, directly influencing the accessibility, intuitiveness, and overall user experience of the operating system.

Concurrency and synchronization mechanisms embedded in the architecture govern how the operating system manages the execution of multiple processes simultaneously. The architecture must provide mechanisms to handle concurrent execution, preventing conflicts and ensuring the correct sharing of resources. Techniques such as locks, semaphores, and inter-process communication mechanisms are integral components of the architecture, maintaining consistency and preventing data corruption in scenarios of concurrent access.

Security is a paramount consideration in operating system architecture, influencing the implementation of access control mechanisms, encryption, and secure boot processes. The architecture defines how the operating system protects against unauthorized access, malware, and other security threats. Access control mechanisms, file permissions, secure communication protocols, and encryption algorithms are intricately woven into the architecture to establish a robust security posture. The design decisions made in the architecture impact the system's ability to isolate processes, prevent unauthorized modifications, and maintain the integrity of sensitive data.

Reliability and fault tolerance are inherent aspects of operating system architecture, ensuring that the system functions predictably and consistently under various conditions. The architecture must incorporate mechanisms for error detection, recovery, and redundancy to enhance the reliability of the system. Fault tolerance mechanisms contribute to the stability of the system, minimizing the impact of hardware failures or unexpected events. Architectural decisions influence how the operating system responds to errors, attempts to recover, and ensures the overall reliability of the computing environment.

Scalability is a key consideration in modern operating system architectures, especially in environments with diverse hardware configurations and varying workloads. The architecture must be designed to accommodate the growth of system resources and adapt to increased demands without compromising performance. The ability to efficiently manage multi-core processors, large memory capacities, and diverse storage configurations is essential for ensuring scalability. Architectural choices determine how well the operating system can leverage advancements in hardware technologies and efficiently utilize available resources.

Real-time capabilities are embedded in the architecture to address time-sensitive requirements in specific applications or embedded systems. Real-time operating system architectures prioritize deterministic behavior, ensuring that tasks are executed within predefined time constraints. Architectural decisions influence how the operating system handles time-critical processes, providing a foundation for applications in industrial control systems, telecommunications, and other domains where timely responses are crucial.

Environmental considerations introduce additional challenges that architecture must address, especially in the context of mobile devices and battery-powered systems. Power consumption during startup, operation, and shutdown needs to be optimized to extend battery life and ensure energy efficiency. Architectural decisions impact how the operating system manages power states, handles transitions between active and low-power modes, and optimizes resource usage in environments with limited power sources.

Moreover, the evolution of operating system architectures is influenced by advancements in hardware technologies, changing computing paradigms, and emerging application requirements. Cloud computing, edge computing, and the Internet of Things (IoT) present new challenges and opportunities that require architectural adaptations. Operating systems designed for these environments must exhibit characteristics such as flexibility, adaptability, and efficient resource utilization to meet the unique demands of distributed and interconnected computing infrastructures.

In conclusion, the key components of operating system architecture collectively shape the organization, behavior, and performance of the entire operating system. From the design of the kernel, device drivers, and system libraries to the user interface, concurrency mechanisms, and security features, each component plays a critical role in defining the capabilities and limitations of the operating system. The decisions made in architecture directly impact aspects such as scalability, reliability, and real-time capabilities, ensuring that the operating system can effectively meet the diverse needs of users and applications in an ever-changing computing landscape.

Explore the functions of the kernel, shell, and other essential elements.

The kernel, the central component of an operating system, is a critical element responsible for managing essential functions that facilitate communication between software applications and hardware. At its core, the kernel is the core executive that governs the allocation of system resources, including CPU time, memory, and input/output operations. Process scheduling, one of its primary responsibilities, ensures that multiple tasks or processes can coexist and execute concurrently, providing the illusion of simultaneous operation. Memory management involves coordinating the allocation and deallocation of memory space for processes, optimizing resource usage and preventing conflicts. Input/output (I/O) operations are orchestrated by the kernel, ensuring that data is efficiently exchanged between the computer's storage, peripherals, and external devices.

The device drivers are integral components closely associated with the kernel, acting as intermediaries between the hardware and the operating system. These drivers facilitate seamless communication by providing a standardized interface for the operating system to interact with a diverse array of hardware devices. Whether it's a printer, graphics card, or network adapter, device drivers enable the kernel to abstract the intricacies of device-specific communication, ensuring compatibility and interoperability across various hardware configurations. The modularity of device drivers allows for their dynamic loading and unloading, accommodating changes in hardware configurations without necessitating a complete system shutdown.

System libraries form a layer above the kernel, providing a collection of standardized functions and routines that applications can leverage. These libraries encapsulate complex and repetitive tasks, offering a simplified interface for software developers. Common system libraries encompass functionalities such as file management, networking, and graphical user interfaces (GUIs). The Application Programming Interface (API) defines the conventions through which applications interact with these libraries, promoting compatibility and ease of development. The use of system libraries facilitates code reuse, streamlining the development process and enhancing the overall efficiency of software applications.

The user interface (UI), an outermost layer of interaction, serves as the bridge between users and the operating system. Command-line interfaces (CLIs) and graphical user interfaces (GUIs) represent two prevalent forms of UIs. CLIs require users to input commands through a text-based interface, providing a powerful and efficient means of interacting with the system. GUIs, on the other hand, present a visual environment with icons, windows, and menus, offering a more intuitive and user-friendly experience. The design and functionality of the UI significantly impact user accessibility, satisfaction, and overall experience with the operating system.

Within the operating system, the shell acts as a command interpreter, serving as the intermediary between users and the kernel. Users interact with the shell by inputting commands, and the shell, in turn, interprets and executes these commands. The shell provides a command-line interface through which users can navigate file systems, launch applications, and perform various tasks. In addition to the command-line interface, some shells offer scripting capabilities, allowing users to automate sequences of commands. The choice of shell can influence the user's experience and workflow, with different shells providing varying features, scripting languages, and customization options.

File systems, another essential element, govern the organization and storage of data on storage devices. The file system manages files, directories, and metadata, ensuring efficient retrieval, storage, and manipulation of data. Hierarchical structures are employed to organize files into directories, facilitating logical grouping and navigation. File systems implement access control mechanisms, determining which users or processes have permission to read, write, or execute specific files. Common file systems include FAT, NTFS, HFS+, and ext4, each with its own characteristics and optimizations suited to different use cases and operating systems.

Processes and process management are fundamental aspects of operating systems, encompassing the execution of programs and applications. A process represents a running instance of a program, including the program's code, data, and resources. Process management involves creating, scheduling, and terminating processes, as well as managing interprocess communication and synchronization. The kernel oversees process execution, allocating CPU time, managing memory space, and coordinating I/O operations. Context switching, the process of switching between different processes, is a critical function that enables multitasking and concurrent execution. Efficient process management contributes to system responsiveness, resource utilization, and overall performance.

Networking functionalities within the operating system enable communication and data exchange between devices within a network. Networking components include protocols, device drivers, and utilities that facilitate the transmission of data over networks. The operating system manages network configurations, handles communication protocols such as TCP/IP, and provides interfaces for network-related operations. Networking capabilities are essential for connecting computers to local area networks (LANs), wide area networks (WANs), and the internet. The seamless integration of networking functionalities into the operating system ensures that users can leverage network resources and services effectively.

Security mechanisms and features are crucial elements embedded within the operating system to protect against unauthorized access, data breaches, and malware. Access control mechanisms regulate user permissions, determining who can access, modify, or execute specific resources. Encryption algorithms safeguard sensitive data during transmission and storage, preventing unauthorized interception or tampering. Secure boot processes ensure that only authenticated and trusted software components are loaded during system startup, mitigating the risk of malicious code execution. Firewalls, antivirus software, and intrusion detection systems contribute to the overall security posture of the operating system, safeguarding against external threats and vulnerabilities.

Error handling and recovery mechanisms are essential components that enhance the robustness and reliability of the operating system. The architecture incorporates error detection, reporting, and recovery mechanisms to address unforeseen events, hardware failures, and software errors. These mechanisms may include error logs, recovery procedures, and redundancy strategies to minimize the impact of errors on system stability. Error handling ensures that the operating system can gracefully recover from unexpected situations, maintaining data integrity and preventing catastrophic failures.

Environmental considerations, particularly in mobile and battery-powered systems, introduce additional challenges that influence operating system elements. Power management features are integrated to optimize power consumption during startup, operation, and shutdown, extending battery life and ensuring energy efficiency. Dynamic power states, sleep modes, and adaptive power management contribute to minimizing power usage during periods of inactivity. The architecture must consider the trade-off between performance and power efficiency, providing mechanisms for users to balance these factors based on their preferences and requirements.

In conclusion, the operating system's key components, including the kernel, device drivers, system libraries, user interfaces, file systems, processes, networking functionalities, security mechanisms, error handling, and environmental considerations, collectively shape the behavior, functionality, and performance of the system. The intricate interplay of these elements ensures that the operating system effectively manages hardware resources, provides a user-friendly interface, facilitates application development, and addresses security and reliability concerns. A well-designed operating system integrates these components seamlessly, offering a stable, efficient, and secure computing environment for users and applications.

Discuss how operating systems manage memory resources.

Operating systems play a critical role in managing memory resources, a fundamental aspect that directly influences the overall performance and efficiency of a computer system. Memory management involves coordinating the allocation, deallocation, and utilization of the system's memory, encompassing physical RAM (Random Access Memory) and, in some cases, virtual memory. The operating system acts as the orchestrator, ensuring that applications have access to the memory they need while efficiently utilizing available resources.

One of the primary functions of memory management is to allocate memory to running processes. When a program is executed, the operating system allocates a portion of the computer's physical memory to the process, allowing it to store and manipulate data. The memory allocation process is dynamic, with the operating system adjusting the size of memory regions based on the changing needs of each process. Efficient memory allocation is crucial for maximizing the use of available RAM and avoiding unnecessary resource wastage.

A key concept in memory management is virtual memory, a technique that extends the available address space beyond the physical RAM. Virtual memory allows processes to use more memory than is physically installed in the system, creating an illusion of vast addressable space. When physical memory becomes scarce, the operating system can transfer portions of data from RAM to the hard disk or other storage devices, making space for new data. This process, known as paging or swapping, enables the system to handle larger and more complex applications without relying solely on the limitations of physical RAM.

Page tables are integral to the functioning of virtual memory. These tables maintain a mapping between the virtual addresses used by applications and the corresponding physical addresses in RAM. When a process accesses a virtual address, the page table translates it to the corresponding physical address, ensuring the correct retrieval of data. Efficient page table management is essential for minimizing memory access times and optimizing the overall system performance.

Memory fragmentation is a challenge that operating systems must contend with, particularly in systems that handle a multitude of processes with varying memory requirements. Fragmentation occurs when free memory is scattered in small, non-contiguous blocks, making it challenging to allocate large contiguous regions of memory to processes. Operating systems employ various techniques to address fragmentation, such as compaction, where the system rearranges memory to create larger free blocks, and memory segmentation, which divides memory into logical segments to minimize fragmentation.

To enhance memory utilization and performance, modern operating systems employ caching strategies. Caches are small, high-speed memory areas that store frequently accessed data and instructions. By keeping frequently used information in the cache, the operating system reduces the need to access slower main memory, improving overall system responsiveness. Cache management involves algorithms that determine which data to retain in the cache, ensuring that the most relevant and frequently accessed information remains readily available.

Concurrency and multitasking further complicate memory management, as multiple processes may run concurrently and share the same physical memory. The operating system must implement mechanisms to prevent processes from interfering with each other's memory space. Address space isolation ensures that each process operates within its allocated memory region, preventing unauthorized access or modification of data. Techniques such as memory protection, segmentation, and virtual memory address spaces contribute to maintaining the integrity and security of individual processes.

Shared memory is another aspect of memory management that facilitates communication and data exchange between concurrent processes. In scenarios where processes need to collaborate or share information, the operating system provides mechanisms for processes to access a common portion of memory. This shared memory region allows processes to exchange data more efficiently than alternative communication methods, such as inter-process communication (IPC). Shared memory is often employed in multiprocessing environments and parallel computing systems.

Memory management is intimately linked to process scheduling, another crucial aspect of operating system functionality. The scheduler determines which processes have access to the CPU at any given time, influencing their execution order and the timing of context switches. Efficient scheduling contributes to optimal memory utilization by ensuring that processes are allocated CPU time in a manner that maximizes memory throughput. Balancing the demands of

CPU scheduling with the requirements of memory management is essential for achieving overall system efficiency.

In the context of virtualization and cloud computing, where multiple virtual machines may run concurrently on the same physical hardware, memory management becomes a complex challenge. Hypervisors, the software responsible for managing virtual machines, must allocate and control memory resources for each virtual machine while ensuring isolation between them. Techniques such as ballooning, where the hypervisor adjusts the memory allocated to virtual machines dynamically, help optimize resource usage in virtualized environments.

The evolution of memory management techniques reflects the ongoing efforts to enhance system performance, accommodate diverse workloads, and adapt to changing computing paradigms. The development of advanced algorithms for page replacement, memory allocation, and caching aims to strike a balance between the conflicting goals of maximizing resource utilization and minimizing access times. As technology advances, with the proliferation of multi-core processors, large memory capacities, and novel memory architectures, memory management continues to be a focal point of innovation in operating system design.

Challenges persist in the quest for optimal memory management. The trade-offs between speed and capacity, the impact of different access patterns on caching effectiveness, and the need to handle diverse workloads underscore the complexity of the task. Operating systems must continuously evolve their memory management strategies to keep pace with advancements in hardware and changes in computing demands.

In conclusion, memory management is a multifaceted and integral function of operating systems, involving the dynamic allocation, deallocation, and utilization of both physical and virtual memory resources. The operating system, acting as the conductor of this intricate symphony, must balance the conflicting goals of optimal resource utilization, efficient process execution, and responsiveness. Techniques such as virtual memory, page tables, caching, and shared memory contribute to the overall effectiveness of memory management, ensuring that modern computing systems can handle diverse workloads and provide a seamless user experience.

Explore memory allocation, virtual memory, and memory protection mechanisms.

Memory allocation, virtual memory, and memory protection mechanisms are integral aspects of memory management in operating systems, playing a crucial role in optimizing the use of physical and virtual memory, ensuring system stability, and safeguarding data integrity.

Memory allocation involves the dynamic assignment of memory space to processes during their execution. Operating systems must efficiently manage memory to accommodate the varying needs of multiple processes running concurrently. One common method of memory allocation is through the use of memory blocks or pages. These blocks can be dynamically assigned and released based on the requirements of running processes. Allocation techniques include contiguous allocation, where processes are allocated contiguous memory blocks, and non-contiguous allocation, which allows for more flexibility in assigning non-contiguous memory regions. Dynamic memory allocation further enhances flexibility by allocating memory at runtime, enabling processes to request and release memory dynamically.

Virtual memory is a critical concept that extends the addressing capabilities of a computer system beyond its physical memory limits. It provides an abstraction layer, allowing processes to use more memory than is physically available. Virtual memory uses a combination of RAM and secondary storage, such as hard drives, to create an illusion of a vast addressable space. When the physical memory becomes insufficient to accommodate all processes, the operating system employs techniques like paging or swapping. In paging, the operating system divides physical memory into fixed-size blocks called pages, and corresponding virtual memory into fixed-size blocks called page frames. Swapping involves transferring portions of a process's data between RAM and secondary storage as needed, facilitating the efficient use of memory resources.

Page tables are central to the functioning of virtual memory, maintaining the mapping between virtual addresses used by applications and the corresponding physical addresses in RAM. Each process has its own page table, and the operating system uses these tables to translate virtual addresses to physical addresses during memory access. Efficient page table management is crucial for minimizing access times and optimizing overall system performance. Techniques like multi-level page tables or inverted page tables are employed to address scalability and efficiency challenges as the size of virtual memory grows.

Memory protection mechanisms are designed to prevent unauthorized access, modification, or execution of memory regions, contributing to the security and stability of the operating system. Access control mechanisms, implemented through a combination of hardware and software, regulate the permissions granted to processes for interacting with specific memory locations. Common access control permissions include read, write, and execute. Memory protection helps isolate processes from one another, preventing unintended interference and enhancing system security. The use of memory protection is particularly critical in multi-user systems where different users or applications may run concurrently.

Segmentation and paging are two fundamental approaches to memory protection. Segmentation involves dividing a program into logical segments, such as code, data, and stack, each with its own access permissions. This allows for fine-grained control over memory access. Paging, as mentioned earlier in the context of virtual memory, involves dividing physical memory into fixed-size blocks. Each process's memory is divided into pages, and the operating system uses page tables to map virtual pages to physical page frames, enabling efficient memory access and providing a mechanism for access control.

Address space layout randomization (ASLR) is a security technique that enhances memory protection by introducing randomness into the memory address space. ASLR randomizes the starting addresses of various memory regions, including the stack, heap, and libraries, making it more challenging for attackers to predict the location of specific functions or data structures. This adds an additional layer of defense against buffer overflow attacks and other security vulnerabilities that exploit predictable memory layouts.

Memory protection extensions in modern processors, such as the NX (No eXecute) bit, contribute to preventing the execution of code in data regions. This feature is especially relevant in thwarting various types of malicious attacks, including buffer overflow exploits. The NX bit designates certain memory regions as non-executable, reducing the risk of executing injected malicious code.

In the realm of shared memory and inter-process communication (IPC), memory protection mechanisms are crucial to ensuring the integrity of shared data. The operating system must facilitate communication between processes while preventing unintended access or modification of each other's memory space. Techniques like memory-mapped files allow processes to share memory regions, and the operating system enforces access control to regulate the permissions of each process.

Dynamic memory allocation and deallocation, a subset of memory allocation, are central to the efficient use of memory resources in programs. In many programming languages, developers use functions like malloc() and free() to allocate and release memory dynamically during program execution. However, improper memory management, such as memory leaks (unreleased memory) or dangling pointers (accessing memory after it has been deallocated), can lead to instability and performance issues. Memory allocators, implemented by the operating system or programming language runtime, manage the heap, where dynamic memory is allocated, to ensure efficient utilization and deallocation.

Garbage collection is a memory management technique used in programming languages with automatic memory management. Instead of relying on manual memory deallocation, garbage collection identifies and automatically reclaims memory that is no longer in use by the program. This helps prevent memory leaks and simplifies memory management for developers. Various garbage collection algorithms, such as mark-and-sweep, generational, and reference counting, are employed to strike a balance between efficiency and overhead.

Memory fragmentation, both internal and external, poses challenges to memory allocation and utilization. Internal fragmentation occurs when allocated memory blocks are larger than required, leading to wasted space within each block. External fragmentation arises when free memory is scattered in non-contiguous blocks, making it difficult to allocate large contiguous regions of memory. Operating systems employ strategies like compaction, where the system rearranges memory to create larger free blocks, and memory pooling, which involves grouping and managing memory blocks of similar sizes to mitigate fragmentation issues.

In conclusion, memory allocation, virtual memory, and memory protection mechanisms are intricately connected components of memory management in operating systems. Efficient memory allocation ensures optimal utilization of physical and virtual memory resources, supporting the dynamic needs of running processes. Virtual memory extends the addressing capabilities of the system, allowing for the execution of larger and more complex programs. Memory protection mechanisms safeguard against unauthorized access and provide a secure environment for concurrent processes. Together, these elements contribute to the stability, security, and performance of modern computing systems.

Explain how the operating system manages processes and schedules tasks.

The management of processes and the scheduling of tasks are integral functions of an operating system, crucial for efficient resource utilization, responsiveness, and overall system performance. A process, in the context of computing, represents the execution of a program and encompasses the program's code, data, and resources. The operating system must orchestrate the creation, scheduling, and termination of processes to enable concurrent execution and ensure a seamless user experience.

The creation of processes begins with the initiation of a program. When a user launches an application or a system service is triggered, the operating system allocates the necessary resources, including memory, CPU time, and I/O resources, to instantiate a process. Each process operates within its own isolated address space, preventing unintended interference between processes and contributing to system stability and security.

Process scheduling is a pivotal aspect of operating system functionality, determining which processes have access to the CPU at any given time. In a multitasking environment, where multiple processes may be competing for CPU time, the scheduler must make decisions that optimize resource usage and provide fair and responsive execution. The operating system employs scheduling algorithms to determine the order in which processes are granted access to the CPU, with the goal of maximizing throughput, minimizing response times, and ensuring fairness.

Schedulers operate at various levels within the operating system, including the long-term scheduler (job scheduler), the mid-term scheduler, and the short-term scheduler (CPU scheduler). The long-term scheduler focuses on selecting processes from the pool of ready processes, deciding which ones to bring into memory for execution. The mid-term scheduler, also known as the swapper, handles processes that are temporarily swapped out of memory to secondary storage to free up space. The short-term scheduler, operating at a higher frequency, determines the sequence in which processes execute on the CPU.

One of the primary challenges in process scheduling is the need to balance conflicting goals. The scheduler must allocate CPU time fairly among competing processes to ensure responsiveness and user satisfaction. Additionally, the scheduler seeks to maximize CPU throughput by minimizing idle time and keeping the CPU busy. Different scheduling algorithms employ various strategies to strike a balance between these goals.

First-Come, First-Served (FCFS), Shortest Job Next (SJN), Priority Scheduling, and Round Robin are examples of common scheduling algorithms, each with its own advantages and limitations. FCFS follows a simple principle of executing processes in the order they arrive, while SJN prioritizes the execution of the shortest jobs to minimize waiting times. Priority Scheduling assigns priorities to processes based on various factors, and Round Robin allocates fixed time slices (quantum) to each process, ensuring fair access to the CPU.

The preemptive and non-preemptive nature of scheduling algorithms introduces another layer of complexity. Preemptive algorithms allow the scheduler to interrupt a running process and allocate the CPU to another process with higher priority. Non-preemptive algorithms, on the other hand, only initiate context switches when a process voluntarily relinquishes the CPU. The choice between preemptive and non-preemptive scheduling depends on factors such as system responsiveness, fairness, and the nature of the applications being executed.

Context switching is a fundamental operation in process scheduling, involving the saving and restoring of a process's state when it transitions between running and waiting states. Context switching imposes an overhead on the system, as it requires saving and restoring registers, program counters, and other essential information. Minimizing the frequency and cost of context switches is a consideration in designing efficient scheduling algorithms.

Real-time scheduling is a specialized domain within process scheduling, catering to applications with stringent timing requirements. Real-time systems must guarantee that critical tasks are executed within specified time constraints. Operating systems designed for real-time applications employ scheduling algorithms that prioritize tasks based on their deadlines, ensuring timely execution and adherence to predefined schedules. Hard real-time systems demand absolute adherence to deadlines, while soft real-time systems tolerate occasional deadline misses.

In multiprocessor systems, where multiple CPUs are available, the operating system must efficiently distribute tasks among processors to maximize parallelism and throughput. Symmetric Multiprocessing (SMP) and Asymmetric Multiprocessing (AMP) are two common architectures in multiprocessor systems. SMP systems provide a symmetric view of the processors, allowing any processor to execute any task. In AMP systems, each processor is assigned specific tasks, and coordination may be required for interprocessor communication.

Parallelism and concurrency present additional considerations in process scheduling. Parallelism involves the simultaneous execution of multiple tasks, leveraging multiple processors to enhance performance. Concurrent execution, on the other hand, involves the interleaved execution of tasks to create the illusion of simultaneous execution. The operating system must manage these aspects to ensure efficient use of available resources and to exploit the benefits of parallel processing.

Interprocess communication (IPC) is another critical aspect of process management, enabling communication and data exchange between concurrently running processes. Shared memory, message passing, and pipes are common mechanisms for IPC. The operating system must provide secure and efficient IPC mechanisms, facilitating collaboration between processes without compromising system integrity.

Deadlocks represent a potential challenge in process management, occurring when two or more processes are unable to proceed because each is waiting for the other to release a resource. The operating system employs various techniques, such as resource allocation graphs and deadlock detection algorithms, to identify and resolve deadlocks. Strategies may involve preemptively terminating processes or releasing resources to break the deadlock.

Security considerations are paramount in process management. The operating system must enforce access controls to prevent unauthorized access or modification of processes and their resources. User authentication, process isolation, and privilege levels contribute to a secure execution environment. In multi-user systems, the operating system ensures that each user's processes are isolated and cannot interfere with one another.

The evolution of process management reflects the changing landscape of computing. As systems become more complex, with diverse workloads, varying hardware architectures, and the advent of cloud computing, process management strategies must adapt to meet new challenges. Emerging technologies, such as containers and virtualization, introduce additional layers of abstraction and introduce novel approaches to process management.

In conclusion, the management of processes and the scheduling of tasks are foundational functions of operating systems, shaping the overall efficiency, responsiveness, and user experience of computer systems. Process creation, scheduling algorithms, context switching, real-time considerations, multiprocessor systems, parallelism, IPC mechanisms, deadlock prevention, and security measures are all integral aspects of process management. The operating system must navigate a complex landscape, balancing conflicting goals to provide a robust and efficient environment for the execution of diverse applications and workloads.

Introduce process scheduling algorithms and their impact on system performance.

Process scheduling algorithms are fundamental components of operating systems, responsible for determining the order in which processes are granted access to the CPU. These algorithms play a crucial role in optimizing system performance, responsiveness, and resource utilization in multitasking environments where multiple processes vie for CPU time. The choice of scheduling algorithm directly influences the overall efficiency, fairness, and user experience of the operating system.

One of the simplest scheduling algorithms is First-Come, First-Served (FCFS), which executes processes in the order they arrive in the ready queue. While FCFS is straightforward, it can lead to the "convoy effect," where short processes are delayed by longer ones, impacting overall system throughput. Shortest Job Next (SJN), also known as Shortest Job First (SJF), prioritizes the execution of the shortest jobs to minimize waiting times and enhance system responsiveness. SJN is optimal in minimizing average waiting times but requires knowledge of the job lengths, which may not be available in real-world scenarios.

Priority Scheduling assigns priorities to processes based on various factors, allowing the scheduler to favor high-priority processes.

This approach is versatile, enabling the system to cater to specific requirements or priorities assigned by the user or the system itself. However, priority scheduling can lead to starvation, where low-priority processes may be indefinitely delayed if higher-priority processes are continually introduced.

Round Robin (RR) scheduling is a preemptive algorithm that allocates fixed time slices, known as quantums, to each process in a cyclic manner. RR ensures fair access to the CPU, preventing any single process from monopolizing it for extended periods. While RR is simple and fair, it may result in high turnaround times for processes with short burst times, leading to inefficient use of CPU resources.

Multilevel Queue Scheduling involves categorizing processes into different priority levels or queues, each with its own scheduling algorithm. This approach accommodates the varying needs of processes and tasks with different priority levels, enhancing both responsiveness and fairness. However, it requires careful tuning of priority levels to avoid potential issues like starvation or excessive execution times for low-priority processes.

Multilevel Feedback Queue Scheduling builds upon multilevel queue scheduling by allowing processes to move between different queues based on their behavior. Processes that use less CPU time may be promoted to higher-priority queues, while those with longer CPU bursts may be demoted. This adaptive mechanism aims to provide responsiveness to interactive processes and fairness to CPU-bound processes, striking a balance between different types of workloads.

Real-time Scheduling is designed for applications with stringent timing requirements, where tasks must be completed within specific deadlines. Hard real-time systems demand absolute adherence to deadlines, while soft real-time systems tolerate occasional misses. Rate Monotonic Scheduling (RMS) is a popular algorithm for real-time systems, assigning priorities based on the inverse of the task period. Earliest Deadline First (EDF) is another real-time scheduling algorithm that prioritizes tasks based on their imminent deadlines.

The impact of process scheduling algorithms on system performance is multi-faceted. Throughput, the number of processes completed in a given time, is a critical metric influenced by scheduling decisions. Efficient scheduling algorithms aim to maximize throughput by minimizing idle CPU time and keeping the CPU busy with productive tasks. Responsiveness is another key factor, especially in interactive systems where users expect swift responses to their inputs. Scheduling algorithms must prioritize tasks with short execution times to reduce waiting times and enhance system responsiveness.

Fairness is a crucial consideration in the design of scheduling algorithms, ensuring that all processes, regardless of their priority or characteristics, have equitable access to the CPU. Unfair scheduling can lead to processes being starved of CPU time, impacting overall system performance and user satisfaction. Striking a balance between fairness and throughput is a continuous challenge in the development of scheduling algorithms.

The impact of scheduling algorithms extends to resource utilization, influencing how effectively system resources are utilized for task execution. Efficient algorithms optimize resource usage, preventing bottlenecks or resource monopolization by specific processes. In contrast, suboptimal scheduling decisions may lead to inefficient use of CPU and other resources, affecting the overall performance of the system.

Context switching overhead is an inherent aspect of scheduling algorithms, representing the cost associated with saving and restoring the state of processes during transitions between running and waiting states. Frequent and resource-intensive context switches can degrade system performance, emphasizing the need for scheduling algorithms that minimize context switching overhead. Preemptive scheduling algorithms, such as Round Robin or Priority Scheduling, may incur more context switches than non-preemptive algorithms, such as FCFS or SJN.

The design of scheduling algorithms is also influenced by the characteristics of the workload and the nature of the applications running on the system. Batch processing systems, characterized by non-interactive tasks, may benefit from algorithms that prioritize throughput over responsiveness. On the other hand, interactive systems, where user interaction is frequent, demand scheduling algorithms that prioritize quick response times to user inputs.

Advancements in hardware architectures, such as the rise of multicore processors, pose additional challenges for scheduling algorithms. While traditional algorithms were designed for single-core systems, modern scheduling must account for the parallelism offered by multiple cores. Load balancing mechanisms become crucial to distribute tasks evenly across cores, preventing underutilization or overutilization of specific CPU cores.

The choice of scheduling algorithm is often context-dependent, with no one-size-fits-all solution. Real-world operating systems may use a combination of scheduling algorithms or employ adaptive strategies to dynamically adjust scheduling decisions based on the characteristics of the workload. The Linux scheduler, for example, uses the Completely Fair Scheduler (CFS) for general-purpose tasks and the Round Robin scheduler for real-time tasks, providing a balanced approach to scheduling in different contexts.

In conclusion, process scheduling algorithms are pivotal elements in operating systems, influencing system performance, responsiveness, fairness, and resource utilization. The design of effective scheduling algorithms involves a trade-off between competing goals, including throughput, responsiveness, fairness, and adaptability to diverse workloads. As computing environments evolve with new technologies and usage patterns, the ongoing refinement and innovation of scheduling algorithms remain essential to meet the challenges of contemporary computing.

Explore the structure of file systems in operating systems.

The structure of file systems in operating systems is a critical aspect of data management, providing the organizational framework for storing, retrieving, and manipulating files. A file system is responsible for managing how data is stored on storage devices, ensuring efficient access, and providing a hierarchical structure that organizes files and directories. The design and structure of file systems have evolved over time to accommodate the increasing complexity of storage devices, diverse data types, and the demands of modern computing.

At the core of any file system is the concept of a file, which serves as a logical unit for organizing and storing data. Files can be documents, programs, images, or any other type of digital information. The file system abstracts the physical storage details, allowing users and applications to interact with files through a user-friendly interface. File systems also facilitate the creation, deletion, and modification of files, providing a mechanism for organizing data in a coherent manner.

The hierarchical structure of file systems is typically represented as a tree-like directory structure. Directories, also known as folders, serve as containers for files and other directories. Each directory can contain multiple files and subdirectories, creating a nested and organized layout. This hierarchical arrangement simplifies the process of locating and managing files, allowing users to navigate through the directory structure to access the desired data.

One of the earliest file systems is the File Allocation Table (FAT), which gained prominence in early Microsoft operating systems such as MS-DOS and Windows. FAT uses a simple table that maps file names to storage locations on the disk. Each file is associated with an entry in the FAT, specifying the clusters or blocks where its data is stored. While straightforward, FAT has limitations, including inefficiencies in space utilization and challenges in handling larger storage capacities.

The New Technology File System (NTFS), developed by Microsoft, represents a more sophisticated and advanced file system. NTFS incorporates features such as improved security, file compression, encryption, and support for larger file sizes and volumes. NTFS also implements a journaling mechanism, which records changes to the file system in a transaction log, enhancing reliability and recovery capabilities. These advancements make NTFS suitable for modern computing environments, supporting both personal computers and servers.

Another widely used file system is the Hierarchical File System (HFS+), developed by Apple Inc. HFS+ is the file system used in Apple's macOS operating system. It features a B-tree structure for directory organization, enabling faster file lookup and access. HFS+ supports journaling for enhanced data integrity and includes features like file compression and encryption. However, as storage technologies and computing demands evolve, Apple has transitioned to the Apple File System (APFS) in more recent macOS versions.

The Linux operating system commonly employs file systems such as ext2, ext3, and ext4. The ext2 file system is an early Linux file system that lacks features like journaling, making it more susceptible to data corruption in the event of system crashes. Ext3 introduced journaling for improved reliability, while ext4 further enhances performance and scalability. Ext4 supports larger file sizes, improved file allocation, and reduced fragmentation, making it a suitable choice for modern Linux distributions.

As storage capacities and data volumes continue to grow, new file systems have emerged to address the challenges posed by evolving technologies. The Z File System (ZFS) is a notable example, developed by Sun Microsystems and later embraced by the open-source community. ZFS introduces features such as pooled storage, copy-on-write snapshots, data integrity checks, and automatic error correction. ZFS is designed to handle large storage capacities efficiently, making it well-suited for file servers and storage appliances.

The concept of distributed file systems has gained prominence with the advent of networked and cloud computing. Distributed file systems, such as the Network File System (NFS) and the Common Internet File System (CIFS), enable file sharing and access over a network. NFS, developed by Sun Microsystems, allows files to be shared among networked computers as if they were local. CIFS, also known as the Server Message Block (SMB) protocol, is commonly used in Windows environments for file and printer sharing. These distributed file systems facilitate collaboration and data sharing among interconnected systems.

Modern file systems also incorporate advanced features to enhance data security and protect against data loss. Encryption mechanisms, both at the file and disk levels, provide a layer of confidentiality for sensitive data. File permissions and access controls regulate user and application access to files, ensuring that only authorized entities can modify or view specific data. These security features are crucial in safeguarding data integrity and preventing unauthorized access.

File systems play a pivotal role in supporting features like file versioning, allowing users to track changes and revert to previous states of a file. This capability is particularly valuable in collaborative environments where multiple users may contribute to a shared set of documents. Versioning mechanisms, integrated into file systems or provided by version control systems, contribute to data resilience and collaborative workflows.

The adoption of solid-state drives (SSDs) and non-volatile memory express (NVMe) storage technologies has prompted the development of file systems optimized for flash-based storage. File systems like F2FS (Flash-Friendly File System) and Btrfs (B-tree file system) are designed to maximize the performance and lifespan of SSDs. F2FS employs log-structured techniques for efficient write operations on flash memory, while Btrfs integrates features like copy-on-write, snapshots, and data deduplication.

The evolution of file systems reflects the dynamic nature of computing environments, responding to the challenges posed by advancements in storage technologies, scalability requirements, and the need for enhanced data management capabilities. Research and development efforts continue to explore novel file system designs that address emerging trends, including the proliferation of data in cloud environments, the rise of edge computing, and the demand for seamless data access across diverse devices.

In conclusion, the structure of file systems in operating systems provides the foundation for organizing, storing, and managing digital data. From hierarchical directory structures to advanced features like journaling, encryption, and distributed file systems, the design and capabilities of file systems have evolved to meet the demands of modern computing. The choice of file system influences factors such as data integrity, access speed, security, and scalability, making it a critical consideration in the design and implementation of operating systems for diverse computing environments.

Discuss file organization, directory structures, and file access methods.

File organization, directory structures, and file access methods are integral components of file systems, playing a crucial role in managing and retrieving data efficiently within operating systems. The organization of files on storage devices involves the arrangement of data to optimize access times, space utilization, and overall system performance. Various directory structures provide a hierarchical framework for organizing files and directories, simplifying the navigation and management of data. File access methods define how applications and users interact with files, influencing the speed and efficiency of read and write operations.

The organization of files within storage devices is a fundamental consideration in file systems. A common approach is sequential file organization, where records are stored consecutively without any specific order. While straightforward, sequential organization may lead to inefficient access times for specific operations, especially when searching for a particular record. To address this limitation, indexed file organization introduces an index that maps key values to the corresponding storage locations. This allows for faster searches and retrieval of specific records, making indexed organization suitable for scenarios where quick access to specific data is essential.

Another approach to file organization is the use of hashing techniques, where a hash function determines the storage location of records based on their key values. Hashing can offer fast access times for certain types of searches, but collisions—occurrences where multiple records map to the same location—need to be carefully managed. Techniques like chaining or open addressing are employed to resolve collisions and ensure the integrity of the hash-based file organization.

In addition to these methods, tree-based file organizations, such as the B-tree and B+ tree structures, provide a balanced and hierarchical approach. These tree structures maintain order and balance within the file organization, enabling efficient search, insertion, and deletion operations. B-trees, for example, are commonly used in file systems and databases to achieve logarithmic time complexity for various operations, making them suitable for large-scale storage scenarios.

Directory structures play a pivotal role in organizing and managing files within file systems. The hierarchical directory structure, commonly represented as a tree, allows for the nesting of directories within other directories. Each directory can contain files and subdirectories, creating a structured and navigable organization. This hierarchical approach simplifies the process of locating and managing files, providing users with an intuitive means of organizing and accessing their data.

One of the earliest and widely used directory structures is the single-level directory, where all files are stored in a single directory. While simple, this structure becomes unwieldy as the number of files increases, leading to difficulties in file management and retrieval. To address this limitation, the two-level directory structure introduces a master directory that contains subdirectories, providing a more organized approach to file organization.

The tree-structured directory is a natural evolution, allowing for the creation of nested subdirectories within parent directories. This hierarchical structure mirrors the organization of files on storage devices and simplifies file management. However, deeper directory hierarchies may lead to longer path names, potentially impacting user experience and file navigation. Balancing depth and breadth within the directory structure is crucial for creating an efficient and user-friendly organization.

The acyclic-graph directory structure, represented as a directed acyclic graph (DAG), introduces a more flexible organization by allowing directories to have multiple parents. This enables shared organization of files without the need for duplication, enhancing efficiency in scenarios where files belong to multiple categories or projects. While offering flexibility, the acyclic-graph structure requires careful management to prevent issues like cycles, which could complicate file access and navigation.

Modern file systems often incorporate a hybrid approach, combining the strengths of different directory structures. For instance, the Unix File System (UFS) and Linux File System (ext4) use a tree-structured directory along with an inode structure to efficiently represent file attributes and manage space allocation. Similarly, the New

Technology File System (NTFS) used in Windows environments employs a B-tree directory structure, providing a balanced and scalable organization.

File access methods define how applications and users interact with files in terms of reading, writing, and updating data. The most basic access method is sequential access, where data is read or written in a linear fashion from the beginning to the end of the file. Sequential access is suitable for scenarios where data is processed in a predefined order and does not require random access. However, it may be inefficient for tasks that involve searching for specific data within the file.

Random access, on the other hand, allows for direct access to any part of the file, enabling efficient retrieval and modification of data at specific locations. This access method is facilitated through techniques like indexing, where a data structure, such as a table or tree, maps logical addresses to physical locations within the file. Random access is essential for applications that require quick access to specific data points without scanning the entire file sequentially.

Relative and direct access methods provide a balance between sequential and random access. Relative access uses record numbers or identifiers to access specific records within a file, offering faster access than sequential methods but not as direct as random access. Direct access, also known as direct file organization, allows direct access to files based on a unique key or identifier. These methods are commonly used in database systems where efficient retrieval of specific records is crucial.

File access methods also incorporate caching mechanisms to optimize data retrieval. Caching involves storing frequently accessed data in a faster, temporary storage area (cache) to reduce access times. This is particularly beneficial for read-intensive operations, enhancing overall system performance by minimizing the need to retrieve data from slower storage devices.

Concurrency control mechanisms are essential in multi-user environments where multiple processes may access and modify the same file simultaneously. Locking mechanisms, such as read and write locks, prevent conflicts and ensure data consistency by restricting access to files during write operations. Transactional file systems, which implement atomicity, consistency, isolation, and durability (ACID) properties, provide a higher level of data integrity and reliability in environments with concurrent access.

In conclusion, file organization, directory structures, and file access methods are foundational elements of file systems, shaping how data is stored, organized, and accessed within operating systems. The choice of file organization and directory structure influences the efficiency of file management, while file access methods define the speed and flexibility of data retrieval and modification. The evolving landscape of computing, with advancements in storage technologies and the rise of distributed computing, continues to drive innovation in file system design to meet the diverse demands of modern computing environments.

Chapter 3: The Role of Drivers in Device Management

Define what device drivers are and their crucial role in device management.

Device drivers are essential software components that facilitate communication between the operating system and hardware devices in a computing system. These drivers serve as intermediaries, translating high-level operating system commands and requests into language and instructions that specific hardware devices can understand and execute. The role of device drivers is crucial in device management, as they bridge the gap between the abstraction provided by the operating system and the unique communication protocols and functionalities of individual hardware components.

At its core, the operating system interacts with devices through a set of standard interfaces and abstractions. These abstractions, such as input/output operations, file systems, and communication protocols, allow the operating system to communicate with devices in a uniform manner, irrespective of the underlying hardware. However, the vast diversity of hardware devices—from graphics cards and network adapters to printers and storage devices—requires specialized software to enable seamless integration with the operating system.

Device drivers act as translators that enable this seamless integration. They encapsulate the intricate details of device-specific operations, hiding the complexities from the rest of the operating system and applications. In doing so, device drivers allow a degree of hardware abstraction, presenting a standardized interface that the operating system and applications can interact with consistently, regardless of the underlying hardware intricacies.

One of the primary functions of device drivers is to facilitate the initialization and configuration of hardware devices during system startup. When a computer boots, the operating system relies on device drivers to identify, initialize, and configure the connected hardware components. This process involves the allocation of resources, such as memory addresses and interrupt request (IRQ) lines, which ensure that each device can operate harmoniously within the system. The device driver communicates with the hardware during this initialization phase, setting parameters and establishing the necessary connections to make the device operational.

In the context of device management, device drivers play a pivotal role in enabling the operating system to manage and control the hardware effectively. This involves the handling of device-specific operations, such as sending and receiving data, managing power states, and responding to various events and signals from the hardware. Device drivers provide a standardized interface for these operations, allowing the operating system to issue commands and retrieve information without needing to understand the intricate details of each device's inner workings.

Moreover, device drivers play a crucial role in ensuring the stability and reliability of the overall system. They are responsible for error handling and recovery mechanisms, managing potential conflicts between devices, and addressing unforeseen issues that may arise during the operation of the hardware. By encapsulating device-specific complexities within the driver, the operating system is shielded from the nuances of different hardware implementations, contributing to a more robust and stable computing environment.

Device drivers are not static entities; they need to be updated and adapted to accommodate changes in hardware, bug fixes, and improvements in performance. Operating systems provide mechanisms for dynamically loading and unloading device drivers to accommodate changes in the system's configuration. This dynamic nature is especially important in modern computing environments where hardware configurations can vary widely, and new devices are regularly introduced to the market.

The device driver ecosystem is vast and diverse, with each hardware component requiring a specific driver tailored to its unique characteristics and functionalities. Graphics drivers, for example, are responsible for facilitating communication between the operating system and the graphics processing unit (GPU), enabling rendering and display functions. Similarly, network drivers enable communication between the operating system and network interface cards (NICs), allowing for data transmission over networks. Without appropriately designed and implemented device drivers, these hardware components would be non-functional within the operating system environment.

The development of device drivers requires a deep understanding of both hardware and software systems. Device driver programmers need to navigate the intricate details of hardware specifications, communication protocols, and data transfer mechanisms. Simultaneously, they must be adept at working within the framework of the operating system, utilizing its provided APIs and abstractions to ensure compatibility and consistency across different hardware platforms.

Device drivers also play a critical role in the performance optimization of hardware components. Through careful design and efficient coding practices, device drivers can enhance the overall efficiency and responsiveness of hardware devices. For instance, graphics drivers can implement optimizations to accelerate rendering processes, network drivers can prioritize data traffic for improved network performance, and storage drivers can implement caching mechanisms to enhance data retrieval speeds.

In the context of device management, device drivers contribute to the overall system's efficiency by enabling the operating system to orchestrate the concurrent operation of multiple devices. Multitasking and parallel processing, which are essential features of modern computing systems, rely on effective device management facilitated by well-designed and well-implemented device drivers. The operating system can delegate tasks to various devices concurrently, optimizing resource utilization and enhancing overall system performance.

Device drivers also play a crucial role in supporting plug-and-play functionality, allowing users to connect new devices to their systems seamlessly. When a user connects a new device, the operating system relies on the appropriate device driver to recognize, configure, and make the device accessible to the user and applications. This plug-and-play capability simplifies the user experience, enabling the straightforward integration of new hardware without requiring intricate manual configurations.

In summary, device drivers serve as indispensable components in the realm of device management within operating systems. Their crucial role lies in mediating between the standardized abstractions provided by the operating system and the specific intricacies of diverse hardware components. Device drivers enable the initialization, configuration, and efficient operation of hardware devices, ensuring stability, reliability, and optimal performance in modern computing environments. The development and maintenance of robust device drivers are essential for the seamless integration and effective management of the diverse array of hardware components that constitute contemporary computer systems.

Explore how drivers act as intermediaries between hardware devices and the operating system.

Device drivers serve as crucial intermediaries between hardware devices and the operating system, playing a pivotal role in facilitating seamless communication and coordination. In the intricate dance of computing, where diverse hardware components need to interact with a standardized operating system environment, drivers act as translators, enabling the two entities to understand and collaborate despite their inherent differences. These software components operate at the interface between the hardware and the operating system, providing a layer of abstraction that shields the OS and applications from the intricate details of individual hardware implementations.

At the most fundamental level, drivers bridge the gap between the abstracted world of the operating system and the tangible, physical realm of hardware. The operating system interacts with hardware through standardized interfaces and abstractions, offering a high-level view that simplifies complex operations into well-defined commands. However, the specific ways in which devices execute these commands, manage resources, and respond to various requests are unique to each piece of hardware. Device drivers step in to interpret these high-level commands and translate them into low-level instructions that the hardware can understand and execute.

Initialization of hardware devices during the system's startup is a critical aspect of the driver's role. As the operating system boots, it relies on device drivers to identify and configure the connected hardware components. This process involves establishing communication channels, allocating memory resources, setting interrupt request (IRQ) lines, and ensuring that each device is initialized in a manner conducive to harmonious operation within the system. Device drivers orchestrate this complex symphony of interactions, communicating directly with the hardware to bring it into a functional state.

A key function of drivers is to provide a standardized interface for the operating system and applications to interact with different types of hardware. Since hardware manufacturers design devices with diverse architectures, communication protocols, and data transfer mechanisms, a universal language is needed for the operating system to manage these devices effectively. Device drivers encapsulate the intricacies of specific hardware implementations, presenting a consistent and abstracted interface that the operating system and applications can utilize without needing to understand the unique details of each device.

In essence, device drivers act as envoys between the operating system and hardware, negotiating the terms of communication. When an application issues a command to, for example, print a document, the operating system forwards this command to the appropriate device driver responsible for managing the printer. The device driver then takes on the responsibility of translating the command into a series of low-level instructions that the printer can comprehend. This might involve specifying the print resolution, color settings, and paper size—all in a language the printer understands.

Error handling and recovery mechanisms are integral aspects of a device driver's responsibilities. Hardware environments are dynamic and unpredictable, and errors or unexpected events can occur during the operation of devices. Device drivers need to anticipate and manage these situations to ensure the stability and reliability of the overall system. Whether it's a communication error with a peripheral device, a malfunctioning sensor, or a power fluctuation affecting a component, device drivers implement protocols for detecting, reporting, and, when possible, recovering from these issues.

The dynamic nature of computing environments requires device drivers to be adaptable and capable of accommodating changes in the system's configuration. Plug-and-play functionality, where users can connect new devices to their systems seamlessly, relies on the ability of device drivers to recognize and integrate new hardware components. When a user plugs in a new device, the operating system relies on the appropriate device driver to identify, configure, and make the device accessible to the user and applications. The driver ensures that the new hardware seamlessly integrates into the existing system, providing a smooth and user-friendly experience.

Device drivers are not static entities; they are subject to updates and modifications to accommodate changes in hardware, fix bugs, and improve performance. Operating systems provide mechanisms for dynamically loading and unloading device drivers to respond to changes in the system's configuration. This dynamic nature is particularly crucial in modern computing environments where hardware configurations can vary widely, and new devices are regularly introduced to the market. Updating drivers allows the operating system to remain compatible with the latest hardware and benefit from improvements in functionality and performance.

The diverse array of hardware components in a typical computing environment—from graphics cards, network adapters, and storage devices to sensors, cameras, and printers—requires an equally diverse set of device drivers. Each device driver is tailored to the unique characteristics and functionalities of a specific hardware component. Graphics drivers, for example, are responsible for managing communication between the operating system and the graphics processing unit (GPU), enabling rendering and display functions. Network drivers facilitate communication between the operating system and network interface cards (NICs), enabling data transmission over networks. Without appropriately designed and implemented device drivers, these hardware components would be non-functional within the operating system environment.

Device drivers are at the forefront of optimizing the performance of hardware components. Through careful design and efficient coding practices, device drivers can enhance the overall efficiency and responsiveness of hardware devices. For instance, graphics drivers can implement optimizations to accelerate rendering processes, network drivers can prioritize data traffic for improved network performance, and storage drivers can implement caching mechanisms to enhance data retrieval speeds. By fine-tuning the interactions between the operating system and hardware, device drivers contribute significantly to the overall performance of computing systems.

Concurrency control mechanisms are essential in multi-user environments where multiple processes may access and modify the same hardware simultaneously. Locking mechanisms, such as read and write locks implemented by device drivers, prevent conflicts and ensure data consistency by restricting access to the hardware during write operations. Transactional device drivers, which implement atomicity, consistency, isolation, and durability (ACID) properties, provide a higher level of data integrity and reliability in environments with concurrent access. These mechanisms ensure that the interactions between the operating system, applications, and hardware are coordinated and free from conflicts that could compromise data integrity.

Device drivers are integral to supporting the plug-and-play functionality that modern users expect. When a user connects a new device, whether it's a USB drive, a printer, or a camera, the operating system relies on the appropriate device driver to recognize, configure, and make the device accessible. This seamless integration of new hardware without intricate manual configurations simplifies the user experience, making it more accessible and user-friendly. Plug-and-play functionality is particularly crucial in scenarios where users frequently connect and disconnect devices, such as in mobile computing environments.

In conclusion, device drivers act as indispensable intermediaries between hardware devices and the operating system, enabling seamless communication and coordination in the dynamic world of computing. By translating high-level operating system commands into instructions that specific hardware devices can understand and execute, device drivers provide a crucial layer of abstraction that ensures compatibility, stability, and optimal performance. As technology continues to advance, the role of device drivers remains pivotal in bridging the ever-expanding gap between diverse hardware implementations and the standardized environments provided by operating systems.

Identify and explain various types of device drivers, such as kernel-mode and user-mode drivers.

Device drivers come in various types, each designed to fulfill specific functions and operate within distinct contexts. One fundamental classification is based on the mode in which they run, distinguishing between kernel-mode and user-mode drivers. Understanding these distinctions is crucial for comprehending the hierarchy and responsibilities within a computing system.

Kernel-mode drivers, also known as system-level drivers, operate in the privileged and protected kernel space of the operating system. This mode grants them direct access to the hardware and core functionalities of the system. Kernel-mode drivers are essential for interacting with critical system components, managing hardware resources, and facilitating efficient communication between the operating system kernel and hardware devices. Their elevated privileges, however, come with increased responsibility, as any error or instability in a kernel-mode driver can potentially compromise the entire system's stability. Examples of kernel-mode drivers include those for managing file systems, memory, and low-level communication with hardware devices.

On the other hand, user-mode drivers operate in a less privileged and isolated space, distinct from the core kernel functions. These drivers run in the user space of the operating system, interacting with applications and providing a bridge between user-level processes and the kernel-mode drivers. Unlike kernel-mode drivers, user-mode drivers lack direct access to hardware and must rely on kernel-mode drivers to perform low-level interactions with the system. While this confinement reduces the risk of catastrophic system failures resulting from errors in user-mode drivers, it also imposes limitations on their capabilities. Common examples of user-mode drivers include those for managing printers, scanners, and other peripheral devices.

Another crucial classification is based on the function or purpose of the device driver. A distinction can be made between file system drivers, which manage the storage and retrieval of data on various storage devices, and network drivers, which facilitate communication between the operating system and network interfaces. File system drivers play a fundamental role in translating high-level file operations issued by the operating system into low-level instructions that interact with storage devices, ensuring proper storage, retrieval, and organization of data. Network drivers, on the other hand, are responsible for handling the communication protocols necessary for data transmission over networks, managing network interfaces, and enabling connectivity.

Graphics drivers constitute another significant category, responsible for facilitating communication between the operating system and graphics hardware, such as GPUs (Graphics Processing Units). These drivers are crucial for rendering graphical content, managing display resolutions, and supporting features like hardware-accelerated graphics. Graphics drivers operate in both kernel and user modes, with the kernel-mode component handling low-level interactions with the hardware, while the user-mode component facilitates communication with graphical applications.

Print drivers, commonly used for printers and multifunction devices, represent yet another type of device driver. These drivers translate print commands issued by the operating system and applications into instructions that printers understand. They manage print queues, handle print job spooling, and ensure the correct interpretation of print data to produce the desired output. Print drivers can operate in both kernel and user modes, depending on the specific requirements of the printing subsystem.

Storage drivers encompass a diverse range of drivers responsible for managing various storage devices, including hard drives, solid-state drives, and external storage. These drivers handle tasks such as disk initialization, partitioning, and formatting, ensuring that the storage devices are properly integrated into the operating system's file system. Storage drivers can also implement features like caching and data retrieval optimization to enhance overall system performance.

Input/output (I/O) drivers play a critical role in managing interactions between the operating system and input or output devices. These drivers facilitate the communication between the system and devices such as keyboards, mice, USB devices, and audio peripherals. I/O drivers interpret user inputs, handle data transfers, and manage the flow of information between the operating system and external devices. Examples include USB drivers that enable the connectivity of various USB devices and audio drivers responsible for processing and transmitting sound data.

Furthermore, bus drivers represent a category of device drivers that manage the communication between the operating system and the system's buses or interconnects. Buses are pathways through which various hardware components, such as processors, memory, and peripheral devices, communicate with each other. Bus drivers ensure that these components can interact seamlessly, managing data transfer, addressing, and other bus-specific operations. Examples include PCI (Peripheral Component Interconnect) bus drivers and USB bus drivers.

Power management drivers are designed to optimize the energy consumption of a computing system. These drivers play a crucial role in managing power states, determining when devices can enter low-power modes, and coordinating the overall power usage of the system. Power management drivers work closely with the operating system's power management features to ensure efficiency and extend the battery life of mobile devices.

Moreover, firmware drivers interact with firmware components embedded in hardware devices. Firmware is software that is permanently stored in hardware and provides essential functionalities for device initialization and operation. Firmware drivers facilitate communication between the operating system and firmware, enabling the system to leverage the capabilities embedded in hardware components. Examples include BIOS (Basic Input/Output System) drivers, which interact with the firmware responsible for initializing the computer's hardware during the boot process.

Each type of device driver serves a specific purpose, contributing to the overall functionality and efficiency of the computing system. The interplay between kernel-mode and user-mode drivers, combined with the diverse functionalities of specific drivers, creates a comprehensive framework that enables the operating system to seamlessly interact with an extensive array of hardware devices. As technology advances, the development and refinement of device drivers remain critical to ensuring compatibility, stability, and optimal performance in the ever-evolving landscape of computing environments.

Discuss the differences and specific use cases for each type.

Natural language processing (NLP), natural language understanding (NLU), and natural language generation (NLG) are three interrelated yet distinct fields within the broader scope of artificial intelligence (AI) that focus on the interaction between computers and human language. NLP involves the development of algorithms and models that enable computers to understand, interpret, and respond to human language in a way that is both meaningful and contextually relevant. It encompasses a wide range of tasks, from simple ones like text classification and sentiment analysis to more complex tasks like machine translation and language generation. NLU, on the other hand, is a subset of NLP that specifically deals with the comprehension of human language, aiming to enable machines to not only recognize patterns in language but also to derive meaning and context from it. This involves parsing and extracting information from text, understanding the relationships between words, and discerning the nuances of human communication.

NLG, distinct from both NLP and NLU, is concerned with the generation of human-like language by machines. It involves creating algorithms and models that can produce coherent and contextually appropriate text based on input data or prompts. While NLP and NLU focus on understanding existing language, NLG is about generating new language that is indistinguishable from what a human might produce. One of the primary use cases for NLP is in information retrieval, where algorithms process large volumes of textual data to extract relevant information or insights. Search engines, for example, heavily rely on NLP to understand user queries and provide relevant search results. Sentiment analysis, another NLP application, involves determining the sentiment expressed in a piece of text, which is valuable for businesses to gauge customer opinions and feedback.

NLU, being a subset of NLP, is integral to applications that require a deeper understanding of language. One significant use case is in virtual assistants like Siri or Alexa, where NLU enables the system to comprehend and respond to user queries in a natural and contextually relevant manner. Another crucial application of NLU is in chatbots, where the system needs to understand user inputs, derive meaning, and generate appropriate responses. By focusing on comprehension, NLU enhances the effectiveness of systems in tasks such as text summarization, where the goal is to condense large amounts of information while retaining the essential meaning.

NLG, with its emphasis on generating human-like language, finds application in various domains. One notable use case is in report generation, where NLG systems can analyze data and automatically produce written reports in a coherent and understandable manner. This is particularly beneficial in industries such as finance, where large datasets can be synthesized into comprehensible narratives. NLG is also employed in content creation, ranging from news articles and marketing copy to creative writing. Automated content generation not only saves time but also ensures consistency and quality in the produced content.

Despite their distinct roles, NLP, NLU, and NLG often collaborate to create more sophisticated AI systems. For instance, in machine translation, NLP is used to understand the source language (NLU), and NLG is employed to generate the corresponding text in the target language. This collaborative approach is evident in the development of conversational AI, where NLU enables understanding user inputs, NLP processes and interprets the information, and NLG generates appropriate and contextually relevant responses. Such integrated systems have paved the way for advanced applications like virtual customer service agents and language translation services.

The challenges within each domain also highlight their differences. NLP often faces difficulties in handling ambiguity and context, as human language is inherently nuanced and context-dependent. NLU, being a more specialized field, grapples with the complexity of understanding semantics, pragmatics, and the intricacies of human communication. NLG, on the other hand, deals with the challenge of generating diverse and contextually appropriate language that mirrors human expression. Addressing these challenges requires continuous advancements in machine learning algorithms, deep neural networks, and language models.

In conclusion, NLP, NLU, and NLG represent integral components of AI that collectively contribute to the development of systems capable of understanding, interpreting, and generating human language. NLP serves as the overarching field, encompassing a wide range of applications focused on language processing. NLU, as a subset, delves deeper into language comprehension, facilitating more nuanced interactions. NLG, distinct in its emphasis on language generation, finds applications in report generation, content creation, and various creative domains. The synergy between these fields is evident in the evolution of conversational AI and other advanced language-centric applications. As technology continues to advance, these three domains will likely continue to converge, leading to more sophisticated AI systems with enhanced language capabilities.

Detail the process of installing and configuring device drivers.

Installing and configuring device drivers is a crucial aspect of setting up and maintaining hardware components in a computer system. The process involves a series of steps that ensure proper communication between the operating system and the hardware devices, enabling them to function seamlessly. To initiate this process, it is essential to understand the role of device drivers. These are specialized software programs that facilitate communication between the operating system and the hardware components, translating generic commands from the OS into specific instructions that the hardware can understand and execute. Device drivers act as intermediaries, bridging the gap between the high-level language of the operating system and the low-level language of the hardware.

The initial step in the installation and configuration of device drivers often begins with the purchase of a new hardware component, such as a graphics card, printer, or network adapter. Most hardware manufacturers provide a CD or downloadable drivers from their official website. These drivers are essential for the proper functioning of the hardware with the specific operating system. In some cases, the operating system itself may include generic drivers for basic functionality, but for optimal performance and access to advanced features, it is recommended to install the manufacturer's drivers.

The installation process typically starts with the insertion of the installation media or running the downloaded driver executable. The installation wizard guides users through the process, prompting them to agree to the terms and conditions, selecting a destination folder, and specifying any additional configuration settings. During this stage, the installer copies necessary files to the system and may prompt for a system reboot to complete the installation. Rebooting is crucial as it allows the operating system to recognize and integrate the newly installed drivers into its configuration.

Once the device driver is installed, the next step involves configuring the driver settings to optimize performance and ensure compatibility with the system. Configuration options vary depending on the type of hardware. For example, graphics card drivers often include settings related to screen resolution, refresh rate, and 3D acceleration. Network adapter drivers may involve configurations for IP addressing, DNS settings, and other network-related parameters. Printers and other peripherals may have specific settings related to print quality, paper type, and other hardware-specific features.

Device Manager, a built-in utility in Windows operating systems, is a central hub for managing device drivers. It provides a graphical interface for viewing and managing installed hardware devices and their associated drivers. Accessible through the Control Panel or by right-clicking on the Start button, Device Manager displays a hierarchical list of hardware categories. By expanding these categories, users can view individual devices and their corresponding drivers. Device Manager also allows users to update, roll back, uninstall, or disable drivers, providing a centralized location for driver management.

Updating device drivers is an essential part of maintaining a stable and secure system. Manufacturers regularly release driver updates to address bugs, enhance performance, and ensure compatibility with the latest operating system updates. Device Manager offers a convenient way to check for driver updates. Users can right-click on a specific device, select "Update driver," and choose between automatic online updates or manual installation using downloaded driver files. Regularly updating drivers helps prevent compatibility issues and ensures that hardware components are running on the latest and most stable software.

In cases where a device is not functioning correctly or conflicts arise between drivers, troubleshooting becomes necessary. Device Manager plays a crucial role in identifying and resolving such issues. Users can access the utility to view devices with missing or outdated drivers, identify hardware conflicts, and troubleshoot error codes related to specific devices. Resolving driver-related issues may involve reinstalling drivers, rolling back to a previous version, or accessing the manufacturer's support resources for additional guidance.

Driver signature enforcement is another aspect that users may encounter, especially in 64-bit versions of Windows. This security feature ensures that only digitally signed drivers, verified by Microsoft, are allowed to load into the kernel. While this enhances system security by preventing the loading of potentially malicious drivers, it can also pose challenges when attempting to install drivers without a valid digital signature. Users may need to disable driver signature enforcement temporarily during the installation process, although caution is advised, as this action involves overriding a security measure.

In Linux-based operating systems, the process of installing and configuring device drivers can vary depending on the distribution and the kernel used. Many Linux distributions include a vast array of open-source drivers within the kernel itself, reducing the need for manual driver installations in most cases. The package management system, such as APT for Debian-based systems or YUM for Red Hat-based systems, simplifies the installation of drivers by automatically resolving dependencies and ensuring that the required components are installed.

For proprietary drivers, such as those for certain graphics cards or wireless network adapters, Linux users may need to download and install drivers manually from the manufacturer's website. Some distributions provide additional tools, like Ubuntu's Additional Drivers utility, which simplifies the process of identifying and installing proprietary drivers. Configuration settings for Linux drivers often involve editing text-based configuration files or using command-line tools. Linux users also benefit from community support and forums where they can seek assistance for specific hardware compatibility or driver-related issues.

In macOS, the process of installing and configuring device drivers is streamlined due to the closed ecosystem and standardized hardware. Apple designs both the hardware and the operating system, allowing for tight integration between the two. In many cases, macOS includes built-in drivers for a wide range of hardware components, minimizing the need for manual installations. Devices like printers, cameras, and external storage are often recognized and configured automatically upon connection.

For third-party hardware that requires additional drivers, macOS prompts users to download and install the necessary software. Apple's App Store may also offer drivers or companion applications for certain peripherals. The System Preferences menu provides a centralized location for configuring hardware settings, including those related to printers, displays, and external devices. Users can access the System Information utility to view detailed information about installed hardware and associated drivers.

In conclusion, the installation and configuration of device drivers are critical steps in ensuring the proper functioning of hardware components within a computer system. The process involves obtaining the necessary drivers from manufacturers, running installation wizards, configuring settings through utilities like Device Manager, and addressing issues through troubleshooting methods. The specific steps and tools used can vary based on the operating system, with Windows providing Device Manager as a central management hub,

Linux relying on package management systems and community support, and macOS benefiting from a closed ecosystem that streamlines driver integration. Regardless of the platform, regular updates, and proactive management of device drivers contribute to system stability, security, and optimal performance.

Discuss best practices for ensuring compatibility and stability during installation.

Ensuring compatibility and stability during the installation process is paramount for the smooth functioning of software and hardware within a computer system. Best practices in this regard encompass various aspects, ranging from pre-installation preparations to post-installation verification, all aimed at minimizing conflicts, addressing potential issues, and optimizing overall system performance. Before initiating the installation, it is crucial to conduct thorough research on the software or hardware requirements. This involves checking the official documentation, system specifications, and compatibility lists provided by the software or hardware manufacturers. Understanding these requirements ensures that the system possesses the necessary resources, such as processor speed, RAM, and disk space, to accommodate the new installation. Additionally, verifying compatibility with the operating system version is essential, as certain software and hardware may be designed for specific OS versions, and mismatched versions can lead to instability and malfunctions.

One effective practice is to create a system backup or restore point before installing any software or hardware. This precautionary measure provides a safety net in case the installation process goes awry or results in unexpected issues. In the event of compatibility problems or system instability post-installation, having a recent backup allows for a swift restoration to a working state, minimizing downtime and potential data loss. The built-in backup tools provided by operating systems or third-party backup solutions can be utilized for this purpose, offering a convenient way to safeguard the system's integrity.

In situations where software installations are concerned, ensuring that the system is free from conflicting applications is crucial. Certain software may share libraries, dependencies, or system resources, and conflicts can arise if incompatible versions or configurations coexist. A comprehensive review of installed software and their dependencies helps identify potential conflicts before initiating the installation. This can be achieved through the use of system monitoring tools, package managers, or dedicated software auditing utilities that provide insights into the existing software landscape. Additionally, checking for the latest updates and patches for the operating system and existing software applications can address known compatibility issues and enhance overall stability.

For hardware installations, especially when adding new components such as graphics cards, network adapters, or storage devices, verifying compatibility with existing hardware is imperative. Compatibility issues may arise due to factors like motherboard chipset support, power supply capacity, or conflicting drivers. Referring to the hardware compatibility lists provided by manufacturers, checking for firmware updates for existing components, and reviewing user forums for compatibility experiences can help anticipate and mitigate potential issues. Additionally, for certain hardware installations, adherence to industry standards, such as PCI Express for expansion cards, ensures that the new hardware aligns with established norms, reducing the likelihood of compatibility conflicts.

During the installation process, selecting custom or advanced installation options provides greater control over the components being installed and their configurations. This approach is particularly beneficial when dealing with software installations that offer bundled components, additional features, or third-party tools. Custom installations allow users to opt-out of unnecessary components, potentially reducing the risk of conflicts and system resource consumption. For hardware installations, following manufacturer-provided installation guidelines and opting for custom configurations, when available, ensures that the hardware is set up according to specific requirements and user preferences.

In the realm of software installations, consideration should be given to the installation directory and file paths. Opting for default installation directories recommended by the software developer ensures consistency and reduces the likelihood of conflicts with other applications or system components. However, for certain software, especially those allowing user-specific configurations, customizing the installation directory may be preferred. It is essential to avoid installation paths that include spaces, special characters, or excessively long names, as these can lead to issues with file access, permissions, and compatibility.

Verification of digital signatures is an often-overlooked yet crucial step to ensure the integrity and authenticity of the installation files, especially when downloading software from the internet. Authentic software developers sign their installation files with digital signatures, providing a cryptographic guarantee of the file's origin and integrity. Verifying digital signatures before installation safeguards against the installation of tampered or malicious software. Operating systems often provide mechanisms for verifying digital signatures, either during the installation process or through file properties. This practice enhances security and ensures that the installed software originates from a legitimate source.

In the context of software installations, users are encouraged to leverage package managers or official distribution channels whenever possible. Package managers, prevalent in Linux and Unix-based systems, simplify the installation, management, and removal of software by handling dependencies, updates, and configurations. Similarly, using official app stores or repositories for software downloads on other platforms provides a level of trust and security, as these platforms vet and distribute software from reputable developers. Avoiding third-party websites or unofficial sources mitigates the risk of downloading compromised or altered software that may introduce compatibility issues or security vulnerabilities.

During the installation process, particularly for software, carefully reviewing and customizing configuration options can contribute to system stability. Some software installations may include default settings that are not optimal for the user's specific requirements. For instance, configuring application preferences related to automatic updates, system resource utilization, or integration with other software can be critical in tailoring the software to the user's needs and preventing potential conflicts. Additionally, opting for manual configuration options when available allows users to control the installation process and tailor settings according to their preferences.

Thoroughly reviewing and understanding the end-user license agreement (EULA) before proceeding with the installation is a vital practice. The EULA outlines the terms and conditions governing the use of the software, including any restrictions, licensing terms, or privacy considerations. While it may be tempting to quickly click through this step, taking the time to read and comprehend the EULA ensures that users are aware of the software's intended use, any limitations imposed, and the implications of the installation on privacy and data usage. Compliance with the EULA is crucial for legal and ethical reasons, and understanding the terms prevents unintentional violations that may lead to issues post-installation.

Post-installation verification involves systematically testing the installed software or hardware to ensure functionality and compatibility. For software, conducting basic functionality tests, such as opening the application, navigating through its interface, and performing common tasks, helps identify any immediate issues. Running the software under varying conditions, such as different user accounts, network environments, or system states, aids in uncovering compatibility concerns that may arise in specific scenarios. Hardware installations, on the other hand, may require more extensive testing, involving stress tests, benchmarking, and compatibility checks with other peripherals. This thorough verification process helps identify and address any lingering issues that may not have been apparent during the installation.

Regularly updating software and drivers after installation is a fundamental best practice for maintaining compatibility and stability. Software developers release updates to address bugs, security vulnerabilities, and compatibility issues with new operating system versions. Ensuring that installed software is up-to-date mitigates potential conflicts and ensures that the latest features and improvements are incorporated. Similarly, updating device drivers, whether for graphics cards, network adapters, or other peripherals, addresses compatibility concerns and enhances the stability of the associated hardware. Automated update mechanisms provided by operating systems or software applications streamline this process, ensuring that users stay current with the latest releases.

In conclusion, best practices for ensuring compatibility and stability during installation span various stages, from pre-installation research and preparation to post-installation verification and ongoing maintenance. Conducting thorough compatibility checks, creating system backups, and understanding software and hardware requirements lay the foundation for a successful installation. During the installation process, customizing configurations, verifying digital signatures, and adhering to best practices for file paths contribute to a stable system environment. Post-installation, testing software functionality and updating both software and drivers regularly are essential steps in maintaining compatibility and stability. By following these practices, users can minimize the risk of conflicts, optimize system performance, and ensure a reliable and secure computing environment.

Explore the importance of keeping device drivers up to date.

The importance of keeping device drivers up to date in a computing environment cannot be overstated, as it directly influences the performance, stability, security, and functionality of hardware components within a system. Device drivers serve as the essential communication link between the operating system and hardware, facilitating seamless interaction and ensuring that the hardware functions optimally. Regularly updating these drivers is crucial for several reasons, the foremost being the resolution of known bugs and issues. Manufacturers continually refine and enhance their drivers, addressing identified software glitches or malfunctions that could affect the performance of connected hardware. By staying up to date with the latest driver releases, users can benefit from bug fixes that contribute to a more stable and reliable computing experience.

Furthermore, updating device drivers is essential for optimizing hardware performance. As technology advances, manufacturers often release driver updates that include performance improvements and optimizations. These enhancements can lead to better efficiency, increased speed, and the utilization of advanced features of the hardware. For instance, graphics card drivers may introduce optimizations for new video games or applications, ensuring a smoother and more responsive user experience. By keeping drivers current, users can unlock the full potential of their hardware, achieving better performance and responsiveness in various tasks and activities.

Compatibility with the latest operating system updates is another critical reason for keeping device drivers up to date. Operating system developers regularly release updates, patches, and new versions to address security vulnerabilities, improve system stability, and introduce new features. Updated drivers are designed to align with these changes, ensuring that hardware components remain compatible with the evolving operating system environment. Failure to update drivers may result in compatibility issues, leading to malfunctions, system crashes, or the inability to take advantage of new OS features. By staying current, users can maintain a harmonious relationship between their hardware and the operating system, preventing potential conflicts.

Security considerations further highlight the importance of timely driver updates. Device drivers, like any software, may contain vulnerabilities that could be exploited by malicious actors. Manufacturers actively work to identify and address security flaws in their drivers, releasing updates that include security patches. Neglecting driver updates could leave systems vulnerable to potential attacks, as outdated drivers may have unpatched vulnerabilities that attackers could exploit to compromise system integrity. In an era where cybersecurity is a growing concern, keeping device drivers up to date is a proactive measure to fortify the overall security posture of a computing environment.

Moreover, device drivers play a pivotal role in ensuring the proper functioning of peripherals and external hardware components. Printers, scanners, cameras, and other external devices rely on specific drivers to communicate effectively with the operating system. Updates to these drivers often include optimizations for device compatibility, improved performance, and support for new features. Failing to update drivers for external devices can result in connectivity issues, limited functionality, or the inability to use the device altogether. Regular driver updates ensure that users can seamlessly integrate new hardware into their systems and enjoy the full range of features offered by external devices.

In the realm of gaming, updated graphics card drivers are crucial for optimal performance and compatibility with the latest video game releases. Gaming enthusiasts often seek the best possible graphics and performance, and manufacturers respond by releasing driver updates that include optimizations for popular games. These optimizations may involve improving graphics rendering, enhancing frame rates, or resolving specific issues related to game compatibility. Staying up to date with graphics card drivers is, therefore, essential for gamers to enjoy a smooth and immersive gaming experience, free from graphical glitches or performance bottlenecks.

The process of updating device drivers has been made increasingly convenient through automated mechanisms provided by operating systems and hardware manufacturers. Operating systems, such as Windows, macOS, and various Linux distributions, often include tools or utilities that can automatically detect outdated drivers and prompt users to install the latest versions. Additionally, manufacturers often provide software applications or services that facilitate the automatic updating of drivers for their specific hardware components. Leveraging these automated update mechanisms simplifies the task for users, ensuring that the latest drivers are installed with minimal effort.

While the benefits of updating device drivers are clear, it's essential to approach the update process with a degree of caution. Users should verify the authenticity of driver updates and obtain them from official sources, such as the manufacturer's website or trusted software repositories. Third-party driver update tools should be used cautiously, as they may introduce risks such as downloading incorrect or outdated drivers or even potentially harmful software. Additionally, before initiating driver updates, creating a system backup or restore point provides a safety net in case unforeseen issues arise during or after the update process, allowing users to revert to a stable system state.

In conclusion, keeping device drivers up to date is a fundamental practice for maintaining the health and performance of a computing environment. The multifaceted benefits, including bug fixes, performance optimizations, compatibility with operating system updates, and enhanced security, underscore the significance of regular driver updates. Whether for internal components like graphics cards and network adapters or external peripherals such as printers and scanners, staying current with the latest drivers ensures optimal functionality and an improved overall user experience. The advent of automated update mechanisms further simplifies this process, making it accessible to a broader range of users. Embracing the practice of timely driver updates is an investment in the longevity, security, and efficiency of the hardware components that form the backbone of modern computing systems.

Discuss methods for updating drivers and potential challenges associated with maintenance.

Updating drivers is a crucial aspect of maintaining a healthy and well-functioning computing environment, and several methods are available to achieve this. One common approach is to leverage the built-in update mechanisms provided by operating systems. For instance, Windows Update in Microsoft Windows and the Software Update feature in macOS offer a streamlined process for automatically identifying and installing the latest drivers. These systems periodically check for updates and present users with a list of available updates, including device drivers, simplifying the update process. Additionally, many Linux distributions incorporate package management systems, such as APT or YUM, which allow users to update all installed software, including drivers, with a single command. These automated update mechanisms are user-friendly and reduce the burden on users by providing a hassle-free way to keep drivers current.

Manufacturers often offer proprietary software or tools specifically designed for updating drivers associated with their hardware components. These tools, commonly provided by graphics card manufacturers, motherboard manufacturers, or other hardware vendors, are intended to streamline the update process for their specific products. Users can download and install these tools from the manufacturer's website, and they typically include features such as automatic driver detection, one-click updates, and additional optimizations for the associated hardware. While these tools can simplify the update process, users should exercise caution and ensure that they are obtaining such tools from official and trustworthy sources to avoid potential security risks or the installation of unnecessary software.

Another method for updating drivers involves manually downloading and installing the latest driver versions from the official websites of hardware manufacturers. This approach is more hands-on and allows users to have direct control over the installation process. Users can navigate to the official website of the hardware component manufacturer, locate the appropriate driver for their specific model, download the installer, and follow on-screen instructions to install the updated driver. This method ensures that users have the latest driver version directly from the source, which can be especially beneficial when the automated update mechanisms are not functioning correctly or when a specific driver needs to be updated outside the regular update cycle.

In the context of gaming, graphics card manufacturers often release new driver versions optimized for the latest video game releases. Gamers who want to ensure optimal performance and compatibility with newly launched games may choose to manually download and install these specialized graphics card drivers. This method allows gamers to stay on the cutting edge of performance enhancements and graphical optimizations, particularly for demanding or newly released titles.

However, despite the variety of methods available for updating drivers, challenges and considerations exist in the maintenance process. One notable challenge is the potential for compatibility issues, especially when dealing with a vast array of hardware components and software applications. An update that works seamlessly on one system configuration may lead to conflicts or unexpected behavior on another. This challenge underscores the importance of verifying the compatibility of driver updates with both the specific hardware component and the overall system environment. Manufacturers often provide release notes or documentation alongside driver updates, offering insights into compatibility, bug fixes, and known issues. Users should review this information before proceeding with an update to mitigate potential challenges.

While automated update mechanisms are designed for user convenience, they may introduce challenges related to timing and control. Automatic updates may occur at inconvenient times, potentially disrupting user activities or triggering updates when network bandwidth is limited. Additionally, automated updates may not provide users with the opportunity to review release notes or customize installation settings. To address these challenges, some users prefer manual control over the update process, allowing them to choose when and how updates are applied. Balancing the need for convenience with the desire for control becomes essential, especially in environments where system stability and uninterrupted workflows are critical.

Security considerations represent another challenge associated with driver maintenance. While keeping drivers up to date is essential for addressing security vulnerabilities, users should exercise caution when obtaining drivers from unofficial sources. Third-party driver update tools or unverified websites may expose users to the risk of downloading incorrect or malicious software. This challenge emphasizes the importance of obtaining drivers directly from official and reputable sources, ensuring that the downloaded files are legitimate and have not been tampered with. Verifying digital signatures, when available, adds an extra layer of security by confirming the authenticity of the downloaded driver files.

Compatibility challenges may also arise when updating drivers in a corporate or enterprise environment with standardized hardware configurations. In such environments, thorough testing of driver updates becomes crucial before deployment to ensure that the updates do not introduce unforeseen issues across a large number of systems. Testing procedures should involve a representative sample of the hardware and software configurations present in the organization to identify potential compatibility challenges early in the update process. Additionally, having a well-defined rollback plan or system backup in place is essential to address any unexpected issues that may arise during or after the deployment of driver updates in an enterprise setting.

Furthermore, users may encounter challenges related to the lack of driver support for legacy or older hardware components. Manufacturers may cease providing updates for older devices, leaving users with outdated drivers that are incompatible with newer operating system versions or applications. In such cases, users may need to explore alternative solutions, such as community-developed drivers or workarounds, to extend the life of their legacy hardware. However, these solutions may come with their own set of challenges, including potential limitations in functionality or stability.

In conclusion, while various methods are available for updating drivers, challenges associated with maintenance persist. Compatibility issues, timing and control concerns with automated updates, security considerations, and challenges in enterprise environments underscore the need for a thoughtful and strategic approach to driver maintenance. Users must weigh the convenience of automated update mechanisms against the desire for manual control, prioritize security by obtaining drivers from official sources, and thoroughly test updates in enterprise environments. Addressing these challenges ensures that the driver update process contributes to a stable, secure, and well-performing computing environment, allowing users to harness the full potential of their hardware components while minimizing risks and disruptions.

Introduce Plug-and-Play (PnP) technology and its impact on device driver management.

Plug-and-Play (PnP) technology has revolutionized the way hardware devices are connected and configured within computing environments. Introduced in the early 1990s, PnP was designed to simplify the process of adding, removing, and configuring hardware components by automating the detection and installation of devices. The primary goal of PnP technology is to enable seamless integration of new hardware into a computer system, minimizing the need for manual intervention and reducing the complexity traditionally associated with device installation. The advent of PnP has had a profound impact on device driver management, fundamentally altering the user experience and streamlining the process of making diverse hardware components work harmoniously with an operating system.

The core principle behind PnP technology is to automate the configuration of hardware devices, eliminating the manual intervention required in the pre-PnP era. Traditionally, users needed to configure hardware settings manually by setting jumpers, switches, or DIP switches on the devices and ensuring that the system's configuration matched these settings. With PnP, devices are designed to automatically communicate their resource requirements, such as interrupt requests (IRQs), memory addresses, and I/O port addresses, to the operating system. This dynamic exchange of information allows the operating system to allocate resources based on the available system configuration, avoiding conflicts and ensuring that multiple devices can coexist without requiring manual configuration adjustments.

One of the significant impacts of PnP on device driver management is the automated detection and installation of device drivers. In a PnP-enabled system, when a new hardware component is connected or installed, the operating system initiates a process to identify the device and locate the appropriate driver. This contrasts with the pre-PnP era, where users had to manually install drivers, often navigating complex installation procedures and dealing with compatibility challenges. PnP streamlines this process, making it more user-friendly and accessible to individuals with varying levels of technical expertise.

The concept of "hot-plugging" or "hot-swapping" is another pivotal aspect of PnP technology. This feature allows users to connect or disconnect hardware devices while the computer is powered on, without requiring a system restart. Hot-plugging is particularly beneficial for peripherals such as USB devices, external hard drives, and cameras. In a PnP environment, when a user plugs in a new device, the system automatically detects and configures it, including the installation of necessary drivers, enabling instant use. Hot-plugging enhances flexibility and convenience, as users can add or remove devices on the fly, reducing downtime and improving the overall user experience.

PnP technology has also played a crucial role in addressing conflicts between hardware devices, a common challenge in computing environments. Conflicts typically arise when two or more devices attempt to use the same system resources, leading to malfunctions or system instability. PnP-enabled systems automatically manage resource allocation, significantly reducing the likelihood of conflicts. The operating system, with assistance from the BIOS (Basic Input/Output System), assigns unique resource addresses to each device based on the information provided during the PnP process. This dynamic resource allocation ensures that devices can coexist harmoniously, contributing to system stability and reliability.

The impact of PnP on device driver management extends to the concept of driver stacks and class drivers. A driver stack refers to a set of drivers that work together to manage a particular device. In PnP environments, the operating system organizes driver stacks to handle devices based on their functionality or class. Class drivers are generic drivers designed to support a particular category of devices, such as printers or keyboards. When a new device is added, the operating system can automatically load the appropriate class driver, minimizing the need for specific device drivers. This simplifies driver management, as class drivers can cater to multiple devices within the same category, further reducing the complexity associated with driver installations.

Moreover, PnP has had a transformative impact on the user experience when dealing with hardware changes or upgrades. In traditional computing environments, users often hesitated to add new hardware or upgrade components due to concerns about compatibility and the intricate process of manual configuration. PnP technology has alleviated these concerns by automating the configuration and driver installation process. Users can confidently add new hardware components, knowing that the system will seamlessly integrate them, automatically configure resources, and install the necessary drivers. This has democratized hardware upgrades, making them accessible to a broader range of users and encouraging a culture of experimentation and customization.

While PnP has undeniably streamlined device driver management, challenges and considerations persist. One challenge arises when dealing with legacy or older hardware that may not fully support PnP. In such cases, users may need to resort to manual configuration or seek alternative solutions to integrate non-PnP devices. Additionally, certain advanced configurations or specialized hardware may still require manual intervention, as PnP technology might not cover all possible scenarios. However, advancements in hardware design and broader industry adoption of PnP standards have significantly reduced the prevalence of these challenges.

The impact of PnP on device driver management is not limited to personal computers but extends to a variety of computing devices, including laptops, servers, and embedded systems. PnP has become a standard feature in modern computing architectures, ensuring a consistent and user-friendly experience across diverse platforms. The ubiquity of PnP has also influenced the design of operating systems, leading to the integration of user interfaces and tools that facilitate driver management. Operating system developers prioritize compatibility with PnP standards to ensure seamless device integration and driver management for end-users.

In conclusion, Plug-and-Play technology has revolutionized the landscape of device driver management, transforming the once complex and manual process into an automated and user-friendly experience. The impact of PnP is evident in the streamlined detection, installation, and configuration of device drivers, making hardware integration more accessible to a broad range of users. The concepts of hot-plugging, dynamic resource allocation, and class drivers have further contributed to the efficiency and convenience of device management in PnP-enabled systems. While challenges may arise, especially with legacy hardware, the overall impact of PnP on device driver management has been overwhelmingly positive, fostering a more inclusive and adaptable computing environment.

Discuss how PnP simplifies the installation and configuration of new hardware.

Plug-and-Play (PnP) technology has profoundly simplified the installation and configuration of new hardware, marking a significant departure from the complex and manual processes that characterized earlier computing environments. PnP's overarching objective is to enable seamless integration of hardware devices into a computer system, minimizing user intervention and reducing the intricacies associated with device installation. One of the fundamental ways PnP achieves this simplification is through its automated detection and configuration of hardware components. Traditionally, users faced the daunting task of manually configuring hardware settings, such as interrupt requests (IRQs), memory addresses, and I/O port addresses, often involving the use of physical jumpers or switches on the devices. PnP revolutionized this process by enabling devices to communicate their resource requirements directly to the operating system, allowing for automatic allocation of resources based on the system's configuration.

The automated detection and installation of device drivers represent a cornerstone of PnP's simplification of new hardware integration. In the pre-PnP era, users were required to manually install drivers for each hardware component, navigating through complex installation procedures and often encountering compatibility challenges. PnP transforms this experience by initiating a seamless process when a new hardware component is added. The operating system, equipped with PnP capabilities, automatically detects the new device and proceeds to locate and install the appropriate driver. This dynamic and automated approach drastically reduces the burden on users, making the installation of new hardware more accessible and user-friendly, even for individuals with limited technical expertise.

Moreover, the concept of "hot-plugging" or "hot-swapping" has been a revolutionary aspect of PnP that simplifies the integration of new hardware. Hot-plugging enables users to connect or disconnect hardware devices while the computer is powered on, eliminating the need for a system restart. In a PnP environment, when a user plugs in a new device, the operating system dynamically detects and configures it, including the installation of necessary drivers. This capability is particularly advantageous for peripherals like USB devices, external hard drives, and cameras. The ability to add or remove devices on-the-fly enhances flexibility, reduces downtime, and significantly contributes to an improved user experience.

The automation of resource allocation is another key aspect of PnP that simplifies the installation and configuration of new hardware. In non-PnP systems, configuring resources manually often led to conflicts between devices attempting to use the same resources. PnP technology addresses this challenge by allowing devices to communicate their resource requirements during the connection process. The operating system, assisted by the BIOS, then dynamically allocates resources to each device based on the available system configuration, minimizing the likelihood of conflicts. This automated resource management ensures that multiple devices can coexist harmoniously within the system, contributing to stability and reliability.

The impact of PnP on device driver management extends to the concept of driver stacks and class drivers, further simplifying the installation process. A driver stack is a set of drivers that work together to manage a specific device, and PnP organizes these stacks to handle devices based on their functionality or class. Class drivers, in particular, are generic drivers designed to support a particular category of devices, such as printers or keyboards. When a new device is added, the operating system can automatically load the appropriate class driver, eliminating the need for specific device drivers for each unique component. This simplification of driver management is especially beneficial as class drivers can cater to multiple devices within the same category, reducing the complexity associated with driver installations.

Additionally, PnP has had a transformative impact on user confidence and the overall experience of dealing with hardware changes or upgrades. In the past, users often hesitated to add new hardware or upgrade components due to concerns about compatibility and the intricate process of manual configuration. PnP has alleviated these concerns by automating the configuration and driver installation process. Users can now confidently add new hardware components, knowing that the system will seamlessly integrate them, automatically configure resources, and install the necessary drivers. This has democratized hardware upgrades, making them accessible to a broader range of users and fostering a culture of experimentation and customization.

Furthermore, the ubiquity of PnP has influenced the design of operating systems, leading to the integration of user interfaces and tools that facilitate the installation and configuration of new hardware. Modern operating systems prioritize compatibility with PnP standards to ensure a consistent and user-friendly experience across diverse platforms. The intuitive interfaces provided by these operating systems guide users through the hardware installation process, offering clear instructions and real-time feedback, further contributing to the overall simplification of the user experience.

Despite the transformative impact of PnP, challenges and considerations persist, particularly when dealing with legacy or older hardware that may not fully support PnP. In such cases, users may need to resort to manual configuration or seek alternative solutions to integrate non-PnP devices. Additionally, certain advanced configurations or specialized hardware may still require manual intervention, as PnP technology might not cover all possible scenarios. However, advancements in hardware design and broader industry adoption of PnP standards have significantly reduced the prevalence of these challenges.

In conclusion, Plug-and-Play technology has simplified the installation and configuration of new hardware in ways that have transformed the landscape of computing. The automated detection and installation of device drivers, the concept of hot-plugging, dynamic resource allocation, and the use of class drivers have collectively contributed to a more accessible and user-friendly experience. PnP has not only eliminated the complexities associated with hardware integration but has also instilled confidence in users to explore and upgrade their computing environments. As a fundamental component of modern computing, PnP continues to shape the user experience, making the addition of new hardware a seamless and straightforward process.

Chapter 4: Optimizing Performance through Device Management

Define performance optimization in the context of device management.

Performance optimization in the context of device management encompasses a comprehensive set of strategies, practices, and methodologies aimed at enhancing the efficiency, responsiveness, and overall functionality of hardware components within a computing environment. At its core, performance optimization seeks to maximize the capabilities of devices, ensuring they operate at their peak potential while minimizing resource consumption. This multidimensional approach involves addressing various facets, including system responsiveness, resource utilization, energy efficiency, and the ability to handle workloads effectively. The ultimate goal is to provide users with a seamless and responsive experience while utilizing hardware resources in an optimal and sustainable manner.

One fundamental aspect of performance optimization in device management involves enhancing system responsiveness. This entails minimizing delays, lags, or latency in the interaction between users and their devices. Optimizing responsiveness is particularly critical for user-centric devices such as input peripherals (e.g., keyboards and mice) and display devices, where any perceptible delay can significantly impact the user experience. Techniques such as reducing input-to-output latency, optimizing data transfer rates, and implementing efficient communication protocols contribute to the responsiveness of devices, ensuring a smooth and instantaneous interaction between users and their computing environment.

Resource utilization is a central focus in performance optimization, as efficient use of system resources directly correlates with overall system performance. This involves managing resources such as CPU (Central Processing Unit), memory (RAM), storage, and network bandwidth in a way that maximizes their potential. Balancing the workload distribution among CPU cores, optimizing memory allocation, and employing efficient caching mechanisms are strategies to enhance resource utilization. Performance optimization also includes minimizing resource contention, where multiple devices or applications compete for the same resources, leading to bottlenecks. By intelligently managing resource allocation and avoiding contention, the system can operate efficiently, preventing resource exhaustion and ensuring a responsive and stable computing environment.

Energy efficiency is a critical consideration in the modern era of computing, given the emphasis on sustainability and the proliferation of portable devices. Performance optimization in device management includes strategies to minimize energy consumption without compromising performance. Power management techniques, such as dynamic frequency scaling and device idle states, enable devices to operate at lower power levels during periods of inactivity, effectively reducing energy consumption. Additionally, optimizing algorithms and processes to execute tasks with minimal energy expenditure contributes to the overall energy efficiency of the system. This approach is particularly relevant for battery-powered devices, such as laptops and mobile devices, where prolonging battery life without sacrificing performance is a key objective.

In the realm of device management, performance optimization extends to the effective utilization of storage resources. This involves streamlining data access, minimizing disk I/O (Input/Output) operations, and implementing efficient file systems. Techniques such as data compression, deduplication, and intelligent caching contribute to faster data retrieval and reduced storage latency. Storage optimization also includes managing disk space to prevent fragmentation and ensuring that data is organized in a manner that facilitates quick access. By optimizing storage performance, devices can read and write data more efficiently, leading to faster application launches, quicker file transfers, and an overall improvement in the responsiveness of the computing environment.

Another facet of performance optimization is the proactive management of device drivers. Device drivers serve as the communication interface between hardware components and the operating system. Ensuring that drivers are up to date, well-maintained, and compatible with the operating system is crucial for optimal device performance. Performance issues, system crashes, or compatibility concerns can arise from outdated or incompatible drivers. Therefore, performance optimization in device management includes practices such as regular driver updates, verification of driver compatibility, and troubleshooting driver-related issues. A well-maintained driver ecosystem contributes to the stability and reliability of the system, ensuring that devices operate seamlessly within the computing environment.

Performance optimization also extends to network devices and communication protocols within a computing environment. Efficient data transmission and network responsiveness are paramount for devices that rely on network connectivity, such as computers accessing the internet, printers in a networked environment, or IoT (Internet of Things) devices. Optimizing network performance involves minimizing packet loss, reducing latency, and maximizing data throughput. This can be achieved through the implementation of efficient communication protocols, network bandwidth management, and Quality of Service (QoS) mechanisms. By optimizing network performance, devices can communicate swiftly and reliably, contributing to a seamless user experience and improved overall system efficiency.

In the context of graphics and multimedia devices, performance optimization becomes particularly critical for applications such as gaming, video editing, and graphic design. Graphics processing units (GPUs) play a central role in rendering high-quality graphics and videos. Performance optimization strategies include optimizing rendering algorithms, leveraging hardware acceleration, and implementing efficient memory management for graphical data. Additionally, ensuring that graphics drivers are up to date and configured for optimal performance is essential. For real-time applications like gaming, frame rate optimization and minimizing input-to-display latency are crucial elements of performance enhancement. These optimizations collectively contribute to a visually appealing and responsive user experience in graphics-intensive applications.

Furthermore, in enterprise environments with a multitude of interconnected devices, performance optimization encompasses efficient device management and monitoring. This involves implementing centralized management solutions to monitor the health, performance, and security of devices across the network. Remote management capabilities enable administrators to identify potential issues, deploy updates, and troubleshoot problems without physically accessing each device. Performance optimization in enterprise device management aims to streamline administrative tasks, reduce downtime, and ensure the reliability of devices across the organization.

Challenges in performance optimization include the complexity of modern computing environments, diverse hardware configurations, and the evolving nature of software applications. Balancing the need for performance with other considerations, such as security and user privacy, adds layers of complexity to optimization efforts. Moreover, the dynamic nature of technology requires ongoing adaptation of optimization strategies to keep pace with advancements in hardware and software. However, the benefits of performance optimization are substantial, leading to improved user experiences, increased productivity, and more sustainable use of resources in computing environments.

In conclusion, performance optimization in the context of device management encompasses a holistic and multifaceted approach aimed at enhancing the efficiency, responsiveness, and overall functionality of hardware components within a computing environment. From streamlining resource utilization and improving energy efficiency to optimizing storage access and managing network performance, the goal is to create a computing environment that delivers optimal performance while minimizing resource consumption. Whether in user-centric devices, enterprise environments, or graphics-intensive applications, performance optimization strategies contribute to a seamless and responsive user experience, ensuring that devices operate at their peak potential within the complexities of modern computing.

Highlight the importance of optimizing device-related processes for overall system performance.

The importance of optimizing device-related processes for overall system performance cannot be overstated, as the efficiency and functionality of hardware components form the bedrock of any computing environment. The seamless interaction between devices and the operating system directly influences the user experience, system responsiveness, and the overall productivity of users. By focusing on the optimization of device-related processes, organizations and individual users can unlock the full potential of their hardware, leading to a more efficient, reliable, and user-friendly computing environment.

At the core of this importance lies the notion of system responsiveness. The speed and agility with which devices interact with the operating system significantly impact the user experience. Whether it's the input responsiveness of a keyboard and mouse, the quick access to files facilitated by optimized storage processes, or the swift rendering of graphics in a high-performance GPU, each device contributes to the overall responsiveness of the system. Optimizing these device-related processes ensures that users can execute commands, launch applications, and perform tasks with minimal delays, fostering a smooth and seamless interaction between humans and machines.

Efficient resource utilization is another critical aspect underscored by the importance of optimizing device-related processes. In any computing environment, resources such as CPU, memory, storage, and network bandwidth are finite and shared among various devices and applications. Optimizing how devices utilize these resources ensures a balanced and equitable distribution, preventing resource contention that can lead to bottlenecks and degraded system performance. By managing resource allocation intelligently, the overall efficiency of the system improves, allowing for optimal performance without exhausting critical resources and minimizing the risk of slowdowns or crashes.

Energy efficiency is increasingly recognized as a pivotal consideration in the realm of device-related processes. With the growing emphasis on sustainability and the proliferation of portable devices, optimizing energy consumption without compromising performance has become a paramount goal. Strategies such as dynamic frequency scaling, which adjusts the power consumption of devices based on workload, and intelligent power management contribute to overall energy efficiency. The importance of energy optimization extends beyond individual devices to encompass the environmental impact of large-scale computing infrastructures, making it a crucial aspect in the quest for sustainable and eco-friendly computing solutions.

In the realm of storage, the importance of optimizing device-related processes is particularly evident. Storage processes directly impact data access speed, file retrieval times, and overall system boot-up times. Efficient storage optimization involves techniques such as data compression, deduplication, and intelligent caching, all contributing to faster data retrieval and reduced storage latency. For both individual users and organizations managing vast amounts of data, optimized storage processes translate to quicker access to information, improved workflow efficiency, and a more responsive computing environment.

Device drivers, serving as the essential communication link between hardware components and the operating system, further highlight the importance of optimization. Keeping device drivers up to date and well-maintained is crucial for system stability and security. Outdated or incompatible drivers can lead to performance issues, system crashes, or security vulnerabilities. The optimization of driver-related processes includes regular updates, compatibility checks, and troubleshooting to ensure that devices operate seamlessly within the computing environment. A well-maintained driver ecosystem contributes to overall system reliability, reducing the risk of disruptions and providing a foundation for enhanced performance.

In enterprise environments, where a multitude of interconnected devices collaboratively contribute to organizational workflows, the importance of optimizing device-related processes becomes even more pronounced. Centralized device management solutions, coupled with optimized processes, enable administrators to monitor the health, performance, and security of devices across the network. Remote management capabilities allow for efficient troubleshooting, updates, and maintenance without physical access to individual devices. The optimization of these processes streamlines administrative tasks, reduces downtime, and ensures that devices within the organization operate at peak efficiency, contributing to overall productivity.

Graphics-intensive applications, such as gaming, design, and video editing, further underscore the importance of optimizing device-related processes. Graphics processing units (GPUs) play a pivotal role in rendering high-quality graphics and videos. Optimization strategies include leveraging hardware acceleration, efficient memory management, and the utilization of optimized rendering algorithms. For users engaged in these demanding applications, the importance of performance optimization directly translates to the quality of visuals, smooth rendering, and a responsive user experience. By ensuring that devices like GPUs are operating optimally, users can extract the maximum performance required for graphics-intensive tasks.

Moreover, the ubiquity of networked devices in modern computing environments highlights the significance of optimizing communication processes. Whether in local area networks (LANs) or wide area networks (WANs), efficient data transmission and network responsiveness are crucial. Optimizing network-related processes involves minimizing packet loss, reducing latency, and maximizing data throughput. These optimizations contribute to a seamless exchange of information between devices, enabling swift and reliable communication. In an era where connectivity is integral to various computing tasks, the importance of network optimization cannot be understated.

Challenges in modern computing, such as the complexity of diverse hardware configurations, the continuous evolution of software applications, and the dynamic nature of technology, underscore the ongoing nature of performance optimization efforts. However, the importance of optimizing device-related processes lies in the tangible benefits reaped by users and organizations alike. Improved system responsiveness, efficient resource utilization, enhanced energy efficiency, and a seamless user experience collectively contribute to a computing environment that is not only high-performing but also adaptable to the evolving landscape of technology.

In conclusion, the importance of optimizing device-related processes for overall system performance is a cornerstone of modern computing. The efficiency and functionality of individual devices collectively shape the user experience and determine the productivity of users and organizations. By prioritizing system responsiveness, resource utilization, energy efficiency, and effective communication between devices, the optimization of device-related processes ensures a computing environment that is not only high-performing but also sustainable, reliable, and user-friendly. As technology continues to advance, the ongoing commitment to optimization remains crucial in harnessing the full potential of hardware components within the complexities of contemporary computing.

Discuss strategies for efficient allocation of system resources to devices.

Efficient allocation of system resources to devices is a cornerstone of optimizing overall system performance, ensuring that each component operates at its peak potential without creating bottlenecks or resource contention. This comprehensive approach involves strategic management of CPU (Central Processing Unit), memory (RAM), storage, and network bandwidth, considering the diverse array of devices within a computing environment. One fundamental strategy for efficient resource allocation is load balancing, a technique aimed at distributing the computational workload evenly across CPU cores. In a multi-core system, load balancing prevents a single core from becoming a bottleneck by dynamically reallocating tasks to available cores. This strategy optimizes CPU utilization, enhances overall system responsiveness, and prevents resource imbalances that could impede the performance of specific devices or applications.

Memory optimization represents another critical aspect of efficient resource allocation. Techniques such as intelligent memory caching, prioritizing frequently accessed data, and minimizing unnecessary memory overhead contribute to effective memory management. By ensuring that memory is allocated judiciously to active processes and that data retrieval is streamlined, the overall efficiency of devices relying on memory-intensive tasks, such as graphics rendering or data analysis, is significantly improved. Moreover, adopting memory compression algorithms and employing virtual memory strategies can prevent memory exhaustion and enhance the system's ability to handle a diverse range of applications concurrently.

Efficient storage resource allocation is imperative for minimizing storage latency and optimizing data access times. Techniques such as dynamic storage tiering, which involves categorizing data based on usage patterns and assigning it to different storage types, contribute to effective storage optimization. Additionally, implementing data deduplication and compression mechanisms reduces the overall storage footprint, optimizing storage space and enhancing access speeds. Furthermore, strategic placement of frequently accessed data on high-speed storage devices, such as SSDs (Solid State Drives), ensures that devices relying on quick data retrieval, such as graphics cards during gaming or video editing, operate with minimal delays.

Network bandwidth management is a key consideration for efficient resource allocation in environments with multiple interconnected devices. Quality of Service (QoS) mechanisms play a vital role in prioritizing network traffic based on the requirements of specific devices or applications. By assigning different levels of priority to network packets, QoS ensures that critical data, such as real-time video streaming or VoIP (Voice over Internet Protocol) calls, receives higher bandwidth allocation. This strategy prevents network congestion, reduces latency, and optimizes communication between devices, particularly in scenarios where uninterrupted data transfer is crucial, such as video conferencing or online gaming.

Power management strategies contribute not only to energy efficiency but also to the effective allocation of system resources. Dynamic frequency scaling, a technique that adjusts the clock frequency and voltage of a device based on its workload, is a key strategy for optimizing power consumption. By dynamically scaling the performance of devices, power management ensures that resources are allocated efficiently, matching the workload demands and minimizing energy consumption during periods of low activity. This approach is particularly relevant in portable devices, where prolonging battery life without sacrificing performance is crucial.

In the context of multi-device environments, such as enterprise networks, centralized device management solutions play a pivotal role in resource allocation. These solutions enable administrators to monitor the health, performance, and resource utilization of devices across the network. By implementing policies for resource allocation and prioritizing critical tasks, administrators can ensure that devices operate within specified performance parameters. Automated provisioning and de-provisioning of resources based on demand further contribute to efficient resource allocation, preventing unnecessary consumption of resources during periods of low activity and optimizing overall system performance.

Virtualization technologies provide advanced strategies for resource allocation by creating virtual instances of physical devices or resources. In virtualized environments, such as server farms or cloud computing infrastructures, hypervisors allocate virtual resources dynamically based on demand. This ensures that each virtual machine receives an equitable share of system resources, preventing resource contention and optimizing overall performance. Moreover, features like live migration allow for the seamless movement of virtual machines between physical servers, enabling efficient resource allocation across the entire virtualized infrastructure.

Machine learning and artificial intelligence (AI) are emerging as innovative approaches to optimize resource allocation dynamically. Predictive analytics and self-learning algorithms analyze historical usage patterns and anticipate future resource demands. By leveraging this predictive capability, systems can preemptively allocate resources to devices or applications that are likely to experience increased demand, enhancing overall efficiency. Machine learning algorithms can adapt and optimize resource allocation strategies based on real-time data, providing a dynamic and responsive approach to managing system resources.

An effective strategy for efficient resource allocation is proactive monitoring and performance tuning. Continuous monitoring of system performance metrics allows administrators to identify potential resource bottlenecks or contention issues. Through performance tuning, administrators can adjust resource allocation parameters, optimize configurations, and fine-tune settings to align with the specific demands of devices and applications. This hands-on approach ensures that resources are allocated judiciously, addressing performance challenges before they impact the overall system.

However, challenges in efficient resource allocation persist, particularly in dynamic computing environments with diverse workloads and constantly evolving technologies. Balancing the need for performance with considerations such as security, data integrity, and regulatory compliance adds complexity to resource allocation decisions. Additionally, achieving optimal resource allocation requires a nuanced understanding of the specific requirements and usage patterns of devices and applications within the computing environment.

In conclusion, efficient allocation of system resources to devices is a multifaceted strategy that involves balancing the demands of diverse hardware components and applications. Load balancing, memory optimization, storage efficiency, network bandwidth management, power management, centralized device management, virtualization technologies, machine learning, and proactive monitoring collectively contribute to effective resource allocation. These strategies ensure that devices operate at their peak potential, preventing resource contention, minimizing latency, and optimizing overall system performance. As technology continues to evolve, the pursuit of efficient resource allocation remains integral to maximizing the capabilities of computing environments and adapting to the ever-changing landscape of hardware and software.

Explore the impact of resource allocation on system responsiveness and stability.

The impact of resource allocation on system responsiveness and stability is fundamental to the overall performance and user experience in any computing environment. Effective resource allocation directly influences how a system responds to user inputs, executes tasks, and maintains stability under varying workloads. The allocation of resources, including CPU (Central Processing Unit), memory (RAM), storage, and network bandwidth, plays a pivotal role in determining the responsiveness of the system, defined by its ability to swiftly and efficiently execute tasks initiated by users or applications.

CPU resource allocation stands as a critical factor in system responsiveness, as the CPU serves as the central hub for processing instructions and executing tasks. Effective allocation involves distributing the computational workload across multiple CPU cores, preventing a single core from becoming a bottleneck. Load balancing strategies dynamically assign tasks to available cores, optimizing CPU utilization and preventing resource contention. In scenarios where CPU-intensive applications or multitasking is prevalent, efficient resource allocation ensures that the system responds promptly to user inputs, reducing latency and enhancing overall responsiveness.

Memory allocation significantly impacts system responsiveness by determining how efficiently the system can store and retrieve data. Optimal memory allocation involves prioritizing active processes, ensuring that frequently accessed data resides in fast-access memory locations. Intelligent memory caching mechanisms contribute to quicker data retrieval, preventing delays in application launches or data processing. Inefficient memory allocation, on the other hand, can lead to memory exhaustion, forcing the system to rely on slower storage devices for data access and thereby compromising responsiveness.

Storage resource allocation directly affects system responsiveness, particularly in tasks involving data retrieval, application launches, and file access. Strategic allocation involves leveraging high-speed storage devices, such as Solid State Drives (SSDs), for frequently accessed data. Techniques like dynamic storage tiering categorize data based on usage patterns and allocate it to different storage types accordingly. Efficient storage resource allocation minimizes storage latency, ensuring that devices relying on quick data access, such as GPUs (Graphics Processing Units) during graphics rendering, experience minimal delays and contribute to a responsive computing environment.

Network bandwidth allocation is paramount for ensuring the responsiveness of devices in networked environments. Quality of Service (QoS) mechanisms play a crucial role in prioritizing network traffic based on the requirements of specific devices or applications. By allocating sufficient bandwidth to critical tasks, such as real-time video streaming or VoIP (Voice over Internet Protocol) calls, QoS prevents network congestion and minimizes latency. Effective network bandwidth allocation is especially crucial in scenarios where seamless data transfer is imperative, such as online gaming or video conferencing, ensuring a responsive and uninterrupted user experience.

Power management strategies impact system responsiveness by dynamically adjusting the performance of devices based on workload demands. Dynamic frequency scaling is a common technique that varies the clock frequency and voltage of a device to match its workload. During periods of low activity, devices can operate at lower frequencies, conserving energy without sacrificing responsiveness. Efficient power management ensures that devices can quickly ramp up performance when needed, contributing to a responsive system while minimizing energy consumption.

Centralized device management solutions play a pivotal role in resource allocation for stability and responsiveness, especially in complex enterprise environments. These solutions monitor the health, performance, and resource utilization of devices across the network. Administrators can allocate resources based on policies, ensuring that critical tasks receive the necessary resources. By automating resource allocation and de-allocation based on demand, administrators can maintain stability during varying workloads, prevent resource contention, and optimize the overall responsiveness of the enterprise computing environment.

Virtualization technologies impact system responsiveness by creating virtual instances of physical devices or resources. In virtualized environments, hypervisors allocate resources dynamically, ensuring that each virtual machine receives a fair share of system resources. Live migration features allow for the seamless movement of virtual machines between physical servers, optimizing resource utilization and maintaining stability. Efficient virtualization strategies contribute to a responsive computing environment by preventing resource contention and adapting to changing workloads.

Machine learning and artificial intelligence (AI) are emerging as innovative approaches to resource allocation, with a profound impact on system responsiveness. Predictive analytics and self-learning algorithms analyze historical usage patterns, anticipate future resource demands, and dynamically allocate resources based on predictions. Machine learning algorithms can adapt to real-time data, optimizing resource allocation strategies dynamically and contributing to a responsive and adaptive system.

Proactive monitoring and performance tuning play a crucial role in maintaining system stability and responsiveness. Continuous monitoring of system performance metrics allows administrators to identify potential resource bottlenecks or contention issues. Through performance tuning, administrators can adjust resource allocation parameters, optimize configurations, and fine-tune settings to align with the specific demands of devices and applications. This hands-on approach ensures that resources are allocated judiciously, addressing performance challenges before they impact the overall system.

However, challenges exist in achieving optimal resource allocation and balancing the trade-offs between performance, stability, and other considerations. Balancing resource allocation decisions with security requirements, data integrity, and regulatory compliance adds complexity to the optimization process. Furthermore, the dynamic nature of technology requires ongoing adaptation of resource allocation strategies to keep pace with advancements in hardware, software, and user demands.

In conclusion, the impact of resource allocation on system responsiveness and stability is profound, shaping the overall user experience in computing environments. Efficient allocation of CPU, memory, storage, network bandwidth, and power directly influences how devices respond to user inputs and maintain stability under varying workloads. Whether through load balancing, memory optimization, storage efficiency, network bandwidth management, power management, centralized device management, virtualization technologies, machine learning, or proactive monitoring, resource allocation strategies collectively contribute to a responsive and stable computing environment. As technology evolves, the pursuit of efficient resource allocation remains integral to maximizing system capabilities and ensuring a computing environment that adapts to the dynamic demands of modern computing.

Introduce scheduling algorithms for managing device access and usage.

Scheduling algorithms play a pivotal role in managing device access and usage within computing systems, determining the order and duration of access for multiple competing tasks or processes. These algorithms are fundamental to optimizing resource utilization, enhancing system responsiveness, and ensuring fair and efficient allocation of computing resources. One of the widely used scheduling algorithms is the First-Come-First-Serve (FCFS) algorithm, which prioritizes tasks based on their arrival time. FCFS is simple to implement, but it may suffer from the "convoy effect," where shorter tasks get delayed by longer ones. Another classic algorithm is the Round Robin (RR) scheduling, commonly employed in time-sharing systems. RR assigns a fixed time quantum to each task in a cyclic manner, promoting fairness in resource access. However, it may lead to inefficiencies in scenarios where tasks have varying execution times, as the fixed quantum may not suit all tasks equally.

Priority Scheduling is another significant algorithm where each task is assigned a priority, and tasks with higher priorities are executed first. While it ensures that high-priority tasks are promptly addressed, it may lead to the starvation of lower-priority tasks if not implemented carefully. To address this, a variation called Aging can be introduced, where the priority of a task increases with time, preventing lower-priority tasks from being indefinitely delayed. Another dynamic scheduling algorithm is Shortest Job Next (SJN) or Shortest Job First (SJF), which selects the task with the shortest burst time for execution. SJN minimizes waiting times and enhances system throughput, yet predicting the burst time accurately can be challenging in practice.

In real-time systems, where tasks have strict deadlines, Earliest Deadline First (EDF) scheduling is often employed. EDF prioritizes tasks based on their closest deadlines, ensuring that tasks with imminent deadlines are executed first. This is critical in applications like avionics or industrial automation, where missing deadlines can have severe consequences. However, EDF doesn't guarantee optimal resource utilization, and task overruns can still occur if not managed carefully. Another real-time scheduling algorithm is Rate-Monotonic Scheduling (RMS), where tasks with shorter periods are assigned higher priorities. RMS ensures that higher-frequency tasks are given precedence but may not be suitable for sporadic or aperiodic tasks.

Multiple-level Queue Scheduling is a versatile approach that organizes tasks into different queues based on priority levels. Each queue follows its scheduling algorithm, such as FCFS or Round Robin, allowing for fine-tuned management of various task types. This approach is particularly useful in systems with diverse task characteristics, catering to both short and long-term task requirements effectively. Another variant is the Multilevel Feedback Queue (MLFQ) scheduling, which dynamically adjusts the priority of tasks based on their behavior. Tasks that use less CPU time may be promoted to higher-priority queues, preventing starvation and adapting to varying task requirements.

The Lottery Scheduling algorithm introduces a unique concept by assigning each task a number of lottery tickets. During each scheduling event, a ticket is randomly drawn, and the corresponding task is selected for execution. This approach ensures a probabilistic distribution of resources, providing equal opportunities for all tasks. However, it introduces an element of randomness, and tasks with more tickets may dominate the CPU, potentially leading to inequalities. Weighted Fair Queuing (WFQ) is another algorithm that aims to provide fairness by assigning weights to tasks based on their resource requirements. Tasks with higher weights receive more CPU time, promoting equitable resource allocation.

In resource-constrained environments, where minimizing turnaround time is crucial, the Guaranteed Scheduling algorithm ensures that each task is allocated a minimum amount of CPU time. This approach prevents task starvation and guarantees a baseline level of service for all tasks. Nevertheless, it may lead to inefficient resource utilization if not adjusted appropriately, as tasks may retain the CPU for longer than necessary.

In modern computing environments, where parallel processing and multi-core architectures are prevalent, Parallel Scheduling algorithms become essential. Work-Stealing is a prominent approach, where idle processors "steal" tasks from busy ones, ensuring a balanced distribution of workload and optimal utilization of available resources. This dynamic strategy is well-suited for applications that can be decomposed into smaller, parallelizable tasks, enhancing overall system throughput. Another parallel scheduling approach is Gang Scheduling, which schedules a set of related tasks simultaneously on different processors. This is particularly beneficial for parallel applications where tasks depend on each other's results or need to synchronize their execution.

Moreover, Global and Local Scheduling strategies are vital in distributed computing environments. Global Scheduling involves coordinating the execution of tasks across multiple processors or nodes in a system. This approach is often used in clusters or cloud computing environments, optimizing resource utilization on a broader scale. Local Scheduling, on the other hand, focuses on managing tasks within an individual processor or node. This can be crucial for load balancing in heterogeneous systems, where each node may have different capabilities and workloads.

Furthermore, Machine Learning-driven Scheduling algorithms are gaining traction, leveraging predictive analytics and self-learning mechanisms. These algorithms analyze historical usage patterns, workload characteristics, and system behaviors to predict future resource demands. By dynamically adjusting scheduling policies based on real-time data, machine learning-driven approaches can optimize resource allocation, enhance system responsiveness, and adapt to evolving workloads.

In conclusion, scheduling algorithms form the backbone of efficient device access and usage management within computing systems. From classic algorithms like FCFS and RR to real-time scheduling strategies such as EDF and RMS, and innovative approaches like Work-Stealing and Machine Learning-driven Scheduling, each algorithm addresses specific requirements and challenges. The choice of a scheduling algorithm depends on the nature of tasks, system characteristics, and performance goals. As technology continues to evolve, the development of new scheduling algorithms and the refinement of existing ones remain critical for optimizing system responsiveness, ensuring stability, and unlocking the full potential of computing resources in diverse and dynamic computing environments.

Discuss how these algorithms contribute to fair and optimal device utilization.

Scheduling algorithms play a pivotal role in achieving fair and optimal device utilization within computing systems, ensuring that available resources are allocated efficiently and equitably among competing tasks or processes. The overarching goal is to strike a balance, promoting fairness in resource access while optimizing system performance. These algorithms contribute to fair and optimal device utilization by addressing various aspects of resource allocation, responsiveness, and adaptability to diverse workloads.

First-Come-First-Serve (FCFS) scheduling, a classic algorithm, contributes to fair utilization by prioritizing tasks based on their arrival time. It ensures that tasks are served in the order they arrive, promoting a sense of fairness. However, FCFS may lead to inefficiencies in optimal utilization, particularly in scenarios where shorter tasks are delayed by longer ones, a phenomenon known as the "convoy effect." While FCFS promotes fairness in terms of task order, it may not always result in optimal device utilization, especially when there is a mix of short and long tasks.

Round Robin (RR) scheduling, another widely used algorithm, contributes to fair device utilization by providing each task with a fixed time quantum. This ensures that tasks are given equal opportunities to access the CPU, promoting fairness in resource allocation. RR is particularly effective in time-sharing systems where multiple users or tasks coexist. However, it may not be optimal for scenarios with varying task execution times, as fixed time quanta may not suit all tasks equally. The fairness achieved by RR comes at the cost of potentially suboptimal resource utilization.

Priority Scheduling introduces fairness by assigning priorities to tasks, ensuring that higher-priority tasks are given precedence over lower-priority ones. This strategy aligns with the importance of specific tasks or the urgency of their execution. However, without proper management, priority scheduling can lead to the starvation of lower-priority tasks, as higher-priority tasks continuously preempt them. To mitigate this, Aging, a variation of Priority Scheduling, increases the priority of tasks with time, preventing indefinite delays for lower-priority tasks.

Shortest Job Next (SJN) or Shortest Job First (SJF) scheduling contributes to optimal device utilization by selecting the task with the shortest burst time for execution. This minimizes waiting times and enhances system throughput, as tasks with shorter execution times are prioritized. SJN is effective in scenarios where the burst time of tasks is accurately known in advance. However, predicting burst times accurately can be challenging in practice, and the overhead of estimating burst times may counteract the benefits in some cases.

In real-time systems, where meeting deadlines is crucial, Earliest Deadline First (EDF) scheduling ensures optimal device utilization by prioritizing tasks based on their closest deadlines. This strategy aligns with the deterministic requirements of real-time applications, where tasks must complete within specified time constraints. However, EDF does not guarantee optimal resource utilization, and task overruns can still occur, especially in situations with high task variability.

Rate-Monotonic Scheduling (RMS) is another real-time scheduling algorithm that contributes to fair and optimal device utilization by assigning higher priorities to tasks with shorter periods. RMS ensures that higher-frequency tasks are given precedence, promoting fairness in time-critical applications. Nevertheless, RMS may not be suitable for sporadic or aperiodic tasks, and its effectiveness relies on a comprehensive understanding of task characteristics.

Multiple-level Queue Scheduling introduces fairness by organizing tasks into different queues based on priority levels. Each queue follows its scheduling algorithm, such as FCFS or RR, allowing for fine-tuned management of various task types. This approach is particularly useful in systems with diverse task characteristics, catering to both short and long-term task requirements effectively. By categorizing tasks based on priority, multiple-level queue scheduling achieves fairness while adapting to varying task needs.

The Multilevel Feedback Queue (MLFQ) scheduling algorithm dynamically adjusts the priority of tasks based on their behavior, contributing to both fairness and optimal device utilization. Tasks that use less CPU time may be promoted to higher-priority queues, preventing starvation and adapting to varying task requirements.

MLFQ combines elements of multiple-level queue scheduling and feedback mechanisms, offering adaptability to dynamic workloads and preventing excessive resource monopolization.

Lottery Scheduling introduces fairness by assigning each task a number of lottery tickets. During each scheduling event, a ticket is randomly drawn, and the corresponding task is selected for execution. This probabilistic approach ensures a balanced distribution of resources, providing equal opportunities for all tasks. However, the randomness introduced by lottery scheduling may lead to inequalities, as tasks with more tickets may dominate the CPU, potentially disadvantaging others.

Weighted Fair Queuing (WFQ) contributes to fair and optimal device utilization by assigning weights to tasks based on their resource requirements. Tasks with higher weights receive more CPU time, promoting equitable resource allocation. WFQ is particularly effective in environments where tasks have varying resource demands, ensuring that tasks with higher resource requirements are allocated proportionally more CPU time. This approach aligns with the notion of fairness based on the relative needs of tasks.

Guaranteed Scheduling ensures fair and optimal device utilization by allocating each task a minimum amount of CPU time. This approach prevents task starvation and guarantees a baseline level of service for all tasks. By ensuring that each task receives a fair share of CPU time, guaranteed scheduling maintains fairness while preventing inefficiencies associated with excessive waiting times.

In parallel processing and multi-core architectures, where balancing workloads is crucial, Work-Stealing contributes to fair and optimal device utilization. This algorithm ensures a balanced distribution of workload by allowing idle processors to "steal" tasks from busy ones. Work-Stealing is particularly effective in scenarios where tasks can be decomposed into smaller, parallelizable units, enhancing overall system throughput while maintaining fairness in resource access.

Global and Local Scheduling strategies are vital in distributed computing environments, ensuring fairness and optimal device utilization. Global Scheduling involves coordinating the execution of tasks across multiple processors or nodes in a system. This approach optimizes resource utilization on a broader scale, considering the global needs of the system. Local Scheduling focuses on managing tasks within an individual processor or node, contributing to fairness and optimal utilization in heterogeneous systems where each node may have different capabilities and workloads.

Machine Learning-driven Scheduling algorithms leverage predictive analytics and self-learning mechanisms to contribute to fair and optimal device utilization. By analyzing historical usage patterns, workload characteristics, and system behaviors, these algorithms predict future resource demands. The dynamic adjustment of scheduling policies based on real-time data allows machine learning-driven approaches to optimize resource allocation, enhance system responsiveness, and adapt to evolving workloads, ultimately contributing to fair and optimal device utilization.

In conclusion, scheduling algorithms are instrumental in achieving fair and optimal device utilization within computing systems. From classic algorithms like FCFS and RR to real-time strategies such as EDF and RMS, and innovative approaches like Work-Stealing and Machine Learning-driven Scheduling, each algorithm addresses specific requirements and challenges. The pursuit of fairness and optimal utilization involves striking a delicate balance, considering the diverse needs of tasks, the dynamic nature of workloads, and the evolving landscape of computing environments. As technology continues to advance, the ongoing development and refinement of scheduling algorithms remain critical for unlocking the full potential of computing resources while ensuring fairness in resource access and optimal device utilization.

Explore the role of caching in optimizing device performance.

Caching plays a pivotal role in optimizing device performance across a wide array of computing systems, from individual devices to complex server architectures. At its core, caching involves the storage of frequently accessed data in a high-speed, easily retrievable location, reducing the need to repeatedly fetch the same information from slower, more distant storage mediums. This strategic use of intermediate storage contributes significantly to enhancing the overall performance, responsiveness, and efficiency of devices in various computing environments.

In storage systems, caching is instrumental in minimizing data retrieval times and reducing latency. By storing frequently accessed data in a cache, such as in-memory cache or Solid State Drives (SSDs), devices can swiftly retrieve information without the delays associated with accessing slower storage mediums like Hard Disk Drives (HDDs). This is particularly critical in scenarios where quick access to data is paramount, such as in gaming applications, database systems, or multimedia editing tools. The utilization of caching transforms the user experience by providing faster data access and minimizing the wait times associated with loading applications or retrieving files.

In the context of operating systems and applications, caching extends beyond storage to include the caching of program instructions and frequently executed code segments. The CPU cache, a small but high-speed memory directly accessible by the processor, stores recently used instructions to accelerate the execution of tasks. This hardware-level caching mechanism significantly reduces the time spent waiting for instructions to be fetched from slower RAM (Random Access Memory) or even more sluggish storage devices. The efficiency gains achieved through CPU caching are particularly noticeable in compute-intensive applications, where the rapid execution of instructions directly correlates with overall system performance.

Web browsers leverage caching to optimize the loading times of websites and web applications. Caching mechanisms, such as browser caches and Content Delivery Networks (CDNs), store static resources like images, stylesheets, and scripts locally on the user's device or in strategically positioned servers. This prevents the need to download these resources anew with each visit to a website, leading to faster page load times and a more responsive browsing experience. Additionally, caching reduces the load on web servers and network bandwidth, contributing to a more efficient and scalable web infrastructure.

In database systems, caching plays a crucial role in enhancing query performance and system responsiveness. Database caching involves storing the results of frequently executed queries or commonly accessed data in a cache, reducing the need to repeatedly query the underlying database. This is especially beneficial in read-heavy applications where certain data remains relatively static. The adoption of caching strategies, such as in-memory caching or database query result caching, accelerates data retrieval, lowers database server load, and contributes to a more responsive and scalable system.

Content caching in Content Delivery Networks (CDNs) is pivotal for optimizing the delivery of web content, especially in scenarios with high user demand or geographically dispersed user bases. CDNs strategically cache static content like images, videos, and web pages in servers distributed across various locations worldwide. When a user requests content, the CDN serves it from the closest cached copy, minimizing latency and reducing the load on origin servers. This not only accelerates content delivery but also enhances the reliability and availability of web services, contributing to an optimized user experience.

The use of caching is also prevalent in networking, where caching proxies store copies of frequently requested content. This is particularly evident in scenarios like content filtering, where proxy servers cache frequently accessed websites, reducing the need to fetch the same content repeatedly from the internet. Caching proxies not only optimize network performance by delivering content more quickly to end-users but also contribute to bandwidth savings and improved network efficiency.

Caching in the realm of graphics and multimedia accelerates rendering and improves the responsiveness of applications that heavily rely on visual elements. Graphics Processing Units (GPUs) utilize texture caching, storing frequently accessed textures in dedicated high-speed memory. This reduces the need to repeatedly fetch textures from system memory or storage, enhancing the rendering speed of graphics-intensive applications such as video games and 3D modeling software. Additionally, caching contributes to smoother video playback by storing previously decoded frames, reducing the impact of fluctuations in network bandwidth or decoding delays.

Operating systems employ file system caching to enhance overall device performance. The file system cache temporarily stores recently accessed file data in memory, reducing the time required to read or write data to slower storage devices. This is particularly advantageous in scenarios where applications frequently access the same files, as the file system cache allows the operating system to fulfill read requests more rapidly. By reducing the reliance on slower storage mediums, file system caching contributes to a more responsive computing environment and improved application performance.

Cache coherence mechanisms in multiprocessor systems are crucial for maintaining data consistency and optimizing shared resource access. In systems with multiple processors or cores, each processor may have its cache, and ensuring that all caches have a coherent view of shared data is essential. Cache coherence protocols, such as MESI (Modified, Exclusive, Shared, Invalid), manage the state of cache lines to prevent data inconsistencies. This contributes to optimized device performance in parallel processing environments by allowing multiple processors to work on shared data without introducing errors or unnecessary delays due to cache conflicts.

The adoption of prefetching techniques in caching further enhances device performance by proactively loading data into the cache before it is explicitly requested. Prefetching algorithms analyze access patterns and predict which data is likely to be accessed next. By loading this data into the cache ahead of time, prefetching mitigates the impact of memory or storage latency, ensuring that the required data is readily available when needed. This is particularly beneficial in scenarios with predictable access patterns, such as sequential data access in file processing or streaming applications.

While caching significantly contributes to optimizing device performance, it is not without challenges. Cache invalidation mechanisms are critical to ensuring that cached data remains consistent with the underlying data source. In scenarios where the source data is frequently updated or modified, effective cache invalidation prevents the delivery of outdated or incorrect information to end-users. Balancing the trade-off between caching and the freshness of data is crucial, and strategies such as time-based expiration or event-driven invalidation are employed to maintain cache coherence.

Cache size and management strategies also play a pivotal role in determining the effectiveness of caching. The size of the cache influences the amount of data that can be stored, and a larger cache can accommodate more frequently accessed data. However, cache management policies, such as Least Recently Used (LRU) or Least Frequently Used (LFU), determine which data is retained in the cache when it reaches its capacity. Choosing an appropriate cache size and management policy requires a nuanced understanding of the specific workload characteristics and access patterns.

In conclusion, caching stands as a cornerstone in optimizing device performance across diverse computing environments. From storage systems and operating systems to web browsers, databases, and graphics processing, caching mechanisms contribute to faster data access, reduced latency, and improved overall system responsiveness. Whether employed in CPU caches, storage caches, web content delivery, or graphics rendering, the strategic use of caching enhances the efficiency of devices, providing users with a more responsive and seamless computing experience. As technology continues to advance, the ongoing refinement and adaptation of caching strategies remain essential for meeting the evolving demands of modern computing.

Discuss how caching reduces latency and improves overall system responsiveness.

Caching serves as a fundamental strategy in reducing latency and enhancing overall system responsiveness across a myriad of computing environments. At its essence, caching involves storing frequently accessed data in a high-speed, easily accessible location, mitigating the need to retrieve the same information from slower, more distant storage mediums. This strategic use of intermediate storage fundamentally transforms the speed at which devices can access critical data, contributing to a more responsive and efficient computing experience.

In the context of storage systems, caching plays a crucial role in minimizing data retrieval times, which directly correlates with reduced latency. By storing frequently accessed data in a cache—be it in-memory cache, Solid State Drives (SSDs), or other high-speed storage devices—devices can swiftly retrieve information without incurring the delays associated with accessing slower storage mediums like Hard Disk Drives (HDDs). This is particularly critical in scenarios where quick access to data is paramount, such as in gaming applications, database systems, or multimedia editing tools. Caching ensures that data is readily available for processing, contributing significantly to reducing the latency associated with data retrieval.

Operating systems and applications leverage caching not only for storage-related purposes but also for storing frequently executed program instructions and code segments. The CPU cache, a high-speed memory directly accessible by the processor, stores recently used instructions, reducing the time spent waiting for instructions to be fetched from slower RAM (Random Access Memory) or storage devices. This hardware-level caching mechanism is instrumental in reducing instruction-fetch latency and improving the overall responsiveness of the system, especially in compute-intensive applications where rapid execution of instructions is crucial.

Web browsers exploit caching strategies to optimize the loading times of websites and web applications, thereby reducing latency. Caching mechanisms, including browser caches and Content Delivery Networks (CDNs), store static resources like images, stylesheets, and scripts locally on the user's device or in strategically positioned servers. This prevents the need to download these resources anew with each visit to a website, leading to faster page load times and a more responsive browsing experience. Additionally, caching reduces the load on web servers and network bandwidth, further contributing to a more efficient and scalable web infrastructure.

Database systems leverage caching to enhance query performance, reducing the latency associated with fetching data from storage. Database caching involves storing the results of frequently executed queries or commonly accessed data in a cache, minimizing the need to repeatedly query the underlying database. This is especially beneficial in read-heavy applications where certain data remains relatively static. The adoption of caching strategies, such as in-memory caching or database query result caching, accelerates data retrieval, lowers database server load, and contributes to a more responsive and scalable system.

Content Delivery Networks (CDNs) employ caching to optimize content delivery, reducing latency for users accessing web content. CDNs strategically cache static content like images, videos, and web pages in servers distributed across various locations worldwide. When a user requests content, the CDN serves it from the closest cached copy, minimizing latency and reducing the load on origin servers. This not only accelerates content delivery but also enhances the reliability and availability of web services, contributing to reduced latency for end-users.

Networking scenarios benefit from caching, particularly with the use of caching proxies that store copies of frequently requested content. This is evident in content filtering applications, where proxy servers cache frequently accessed websites, reducing the need to fetch the same content repeatedly from the internet. Caching proxies optimize network performance by delivering content more quickly to end-users, thereby reducing latency. Additionally, they contribute to bandwidth savings and improved network efficiency by reducing the volume of redundant data traversing the network.

In graphics and multimedia applications, caching accelerates rendering processes and improves overall responsiveness. Graphics Processing Units (GPUs) utilize texture caching, storing frequently accessed textures in dedicated high-speed memory. This reduces the need to repeatedly fetch textures from system memory or storage, enhancing the rendering speed of graphics-intensive applications such as video games and 3D modeling software. Additionally, caching contributes to smoother video playback by storing previously decoded frames, reducing the impact of fluctuations in network bandwidth or decoding delays.

File system caching in operating systems plays a crucial role in reducing latency associated with file access. The file system cache temporarily stores recently accessed file data in memory, reducing the time required to read or write data to slower storage devices. This is particularly advantageous in scenarios where applications frequently access the same files, as the file system cache allows the operating system to fulfill read requests more rapidly. By minimizing reliance on slower storage mediums, file system caching contributes to a more responsive computing environment and improved application performance.

Cache coherence mechanisms in multiprocessor systems further reduce latency and maintain data consistency in shared-memory architectures. In systems with multiple processors or cores, each processor may have its cache, and ensuring that all caches have a coherent view of shared data is essential. Cache coherence protocols, such as MESI (Modified, Exclusive, Shared, Invalid), manage the state of cache lines to prevent data inconsistencies. By maintaining cache coherence, these mechanisms ensure that data can be accessed with minimal latency and without introducing errors or unnecessary delays due to cache conflicts.

Prefetching techniques in caching proactively reduce latency by loading data into the cache before it is explicitly requested. Prefetching algorithms analyze access patterns and predict which data is likely to be accessed next. By loading this data into the cache ahead of time, prefetching mitigates the impact of memory or storage latency, ensuring that the required data is readily available when needed. This is particularly beneficial in scenarios with predictable access patterns, such as sequential data access in file processing or streaming applications.

While caching substantially reduces latency and improves system responsiveness, it is not without its challenges. Cache invalidation mechanisms are crucial to ensuring that
cached data remains consistent with the underlying data source. In scenarios where the source data is frequently updated or modified,

effective cache invalidation prevents the delivery of outdated or incorrect information to end-users. Balancing the trade-off between caching and the freshness of data is crucial, and strategies such as time-based expiration or event-driven invalidation are employed to maintain cache coherence.

Cache size and management strategies also play a pivotal role in determining the effectiveness of caching in reducing latency. The size of the cache influences the amount of data that can be stored, and a larger cache can accommodate more frequently accessed data. However, cache management policies, such as Least Recently Used (LRU) or Least Frequently Used (LFU), determine which data is retained in the cache when it reaches its capacity. Choosing an appropriate cache size and management policy requires a nuanced understanding of the specific workload characteristics and access patterns.

In conclusion, caching stands as a linchpin in the quest to reduce latency and enhance overall system responsiveness across diverse computing environments. Whether employed in storage systems, operating systems, web browsers, databases, networking, graphics processing, or multiprocessing architectures, the strategic use of caching substantially contributes to faster data access, minimized latency, and an improved computing experience. As technology continues to advance, the ongoing refinement and adaptation of caching strategies remain essential for meeting the evolving demands of modern computing and delivering optimal responsiveness to end-users.

Discuss the integration of parallel processing techniques for enhanced device handling.

The integration of parallel processing techniques stands as a transformative approach to enhance device handling across a spectrum of computing applications, ranging from individual devices to high-performance computing clusters. Parallel processing, at its core, involves the simultaneous execution of multiple tasks or subtasks to achieve a collective goal, offering a pathway to overcome the limitations of sequential processing and unlock the full potential of modern computing devices. The multifaceted integration of parallel processing encompasses diverse strategies, including task parallelism, data parallelism, and model parallelism, each contributing to improved performance, scalability, and efficiency in handling complex computational workloads.

In the realm of central processing units (CPUs), the adoption of multicore architectures represents a foundational step in integrating parallel processing techniques. Multicore processors feature multiple independent processing units, or cores, on a single chip, enabling concurrent execution of tasks. This architecture harnesses task parallelism, allowing different cores to work on separate tasks simultaneously. Applications that can be decomposed into distinct threads or processes benefit significantly from multicore processors, experiencing accelerated performance and reduced execution times. The integration of multicore architectures has become ubiquitous, from personal computers and laptops to servers and high-performance computing clusters, marking a paradigm shift in how devices handle compute-intensive workloads.

Graphics Processing Units (GPUs) exemplify a specialized form of parallel processing integration that focuses on data parallelism, particularly suited for computationally intensive tasks such as graphics rendering, scientific simulations, and machine learning. GPUs consist of numerous parallel processing units, commonly organized into a large number of cores, designed to efficiently handle parallelizable tasks by concurrently processing data elements in parallel. The widespread adoption of GPUs for general-purpose computing, known as General-Purpose GPU (GPGPU) computing, has revolutionized the landscape of parallel processing. Through frameworks like CUDA (Compute Unified Device Architecture) and OpenCL (Open Computing Language), developers can leverage the immense parallel processing power of GPUs to accelerate a diverse range of applications, from scientific simulations to deep learning algorithms.

In distributed computing environments, the integration of parallel processing extends to clusters of interconnected devices working collaboratively to tackle large-scale computational challenges. Task parallelism is a cornerstone in this context, where different devices within the cluster contribute to the execution of distinct tasks or subtasks. High-Performance Computing (HPC) clusters, often used for scientific simulations and data-intensive computations, exemplify the integration of parallel processing techniques at an extensive scale. Message Passing Interface (MPI) and parallel programming models such as OpenMP enable the seamless coordination of parallel tasks across distributed nodes, allowing for enhanced scalability and performance in handling complex simulations and analyses.

The emergence of parallel file systems is another facet of parallel processing integration that addresses the challenges associated with handling vast amounts of data in parallel. In traditional file systems, a single storage device may become a bottleneck, limiting the overall throughput. Parallel file systems, designed for concurrent access by multiple nodes, distribute data across multiple storage devices and enable parallel read and write operations. This approach aligns with data parallelism, enhancing the efficiency of data-intensive applications that require simultaneous access to large datasets. Parallel file systems, such as Lustre and GPFS (General Parallel File System), have become integral components in HPC environments, providing high-performance storage solutions for parallel workloads.

Parallel processing techniques are pivotal in the context of database management systems, where the demands for handling large datasets and complex queries necessitate efficient concurrency and parallel execution. Parallel database systems leverage both task and data parallelism to enhance query performance. Tasks can be decomposed into parallelizable units, and data can be partitioned across multiple nodes for concurrent processing. This approach accelerates query execution times and improves the responsiveness of database systems, making them well-suited for applications with demanding data processing requirements.

In the context of parallel processing for enhanced device handling, the adoption of parallel algorithms plays a crucial role. Parallel algorithms are designed to exploit the parallel nature of the underlying architecture, ensuring that computations can be distributed across multiple processing units for improved efficiency. Parallel sorting algorithms, parallel matrix multiplication, and parallel search algorithms are examples of how parallel processing techniques are applied to foundational computational tasks. These algorithms, often implemented using parallel programming frameworks like OpenMP or MPI, showcase the potential for significant speedup and improved performance in handling diverse computational workloads.

Machine learning and artificial intelligence applications benefit extensively from the integration of parallel processing techniques. Training deep neural networks, a computationally intensive task, involves processing vast amounts of data through complex mathematical operations. GPUs, with their parallel processing capabilities, have become indispensable for accelerating the training of deep learning models. Additionally, parallelization techniques such as model parallelism, where different parts of a neural network are processed in parallel, contribute to handling increasingly complex and larger models. The integration of parallel processing has been instrumental in democratizing access to advanced machine learning capabilities, making it feasible to train sophisticated models even on consumer-grade GPUs.

The integration of parallel processing techniques extends into real-time and embedded systems, where responsiveness and efficiency are critical. In these systems, task parallelism ensures that different components or processes can operate concurrently, meeting stringent timing requirements. Parallelization in real-time systems may involve the use of multicore processors, hardware accelerators, or custom-designed parallel architectures. The automotive industry, for instance, leverages parallel processing in embedded systems for tasks such as sensor data fusion, image processing for advanced driver assistance systems (ADAS), and control algorithms for autonomous vehicles.

Furthermore, the integration of parallel processing techniques in scientific simulations and computational modeling has led to breakthroughs in fields such as weather forecasting, fluid dynamics, and materials science. Numerical simulations that require solving complex equations or simulating physical phenomena can benefit significantly from parallel processing. High-fidelity simulations, previously impractical due to computational demands, become feasible with the ability to distribute the workload across multiple processing units. This not only accelerates simulation times but also enables scientists and researchers to explore more intricate models and gain deeper insights into complex systems.

Challenges associated with the integration of parallel processing techniques include the need for effective load balancing, minimizing communication overhead, and ensuring data consistency in distributed environments. Load balancing is critical to distributing computational tasks evenly across processing units, preventing situations where some units are idle while others are overloaded. Efficient communication patterns and data sharing mechanisms are essential to minimize the overhead associated with synchronizing parallel tasks. Additionally, ensuring data consistency across distributed nodes is crucial, especially in scenarios where multiple nodes may be working on shared datasets. These challenges underscore the importance of careful algorithm design, parallel programming models, and system architectures to fully realize the benefits of parallel processing.

In conclusion, the integration of parallel processing techniques stands as a cornerstone for enhanced device handling across a diverse range of computing applications. From multicore processors and GPUs to distributed clusters and parallel algorithms, the strategic use of parallelism addresses the ever-growing demands for performance, scalability, and efficiency in handling complex computational workloads. Whether applied in scientific simulations, machine learning, database systems, or embedded systems, parallel processing techniques continue to push the boundaries of what devices can achieve, unlocking new possibilities and contributing to the evolution of modern computing paradigms. As technology advances, the ongoing refinement and adaptation of parallel processing strategies remain paramount for meeting the challenges of an increasingly parallel and data-intensive computing landscape.

Explore how multi-core architectures impact device management strategies.

The advent of multi-core architectures has significantly reshaped device management strategies, ushering in a new era of computing where parallelism is harnessed to address the growing demands for performance, efficiency, and responsiveness. Multi-core architectures, featuring multiple independent processing units (cores) on a single chip, represent a departure from traditional single-core designs and introduce a paradigm shift in how devices are managed and optimized to handle diverse workloads. This transformation is evident across a spectrum of computing devices, from personal computers and servers to embedded systems and mobile devices, each grappling with the challenges and opportunities presented by the integration of multiple processing cores.

One of the primary impacts of multi-core architectures on device management strategies lies in the realm of parallel processing. Multi-core processors allow for concurrent execution of tasks, enabling the exploitation of task parallelism in applications. Device management strategies must now be tailored to leverage this parallelism effectively, distributing tasks across available cores to maximize overall system throughput. The design and optimization of software applications become paramount, as traditional sequential algorithms need to be restructured or replaced with parallel counterparts to fully capitalize on the capabilities of multi-core architectures. Programming models like OpenMP and CUDA facilitate the development of parallel applications, enabling developers to harness the power of multi-core processors efficiently.

Task scheduling, a critical aspect of device management, undergoes a paradigm shift with the introduction of multi-core architectures. Traditional scheduling strategies, which focused on optimizing the execution of tasks sequentially, must evolve to handle the intricacies of concurrent task execution on multiple cores. Load balancing becomes a key consideration, ensuring that the computational workload is evenly distributed across cores to prevent situations where some cores remain idle while others are overloaded. Dynamic task scheduling algorithms, capable of adapting to varying workloads and core availability, emerge as essential components of device management strategies in multi-core environments. Efficient task scheduling directly impacts system responsiveness, throughput, and the overall utilization of processing resources.

Cache management strategies also experience significant changes in the context of multi-core architectures. Each core typically comes with its cache, introducing the potential for cache coherency issues when multiple cores access shared data. Cache coherence protocols, such as MESI (Modified, Exclusive, Shared, Invalid), are employed to maintain consistency among caches, ensuring that all cores have a coherent view of shared data. Device management strategies need to account for the intricacies of cache coherence, optimizing data access patterns to minimize the impact of cache invalidations and coherence-related overhead. The efficient utilization of caches is crucial for reducing memory access latencies and enhancing overall system performance in multi-core environments.

Parallelism, however, introduces new challenges related to synchronization and inter-core communication. Device management strategies must grapple with the intricacies of coordinating parallel tasks to avoid data races, deadlocks, and other synchronization-related issues. Techniques such as locks, semaphores, and atomic operations become integral components of managing shared resources among multiple cores. Furthermore, inter-core communication mechanisms, such as message passing or shared-memory models, require careful consideration to minimize latency and contention. Device managers and system architects need to implement strategies that strike a balance between maximizing parallelism and minimizing synchronization overhead, ensuring efficient cooperation among multiple cores.

Power management strategies are also significantly impacted by the introduction of multi-core architectures. While multi-core processors offer increased processing power, they may also lead to higher power consumption, particularly when all cores are active. Dynamic Voltage and Frequency Scaling (DVFS) techniques become crucial in managing power consumption by adjusting the voltage and frequency of individual cores based on workload requirements. Device management strategies must intelligently leverage DVFS and other power management techniques to optimize the trade-off between performance and power consumption, ensuring that devices operate efficiently while minimizing energy consumption and heat dissipation.

The integration of multi-core architectures has implications for real-time and embedded systems, where predictability and responsiveness are paramount. Real-time operating systems (RTOS) and embedded device managers need to account for the parallel nature of multi-core processors while ensuring that real-time constraints are met. Scheduling strategies in real-time systems must evolve to handle multiple concurrent tasks, with considerations for task priorities, deadlines, and resource access. Moreover, embedded systems, which often operate in resource-constrained environments, must carefully manage power consumption and thermal considerations while delivering optimal performance through parallelism.

Multi-core architectures also influence memory management strategies, introducing considerations for shared memory access and data locality. Efficient memory allocation and access patterns become critical in maximizing the benefits of multi-core processors. Device management strategies need to optimize memory layouts, minimize cache misses, and ensure that data is efficiently shared among cores when necessary. Memory hierarchy considerations, including the interplay between caches and main memory, play a central role in managing data access patterns and influencing overall system performance.

Software development practices are profoundly impacted by the prevalence of multi-core architectures. Parallel programming becomes a requisite skill as developers aim to extract optimal performance from multi-core processors. Traditional sequential programming approaches are no longer sufficient, and developers need to embrace parallel programming models and frameworks. Device management strategies extend beyond the operating system level, requiring collaboration between hardware and software developers to design applications that exploit parallelism effectively. This shift in software development practices underscores the importance of interdisciplinary collaboration and a holistic approach to device management in a multi-core ecosystem.

The evolution of multi-core architectures intersects with the broader trends in cloud computing and virtualization. Cloud service providers leverage multi-core processors to deliver scalable and high-performance computing resources to users. Virtualization technologies, such as hypervisors, need to efficiently manage multiple virtual machines running on multi-core hosts. Device management strategies in cloud environments involve dynamic allocation and deallocation of resources based on workload demands, efficient scheduling of virtual machines on multi-core hosts, and optimization of resource utilization to achieve cost-effective and responsive cloud services.

In conclusion, the impact of multi-core architectures on device management strategies is profound and far-reaching. The shift from single-core to multi-core processors necessitates a reevaluation and evolution of traditional device management approaches. Strategies for parallelism, task scheduling, cache management, synchronization, power management, and memory allocation must be tailored to the intricacies of multi-core architectures. The advent of multi-core processors not only demands changes in hardware and software design but also calls for a paradigm shift in how devices are managed and optimized to meet the challenges and opportunities presented by the era of parallel computing. As technology continues to advance, the ongoing refinement and adaptation of device management strategies will remain essential for harnessing the full potential of multi-core architectures and delivering optimal performance across a diverse range of computing devices.

Chapter 5: Security Measures in Device Management

Define the importance of security in device management within operating systems.

Security in device management within operating systems stands as a cornerstone in the overall framework of ensuring the integrity, confidentiality, and availability of computing systems. Operating systems serve as the fundamental layer that facilitates communication and coordination between hardware devices and higher-level software applications. The importance of security in this context lies in safeguarding these interactions, protecting against unauthorized access, preventing malicious attacks, and ensuring the stability and reliability of the entire computing environment.

One of the primary imperatives of security in device management is to control and authenticate access to critical system resources. Operating systems often manage a diverse array of devices, including storage drives, network interfaces, and input/output peripherals. Proper authentication mechanisms and access controls must be in place to ensure that only authorized users or processes can interact with these devices. Unauthorized access to sensitive devices can lead to data breaches, system instability, or the exploitation of vulnerabilities, emphasizing the critical role that security mechanisms play in protecting the underlying hardware components.

In the realm of data security, the encryption of communication between the operating system and devices becomes paramount. Many devices, especially in the context of networks and storage, transmit sensitive information. Security protocols and encryption algorithms help safeguard the confidentiality of this data, ensuring that even if intercepted, it remains unintelligible to unauthorized entities. The integration of secure communication protocols in device management within operating systems is crucial for protecting against eavesdropping, data tampering, and unauthorized data access, contributing to the overall robustness of the system.

Device drivers, integral components of device management, pose a potential security risk if not rigorously managed. Ensuring the integrity of device drivers is imperative to prevent the injection of malicious code into the operating system kernel. The installation and execution of drivers should follow secure practices, and mechanisms such as driver signing can be employed to verify the authenticity and integrity of drivers before allowing them to interact with the kernel. Security-conscious device management involves continuous monitoring and auditing of drivers to detect and mitigate any potential vulnerabilities or malicious activities.

The protection of system resources from malicious software, including viruses, malware, and ransomware, is a paramount aspect of security in device management. Operating systems must employ robust security measures to prevent unauthorized software from interacting with devices in a harmful manner. This involves implementing access controls, sandboxing mechanisms, and intrusion detection systems to identify and mitigate potential threats. Security updates and patches are crucial for addressing vulnerabilities that could be exploited by malicious software, underscoring the importance of timely and comprehensive device management security practices.

Network security is a critical facet of device management within operating systems, especially in the context of connected devices and the Internet of Things (IoT). Operating systems must manage network interfaces securely, implementing protocols such as firewalls, intrusion detection/prevention systems, and secure communication protocols to protect against unauthorized access and cyberattacks. With the proliferation of interconnected devices, security in device management becomes increasingly complex, necessitating a comprehensive approach to mitigate the risks associated with network-based threats.

Secure boot mechanisms play a pivotal role in ensuring the integrity of the operating system itself. By verifying the authenticity and integrity of the operating system kernel during the boot process, secure boot mechanisms prevent the execution of tampered or malicious code. This foundational security measure protects against attacks that attempt to compromise the operating system at its core, emphasizing the significance of secure boot in device management for establishing a trusted computing environment.

Device management security is closely linked to the concept of least privilege, where users and processes are granted only the minimum level of access necessary to perform their functions. This principle is particularly relevant in device management, where limiting access rights helps mitigate the impact of potential security breaches. Implementing least privilege principles in the context of device management involves fine-grained access controls, user privilege management, and process isolation to minimize the attack surface and limit the potential damage caused by security incidents.

The secure handling of input and output devices is essential in mitigating the risks associated with input-based attacks, such as keyloggers or injection attacks. Secure input handling mechanisms within the operating system prevent malicious manipulation of input data and protect against attempts to compromise the integrity of user interactions. Additionally, secure output handling ensures that sensitive information is not inadvertently leaked through output devices, reinforcing the importance of comprehensive security measures in device management.

Security in device management extends to the realm of physical security, particularly in scenarios where devices can be physically accessed by unauthorized individuals. Protecting against physical tampering, theft, or unauthorized removal of devices is critical for maintaining the overall security posture of the system. Security features such as secure boot, tamper-evident seals, and physical access controls contribute to the safeguarding of devices against physical threats, highlighting the holistic nature of security in device management.

In the context of mobile and embedded systems, where devices often have limited resources and operate in diverse and potentially hostile environments, security becomes even more challenging. Operating systems for mobile devices must implement robust security measures to protect against mobile-specific threats, including unauthorized access to sensitive data, malware, and device theft. Secure device management practices in mobile and embedded systems encompass secure boot, encryption, secure communication protocols, and mobile device management solutions to enforce security policies and protect against a wide range of potential threats.

Compliance with industry standards and regulations further underscores the importance of security in device management. Various sectors, including finance, healthcare, and critical infrastructure, are subject to regulatory frameworks that mandate stringent security measures to protect sensitive data and ensure the reliability of systems. Device management within operating systems must adhere to these standards, implementing security controls, conducting regular audits, and maintaining documentation to demonstrate compliance with regulatory requirements.

The resilience of device management security also hinges on the ability to detect and respond to security incidents promptly. Intrusion detection systems, security event logging, and real-time monitoring play critical roles in identifying anomalous activities or potential security breaches. The operating system, as the central orchestrator of device management, must integrate robust security incident response mechanisms to isolate and mitigate security threats effectively.

User awareness and education are integral components of device management security. Users play a crucial role in maintaining the security of devices, and awareness programs can help educate them about best practices, the importance of strong authentication, and the potential risks associated with insecure device usage. Secure device management strategies include user training, awareness campaigns, and the promotion of security hygiene practices to empower users to contribute actively to the overall security posture.

In conclusion, security in device management within operating systems is a multifaceted and critical aspect of modern computing. The holistic approach to security involves protecting against a wide array of threats, encompassing unauthorized access, data breaches, malware, network attacks, and physical tampering. The operating system, as the central orchestrator of device management, plays a pivotal role in implementing and enforcing security measures to create a trusted and resilient computing environment. From access controls and encryption to secure boot mechanisms and incident response, the comprehensive security framework ensures the integrity, confidentiality, and availability of computing systems, fostering a secure foundation for the diverse devices that operate within the ecosystem. As technology evolves and cyber threats continue to advance, the ongoing refinement and adaptation of security measures in device management remain essential to stay ahead of the evolving threat landscape and protect the integrity of computing environments.

Explore the potential risks and consequences of insecure device configurations.

Insecure device configurations represent a significant and pervasive threat in the landscape of modern computing, encompassing a multitude of devices ranging from computers and servers to network infrastructure, Internet of Things (IoT) devices, and beyond. The potential risks associated with insecure device configurations are diverse, with consequences that span security, privacy, financial, operational, and reputational domains. Understanding the depth and breadth of these risks is crucial for devising effective strategies to mitigate vulnerabilities and safeguard the integrity of digital ecosystems.

Security risks are perhaps the most immediate and severe consequences of insecure device configurations. Misconfigurations in security settings, such as default passwords, open ports, and weak authentication mechanisms, create entry points for malicious actors to exploit. Attackers can leverage these vulnerabilities to gain unauthorized access to devices, compromise sensitive data, or launch further attacks within the network. Insecure configurations may lead to unauthorized privilege escalation, allowing attackers to assume higher levels of access than intended, potentially compromising the entire system. The consequence of such security breaches extends beyond the device itself, as compromised devices may be used as launchpads for broader attacks, including Distributed Denial of Service (DDoS) attacks, data exfiltration, or the propagation of malware.

Privacy risks are closely intertwined with insecure device configurations, particularly in an era where data collection and processing are ubiquitous. Insecurely configured devices may inadvertently expose sensitive user information or enable unauthorized surveillance. IoT devices, in particular, often handle personal data and may be susceptible to privacy breaches if not configured securely. Unauthorized access to surveillance cameras, smart home devices, or wearable technologies can compromise individuals' privacy, leading to unintended data exposure or misuse. The consequences of privacy breaches extend beyond immediate harm, potentially eroding trust in digital technologies and the responsible entities deploying these devices.

Financial risks arise from the potential economic impact of insecure device configurations. Organizations may incur substantial financial losses due to data breaches, legal liabilities, and regulatory fines resulting from insecurely configured devices. The costs associated with investigating and remediating security incidents, as well as potential lawsuits from affected parties, contribute to the financial consequences of inadequate device configuration security. Moreover, the loss of intellectual property, trade secrets, or proprietary information due to insecure configurations can have lasting financial implications, affecting an organization's competitiveness and market position.

Operational risks manifest in the disruption of essential business functions and processes due to insecure device configurations. Devices with inadequate security measures are more susceptible to exploitation, leading to service interruptions, downtime, or the compromise of critical systems. Insecurely configured network devices, such as routers and firewalls, may open avenues for attackers to manipulate network traffic, redirect communications, or launch man-in-the-middle attacks. The operational consequences of insecure configurations extend to supply chain risks, where compromised devices within the supply chain may introduce malicious elements, impacting the overall reliability and continuity of operations.

Reputational risks are significant and often underestimated outcomes of insecure device configurations. Security incidents resulting from misconfigurations can tarnish the reputation of organizations, manufacturers, and service providers. Public perception of trust and confidence in the security of devices is paramount, and a breach resulting from insecure configurations can lead to reputational damage that is challenging to repair. Customers, clients, and partners may lose faith in the ability of an organization to protect sensitive information, undermining the trust that is essential for sustained relationships. Rebuilding a damaged reputation requires substantial effort, transparency, and a commitment to implementing robust security measures.

Compliance risks loom large in industries and sectors subject to regulatory frameworks and legal requirements. Insecure device configurations may lead to violations of data protection laws, industry standards, or specific regulatory mandates. Non-compliance with these regulations can result in severe penalties, fines, and legal action. Additionally, organizations may face reputational damage as a consequence of publicized regulatory violations, further compounding the adverse effects. The evolving landscape of data protection and privacy regulations, such as the General Data Protection Regulation (GDPR), underscores the importance of secure device configurations in maintaining compliance and avoiding legal repercussions.

Vulnerabilities in insecurely configured devices contribute to the proliferation of malware and the expansion of botnets. Malicious actors actively seek out devices with weak or default configurations to compromise and enlist them into botnets, which can be used for various malicious purposes. Botnets formed from insecurely configured devices can participate in coordinated DDoS attacks, spam campaigns, or serve as platforms for launching further cyberattacks. The consequences of widespread botnet activities include network congestion, service disruptions, and the potential for large-scale data breaches.

Supply chain risks emerge as a consequence of insecure device configurations, especially in scenarios where devices are sourced from third-party manufacturers or vendors. Insecurely configured devices within the supply chain can introduce vulnerabilities that propagate through the entire ecosystem. Adversaries may exploit weak links in the supply chain to compromise devices before they even reach end-users. The compromise of devices during the manufacturing, shipping, or installation phases can have cascading effects, affecting multiple stakeholders within the supply chain and posing a substantial challenge in ensuring the security and integrity of devices.

Insecure configurations also amplify the risks associated with insider threats. Malicious insiders or employees with access to devices may exploit insecure configurations to carry out unauthorized activities, including data theft, sabotage, or the introduction of backdoors. Inadequate access controls, weak authentication mechanisms, or misconfigurations that grant excessive privileges can facilitate insider threats and significantly amplify the potential damage they can inflict.

Environmental risks are pertinent in scenarios where insecure device configurations lead to energy inefficiencies or contribute to electronic waste. Devices configured without proper power management settings may consume excessive energy, leading to environmental impacts such as increased carbon emissions and higher energy costs. Additionally, insecurely configured devices may be more prone to premature obsolescence, resulting in the disposal of electronic waste that poses environmental challenges. Addressing environmental risks requires holistic considerations in device configurations, including energy-efficient settings and sustainable design practices.

Operational overhead and complexity increase as a result of managing and mitigating the consequences of insecure device configurations. Organizations must invest significant resources in monitoring, vulnerability assessments, and remediation efforts to address the ongoing challenges posed by insecurely configured devices. The complexity of managing diverse devices across an ecosystem becomes a substantial burden, requiring comprehensive device management strategies to navigate the intricacies of identifying and rectifying insecure configurations.

In conclusion, the potential risks and consequences of insecure device configurations are broad-reaching and multifaceted, affecting security, privacy, financial stability, operational continuity, reputation, and regulatory compliance. The dynamic and evolving nature of the threat landscape underscores the importance of proactive measures to secure devices, including robust configuration practices, continuous monitoring, and the implementation of security best practices. As technology advances and the number of interconnected devices continues to grow, addressing the risks associated with insecure configurations remains an ongoing challenge that demands vigilant attention, collaboration, and a commitment to creating a secure and resilient digital ecosystem.

Discuss access control mechanisms for regulating device access.

Access control mechanisms play a pivotal role in the realm of device management, serving as the bedrock for enforcing security policies, safeguarding sensitive information, and mitigating unauthorized access to computing resources. These mechanisms, ranging from traditional access control lists (ACLs) to more advanced role-based access control (RBAC) and attribute-based access control (ABAC) systems, provide a comprehensive framework for regulating device access across diverse computing environments.

At its core, access control is about determining who or what can access a device, what actions they are permitted to perform, and under what circumstances these actions are allowed. Discretionary Access Control (DAC) is a widely used model where owners of resources have the discretion to control access to their resources. In this model, each device or resource has an associated access control list, specifying the users or groups and the permissions they hold. While DAC provides flexibility, it relies heavily on the owner's decisions, which may lead to challenges in managing large-scale systems or ensuring consistency in access policies.

Role-Based Access Control (RBAC) offers a more structured approach by organizing users into roles based on their responsibilities within an organization. Each role is associated with specific permissions, and users inherit these permissions by virtue of their role. RBAC simplifies access control management by linking permissions to job functions, making it easier to assign and revoke access rights. This model is particularly effective in large organizations with complex access requirements, as it streamlines the administration of access policies and enhances the overall manageability of device access.

Attribute-Based Access Control (ABAC) extends access control capabilities by considering a broader set of attributes, such as user attributes, environmental conditions, and resource attributes, to make access decisions. ABAC allows for more fine-grained control, as access decisions can be based on multiple factors. Policies in ABAC are expressed as rules that evaluate these attributes, enabling a dynamic and context-aware access control system. For example, access to a device may depend on the user's role, location, and time of day, providing a nuanced approach to access management that aligns with dynamic and evolving computing environments.

Mandatory Access Control (MAC) enforces access policies based on system-wide rules that are defined by administrators or security policies. Unlike DAC, where owners have control over access decisions, MAC is centrally administered and is often used in environments where security is of utmost importance, such as military or government systems. The model restricts users and processes based on predefined labels or security classifications, ensuring a high level of control over data and device access. While MAC provides strong security guarantees, it may be perceived as less flexible compared to DAC, as access decisions are determined by system-wide policies rather than individual users.

Access control mechanisms are not limited to a single model, and hybrid approaches often combine elements from different models to meet specific requirements. For instance, Attribute-Based RBAC (AB-RBAC) integrates attributes into the RBAC framework, allowing for more dynamic role assignments based on user attributes and contextual factors. This hybrid model leverages the strengths of both RBAC and ABAC, offering a balance between simplicity and flexibility in access control management.

In the context of operating systems, discretionary access control is commonly implemented through access control lists (ACLs). ACLs specify the permissions associated with each user or group for a particular resource. For example, a file in a file system may have an ACL that grants read and write permissions to the file owner, read-only access to a specific group, and no access to other users. This approach empowers resource owners with control over access, allowing them to specify who can interact with their devices and what actions are permitted.

Network devices, such as routers and firewalls, rely on access control mechanisms to regulate traffic flow and secure network communications. In these devices, access control lists (ACLs) are commonly used to define rules that dictate which network packets are permitted or denied. ACLs can filter traffic based on source and destination IP addresses, port numbers, and other packet attributes. This helps network administrators define and enforce policies that control the flow of data within the network, preventing unauthorized access and enhancing network security.

In cloud computing environments, access control becomes a critical component due to the dynamic and distributed nature of resources. Cloud providers often implement RBAC mechanisms that allow organizations to define roles and associated permissions for their users. This facilitates the efficient management of access to cloud resources, ensuring that users have the appropriate level of access based on their roles within the organization. Additionally, cloud environments may incorporate ABAC principles to accommodate dynamic resource provisioning, enabling access decisions based on contextual factors and attributes.

The Internet of Things (IoT) introduces new challenges and opportunities for access control, given the proliferation of interconnected devices with diverse functionalities. In IoT ecosystems, access control mechanisms must address the unique characteristics of constrained devices, varying communication protocols, and the need for scalable and adaptable access policies. Role-based models can be extended to IoT environments, where devices are assigned roles based on their functions or responsibilities within the network. Furthermore, attribute-based access control becomes crucial in IoT, allowing for context-aware decisions based on device attributes, user attributes, and environmental conditions.

Authentication and authorization are integral components of access control mechanisms. Authentication verifies the identity of users or devices attempting to access resources, ensuring that only legitimate entities are granted access. This process often involves the use of credentials, such as usernames and passwords, or more advanced authentication methods like biometrics or multifactor authentication. Once authenticated, authorization comes into play, determining the level of access that the authenticated entity is granted. Strong authentication mechanisms are essential for building a secure foundation for access control, preventing unauthorized entities from masquerading as legitimate users.

Access control extends beyond user-based access to include programmatic access in the form of application programming interfaces (APIs) and service-to-service communication. API access control mechanisms ensure that only authorized applications or services can interact with specific APIs, protecting against unauthorized access and potential misuse. This is particularly crucial in modern software architectures, where microservices and APIs play a central role in facilitating communication between diverse components.

Fine-grained access control becomes increasingly important in scenarios where sensitive or regulated data is involved. This level of control allows administrators to define access policies at the attribute or data level, ensuring that users or processes can only access specific subsets of data based on their permissions. Database management systems often incorporate fine-grained access control mechanisms to enforce data confidentiality and privacy, allowing organizations to meet compliance requirements and protect sensitive information.

The evolution of access control mechanisms is influenced by advancements in technologies such as blockchain. Blockchain-based access control introduces decentralized and immutable methods for managing access permissions. Smart contracts, which are self-executing contracts with the terms of the agreement directly written into code, can be leveraged to automate and enforce access control rules. Blockchain's distributed and tamper-resistant nature enhances the transparency and auditability of access decisions, providing a novel approach to secure and transparent access control.

Access control auditing and monitoring play critical roles in ensuring the effectiveness of access control mechanisms. Auditing allows organizations to track and review access events, providing insights into who accessed what resources, when, and with what permissions. Monitoring helps detect and respond to anomalous access patterns or potential security incidents. By continuously evaluating access logs and monitoring access patterns, organizations can identify and mitigate unauthorized access attempts, enhancing the overall security posture.

Challenges in access control include the need to balance security requirements with usability, especially in environments with diverse user roles and complex access scenarios. Striking the right balance between restrictive access policies and user productivity is essential to avoid hindering legitimate activities. Additionally, the dynamic nature of modern computing environments, with frequent changes in user roles, device configurations, and access requirements, poses challenges in maintaining accurate and up-to-date access control policies.

In conclusion, access control mechanisms constitute a foundational aspect of device management, shaping the security posture of computing systems across various domains. From traditional discretionary access control to more advanced models like RBAC and ABAC, access control mechanisms provide the framework for regulating device access, ensuring that users and processes interact with devices in a secure and controlled manner. The evolution of access control reflects the dynamic nature of computing environments, adapting to the challenges posed by diverse devices, interconnected systems, and evolving security threats. As technology continues to advance, access control mechanisms will remain pivotal in establishing and maintaining secure, resilient, and compliant device management practices.

Explore how permissions are assigned and managed to ensure secure device interactions.

The assignment and management of permissions are integral components of ensuring secure device interactions within computing systems. Permissions dictate what actions users, processes, or entities are allowed to perform on devices, influencing the overall security posture and protecting sensitive information. The process involves defining, assigning, and enforcing permissions in a granular manner to strike a balance between providing necessary access and mitigating potential security risks. As computing environments become increasingly complex and interconnected, the robust management of permissions becomes paramount for regulating device interactions securely.

Permissions are typically associated with resources such as files, directories, devices, or network services. In the context of file systems, the assignment of permissions governs who can read, write, execute, or delete specific files or directories. These permissions are often categorized for three distinct user groups: the owner of the resource, a designated group, and others. The management of file permissions in operating systems, such as Unix-like systems, involves setting permission bits using symbolic or numeric representations. For example, the command "chmod 755 filename" assigns read, write, and execute permissions to the owner, and read and execute permissions to the group and others. This granular approach allows administrators to tailor access rights based on user roles and requirements, ensuring that only authorized individuals or processes can interact with specific files.

In the realm of network devices and services, permissions are managed through access control lists (ACLs) and authorization policies. Network ACLs define rules that control traffic flow, specifying which IP addresses, protocols, or ports are permitted or denied. By configuring ACLs on routers, firewalls, or network appliances, administrators can regulate device interactions at the network level, preventing unauthorized access and enhancing overall security. Additionally, authorization policies play a crucial role in managing permissions for accessing services or resources. In a web server, for instance, permissions may be configured to allow certain users or groups to access specific directories or execute certain operations, while denying access to others. The management of these permissions ensures that only authenticated and authorized entities can interact with network services securely.

In the context of cloud computing, the management of permissions is a fundamental aspect of ensuring secure interactions with cloud resources. Cloud service providers implement identity and access management (IAM) systems that allow organizations to define and manage permissions for users, groups, and roles. IAM policies specify what actions are allowed or denied on specific resources within the cloud environment. For example, an IAM policy might grant a user the permission to launch virtual machines but restrict access to modify network configurations. The hierarchical and role-based nature of IAM systems enables organizations to implement fine-grained control over access, aligning with the principle of least privilege to minimize security risks.

Permissions are often associated with roles in access control mechanisms, providing a scalable and manageable approach to authorization. Role-Based Access Control (RBAC) models streamline the assignment and management of permissions by grouping users into roles based on their responsibilities within an organization. Each role is associated with specific permissions, and users inherit these permissions by virtue of their role. The management of roles and their associated permissions simplifies the administration of access policies, making it easier to assign, modify, or revoke access rights. RBAC models enhance the overall manageability of permissions, especially in large organizations with diverse access requirements and user roles.

Attribute-Based Access Control (ABAC) introduces a more dynamic and context-aware approach to managing permissions. In ABAC systems, access decisions are based on a combination of attributes related to users, devices, resources, and environmental conditions. For instance, access to a file may depend on the user's role, location, time of day, or specific attributes associated with the file itself. ABAC provides a flexible and nuanced framework for managing permissions, allowing organizations to tailor access policies to dynamic and evolving scenarios. The ability to consider multiple attributes in access decisions enhances the adaptability of permissions management, especially in modern computing environments where contextual factors play a significant role in security.

The assignment of permissions is closely tied to the process of authentication, where the identity of users, devices, or entities is verified. Authentication mechanisms, such as username/password combinations, biometrics, or multifactor authentication, ensure that individuals or processes attempting to interact with devices are who they claim to be. Once authenticated, the assignment of permissions comes into play during the authorization process. Authorization mechanisms determine the level of access that authenticated entities are granted, ensuring that permissions align with the roles, attributes, or policies associated with the identity.

In operating systems, access control mechanisms are implemented through security models that enforce permissions at the kernel level. Discretionary Access Control (DAC) is a common model where resource owners have discretion over access decisions. The assignment of permissions is managed through access control lists (ACLs) or other mechanisms that specify the rights associated with each user or group. DAC allows resource owners to define who can access their devices and what actions are permitted, providing a decentralized approach to permissions management.

Mandatory Access Control (MAC) models, on the other hand, enforce permissions based on system-wide policies and labels. MAC is often employed in high-security environments where centralized control over access decisions is deemed necessary. Labels or security classifications are assigned to devices, users, or processes, and access decisions are determined by predefined rules that consider these labels. MAC models provide a robust means of enforcing permissions in scenarios where a more rigid and centrally managed approach to security is required.

Access control in databases involves managing permissions at the level of tables, views, and stored procedures. Database management systems (DBMS) incorporate mechanisms for defining, assigning, and revoking permissions to ensure that only authorized users or applications can interact with specific data. For example, a database administrator may grant SELECT and UPDATE permissions on a table to a particular user, restricting other users from modifying or accessing that table. Database permissions are crucial for maintaining data integrity, confidentiality, and compliance with regulatory requirements.

The assignment and management of permissions become particularly challenging in scenarios where devices are part of dynamic and evolving ecosystems, such as the Internet of Things (IoT). In IoT environments, diverse devices with varying capabilities and functions interact within interconnected networks. Permissions for IoT devices may be based on contextual factors, device attributes, or the specific role a device plays within the IoT ecosystem. Managing permissions for a diverse array of IoT devices requires scalable and adaptable mechanisms that can accommodate the unique characteristics of each device and the dynamic nature of IoT environments.

Cloud-based applications and services often rely on OAuth (Open Authorization) and similar protocols for managing permissions. OAuth allows users to grant specific permissions to third-party applications without sharing their credentials. For example, a user may grant a cloud-based application the permission to access their calendar but not their emails. OAuth's token-based approach facilitates the delegation of specific permissions, enhancing security and user control over access to cloud resources.

The management of permissions also extends to programmatic access through APIs (Application Programming Interfaces). API access control mechanisms ensure that only authorized applications or services can interact with specific APIs, preventing unauthorized access and potential misuse. This is crucial in modern software architectures, where microservices and APIs facilitate communication between diverse components. Managing permissions for API access involves defining authentication mechanisms, specifying the level of access granted to different applications, and enforcing secure communication protocols.

Fine-grained access control is essential in scenarios where sensitive or regulated data is involved. This level of control allows administrators to define access policies at the attribute or data level, ensuring that users or processes can only access specific subsets of data based on their permissions. Database management systems often incorporate fine-grained access control mechanisms to enforce data confidentiality and privacy, allowing organizations to meet compliance requirements and protect sensitive information.

Permissions management is an ongoing and dynamic process, especially in environments where user roles, device configurations, and access requirements change frequently. Effective permissions management requires regular audits, reviews, and updates to ensure that permissions align with the principle of least privilege. The principle of least privilege advocates granting only the minimum level of access necessary for users or processes to perform their functions. Adhering to this principle reduces the potential attack surface, minimizes security risks, and enhances the overall security posture of device interactions.

Auditing and monitoring play crucial roles in validating and enhancing the effectiveness of permissions management. Auditing involves tracking and reviewing access events, providing insights into who accessed what resources, when, and with what permissions. Regular audits help identify and rectify inconsistencies, unauthorized access, or potential security incidents. Monitoring, on the other hand, involves real-time evaluation of access patterns and activities. Continuous monitoring enables organizations to detect and respond promptly to anomalous access behaviors, enhancing the overall security and accountability of device interactions.

In conclusion, the assignment and management of permissions constitute a foundational aspect of secure device interactions within computing systems. From file systems and network devices to cloud environments and IoT ecosystems, effective permissions management involves defining, assigning, and enforcing access rights in a granular and context-aware manner. The evolution of access control mechanisms, from traditional discretionary access control to more advanced models like RBAC and ABAC, reflects the dynamic nature of computing environments and the need for adaptable, scalable, and secure permissions management. As technology continues to advance, the ongoing refinement and adaptation of permissions management practices remain essential to meet the challenges posed by diverse devices, interconnected systems, and evolving security threats.

Introduce authentication protocols for verifying the identity of devices.

Authentication protocols play a critical role in the realm of device management, serving as the cornerstone for verifying the identity of devices within computing systems. These protocols provide a systematic and secure framework for ensuring that devices attempting to access resources or services are legitimate and authorized entities. The landscape of authentication protocols is diverse, ranging from traditional methods like username-password combinations to more advanced techniques such as public key cryptography and multifactor authentication. As the digital ecosystem continues to evolve, authentication protocols become increasingly pivotal in establishing a secure foundation for device interactions, safeguarding sensitive information, and mitigating unauthorized access.

One of the most prevalent and longstanding authentication methods is based on the use of username and password combinations. This approach requires users or devices to provide a unique identifier, typically a username, and a secret passphrase to prove their identity. While widely adopted, username-password authentication has its limitations, including susceptibility to password-related vulnerabilities such as brute-force attacks, password reuse, and the challenge of managing complex and frequently changing passwords. Nonetheless, it remains a fundamental authentication protocol, especially in scenarios where simplicity and ease of implementation are paramount.

Public key cryptography introduces a more robust and secure authentication paradigm, particularly prevalent in secure communication protocols such as SSL/TLS. In this approach, devices possess a pair of cryptographic keys: a public key, which is widely shared, and a private key, which is kept confidential. During the authentication process, a device can prove its identity by presenting a digital signature generated with its private key. The recipient can then verify the signature using the device's public key, establishing a high level of confidence in the device's authenticity. Public key cryptography enhances security by eliminating the need to share secret keys over the network, reducing the risk of eavesdropping and man-in-the-middle attacks.

Multifactor authentication (MFA) represents a significant advancement in authentication protocols, addressing the vulnerabilities associated with single-factor methods. MFA requires devices to authenticate using two or more independent factors, typically categorized as "something you know" (e.g., passwords), "something you have" (e.g., security tokens or mobile devices), and "something you are" (e.g., biometrics). By combining multiple factors, MFA significantly enhances the robustness of authentication, making it more challenging for adversaries to compromise devices and gain unauthorized access. MFA is widely adopted in various domains, including online banking, cloud services, and enterprise systems, where an additional layer of security is crucial to protect sensitive data and resources.

OAuth (Open Authorization) is an authentication protocol designed for secure authorization in distributed systems. While OAuth is primarily focused on authorization, it incorporates authentication as part of its workflow. OAuth enables devices or applications to obtain limited access to a resource on behalf of a user without exposing the user's credentials. This is achieved through the delegation of access tokens, allowing devices to authenticate and access resources on behalf of the user without requiring the user's credentials to be shared directly. OAuth is extensively used in scenarios such as social media logins, where third-party applications are granted access to user accounts without exposing login credentials.

Security Assertion Markup Language (SAML) is a widely adopted standard for exchanging authentication and authorization data between parties, particularly in web-based single sign-on (SSO) scenarios. SAML enables the secure transfer of authentication assertions between an identity provider (IdP) and a service provider (SP). During the authentication process, the device interacts with the IdP to obtain a digitally signed SAML assertion, which is then presented to the SP to gain access. SAML enhances security by facilitating the exchange of trusted assertions, enabling seamless and secure authentication across different web applications without the need for users to repeatedly log in.

OpenID Connect (OIDC) builds upon OAuth 2.0 to provide a standardized authentication layer. OIDC is designed to enable secure authentication in web and mobile applications, providing a simple and scalable mechanism for verifying the identity of devices. By leveraging JSON Web Tokens (JWTs) and OAuth 2.0 flows, OIDC allows devices to authenticate and obtain identity information from an authorization server. OIDC enhances interoperability and simplifies the integration of authentication mechanisms into diverse applications, making it a popular choice for scenarios where a standardized approach to authentication is essential.

FIDO (Fast Identity Online) Alliance specifications, including FIDO2 and WebAuthn, introduce a passwordless authentication paradigm. FIDO protocols leverage public key cryptography to enable secure and convenient device authentication without the need for traditional passwords. Devices are equipped with biometric sensors, USB security keys, or other authenticators that generate cryptographic keys for authentication. FIDO protocols provide a higher level of security by eliminating the reliance on passwords, reducing the risk of credential theft and unauthorized access. FIDO-based authentication is gaining traction across various applications and services, contributing to the evolution of secure and user-friendly authentication experiences.

Kerberos is a network authentication protocol developed by MIT that uses symmetric key cryptography to secure communications over a non-secure network. Kerberos provides a trusted third-party authentication service, known as the Key Distribution Center (KDC), which issues tickets to devices and services. Devices requesting access to a service present their ticket to prove their identity, and the service can verify the ticket's authenticity with the KDC. Kerberos enhances security by preventing replay attacks and eavesdropping on authentication exchanges, making it a widely used protocol in enterprise environments for authenticating devices and users.

Device-based authentication protocols, such as Device Identity Composition Engine (DICE) and Trusted Platform Module (TPM), focus on establishing the authenticity and integrity of the devices themselves. DICE defines a standard for creating a unique identity for each device based on its hardware components and the manufacturing process. This identity is used for authentication and attestation, ensuring that only devices with a valid and trusted identity can access resources. TPM, on the other hand, is a hardware-based solution that provides a secure enclave for storing cryptographic keys and performing secure operations. TPM enhances device security by enabling devices to prove their identity and integrity during authentication processes.

Time-based One-Time Passwords (TOTPs) and Counter-based One-Time Passwords (HOTPs) are commonly used in two-factor authentication (2FA) scenarios. TOTPs generate unique passwords based on the current time, typically using a mobile app or hardware token. HOTPs generate passwords based on a counter value, ensuring that each password is unique and time-independent. These one-time passwords are used in conjunction with traditional credentials to provide an additional layer of security during the authentication process. TOTPs and HOTPs are widely employed in scenarios where an extra layer of authentication is necessary to mitigate the risk of credential theft.

Biometric authentication leverages unique physical or behavioral traits of individuals to verify their identity. Common biometric modalities include fingerprint recognition, facial recognition, iris scanning, and voice recognition. Biometric authentication protocols capture and analyze these biometric traits, converting them into digital representations for comparison during the authentication process. Biometrics provide a high level of security and user convenience, as they are inherently tied to the individual and difficult to replicate. However, challenges such as privacy concerns, potential biases, and the risk of biometric data breaches must be addressed to ensure the ethical and secure implementation of biometric authentication.

In the Internet of Things (IoT), authentication protocols face unique challenges due to the diverse nature of connected devices, resource constraints, and the need for scalability. Lightweight protocols like MQTT (Message Queuing Telemetry Transport) and CoAP (Constrained Application Protocol) are commonly used in IoT environments to enable secure device communication. These protocols often incorporate authentication mechanisms based on pre-shared keys or digital certificates, ensuring that only authorized devices can participate in IoT networks. Additionally, protocols like OAuth and OIDC are adapted for IoT scenarios to provide secure and standardized authentication flows.

The ongoing evolution of authentication protocols is shaped by advancements in cryptography, security standards, and the evolving threat landscape. As computing systems continue to embrace decentralized and distributed architectures, the need for secure, interoperable, and user-friendly authentication solutions becomes paramount. The synergy between authentication protocols and emerging technologies, such as blockchain and decentralized identity systems, holds the promise of further enhancing the security, privacy, and usability of device authentication in the digital age. In conclusion, authentication protocols form the bedrock of secure device interactions, ensuring the trustworthiness and integrity of devices within the dynamic and interconnected landscape of modern computing.

Discuss the role of secure authentication in preventing unauthorized access.

The role of secure authentication is paramount in preventing unauthorized access within the intricate fabric of modern computing systems. Authentication serves as the linchpin for establishing the legitimacy of users, devices, or entities attempting to access resources, applications, or services. By demanding proof of identity through a multifaceted and robust process, secure authentication acts as the primary barricade against unauthorized entry, fortifying the defenses of digital ecosystems and safeguarding sensitive information from malicious actors.

At its core, the purpose of authentication is to verify that the entity seeking access is who it claims to be. This foundational principle addresses the fundamental challenge of distinguishing legitimate users or devices from potential adversaries. The ramifications of unauthorized access are profound, ranging from the compromise of sensitive data and intellectual property to disruptions in critical services and potential financial losses. Secure authentication stands as the initial sentinel, diligently scrutinizing each attempt to gain entry and allowing only those with verified identities to traverse the digital threshold.

Traditional authentication methods, such as username and password combinations, have long been the workhorses of digital access control. While effective when coupled with best practices like strong password policies, these methods face inherent vulnerabilities. Password-related challenges, including weak passwords, password reuse, and susceptibility to phishing attacks, underscore the need for more sophisticated authentication mechanisms. Secure authentication protocols, such as multifactor authentication (MFA), transcend the limitations of single-factor methods, requiring users or devices to provide two or more independent pieces of evidence to establish their identity. MFA adds an extra layer of resilience, making it exponentially more difficult for unauthorized entities to bypass authentication barriers.

Public key cryptography, a cornerstone of secure communication protocols like SSL/TLS, injects a robust layer of security into the authentication landscape. This method employs a pair of cryptographic keys – a public key disseminated widely and a private key safeguarded by the device or user. During authentication, the device uses its private key to generate a digital signature, which the recipient can verify using the device's public key. This process, known as asymmetric authentication, not only verifies identity but also ensures the integrity of the communication channel. Public key cryptography mitigates the risks associated with eavesdropping and man-in-the-middle attacks, offering a formidable defense against unauthorized access attempts.

Multifactor authentication, with its multifaceted approach, addresses the imperfections of single-factor methods and provides a robust defense against unauthorized access. By combining factors such as something the user knows (e.g., passwords), something the user has (e.g., security tokens), and something the user is (e.g., biometrics), MFA erects multiple barriers that potential adversaries must overcome. This layered defense dramatically reduces the likelihood of unauthorized access, even in the event of compromised credentials. The implementation of MFA has become increasingly prevalent across diverse domains, from online banking and e-commerce to enterprise systems, underscoring its effectiveness in fortifying authentication processes.

OAuth (Open Authorization), designed for secure authorization in distributed systems, incorporates authentication as an integral part of its workflow. OAuth allows entities, such as devices or applications, to obtain limited access to a resource on behalf of a user without exposing the user's credentials. This delegation of access is facilitated through the exchange of tokens, ensuring that the entity seeking access is authorized and authenticated. OAuth's role in preventing unauthorized access lies in its ability to securely delegate and manage access permissions, reducing the risk of compromised credentials and enhancing the overall security posture.

Security Assertion Markup Language (SAML) is a standard used for exchanging authentication and authorization data between parties, particularly in web-based single sign-on (SSO) scenarios. SAML enables the secure transfer of authentication assertions between an identity provider (IdP) and a service provider (SP). During the authentication process, the device interacts with the IdP to obtain a digitally signed SAML assertion, which is then presented to the SP to gain access. SAML ensures that only authenticated and authorized devices can seamlessly access multiple services without the need for repeated logins. Its role in preventing unauthorized access lies in the secure and standardized exchange of trusted assertions, establishing a robust mechanism for digital identities to navigate interconnected online services securely.

OpenID Connect (OIDC), an authentication layer built on top of OAuth 2.0, offers a standardized approach to secure authentication in web and mobile applications. OIDC leverages JSON Web Tokens (JWTs) and OAuth 2.0 flows to enable devices to authenticate and obtain identity information from an authorization server. The standardized nature of OIDC facilitates interoperability and simplifies the integration of authentication mechanisms into various applications. By ensuring that only authenticated devices gain access to identity information and services, OIDC plays a crucial role in preventing unauthorized access in the digital landscape.

The FIDO (Fast Identity Online) Alliance specifications, including FIDO2 and WebAuthn, usher in a passwordless era of authentication. The FIDO protocols utilize public key cryptography and authenticators, such as biometric sensors or USB security keys, to provide secure and convenient authentication without relying on traditional passwords. FIDO protocols aim to eliminate the vulnerabilities associated with passwords, offering a resilient defense against unauthorized access attempts. The role of FIDO in preventing unauthorized access lies in its ability to provide a higher level of security while simultaneously enhancing user experience through passwordless authentication mechanisms.

Kerberos, a network authentication protocol, employs symmetric key cryptography to secure communications over non-secure networks. Kerberos provides a trusted third-party authentication service known as the Key Distribution Center (KDC). During authentication, devices request access tickets from the KDC, and these tickets are used to prove their identity to services within the network. Kerberos enhances security by preventing replay attacks and eavesdropping on authentication exchanges. Its role in preventing unauthorized access is rooted in the robustness of its authentication process, ensuring that only devices with valid tickets gain access to network services.

Device-based authentication protocols, such as Device Identity Composition Engine (DICE) and Trusted Platform Module

(TPM), are designed to establish the authenticity and integrity of devices themselves. DICE creates a unique identity for each device based on its hardware components and manufacturing process, using this identity for authentication and attestation. TPM, a hardware-based solution, provides a secure enclave for storing cryptographic keys and performing secure operations. Device-based authentication enhances security by ensuring that only devices with valid and trusted identities can access resources. The role of these protocols in preventing unauthorized access lies in their focus on the integrity of the devices involved, creating a robust foundation for secure interactions.

Time-based One-Time Passwords (TOTPs) and Counter-based One-Time Passwords (HOTPs) play a pivotal role in two-factor authentication (2FA). TOTPs generate unique passwords based on the current time, while HOTPs generate passwords based on a counter value. These one-time passwords, combined with traditional credentials, provide an additional layer of security during the authentication process. TOTPs and HOTPs thwart unauthorized access attempts by introducing dynamic and time-sensitive elements into the authentication workflow.

Biometric authentication leverages unique physical or behavioral traits of individuals to verify their identity. Common biometric modalities include fingerprint recognition, facial recognition, iris scanning, and voice recognition. Biometric authentication protocols capture and analyze these biometric traits, converting them into digital representations for comparison during the authentication process. The role of biometric authentication in preventing unauthorized access lies in its ability to provide a high level of security by tying authentication to inherent and difficult-to-replicate characteristics of individuals.

In the Internet of Things (IoT), authentication protocols face distinctive challenges due to the diverse nature of connected devices, resource constraints, and the need for scalability. Lightweight protocols like MQTT (Message Queuing Telemetry Transport) and CoAP (Constrained Application Protocol) are commonly used in IoT environments, incorporating authentication mechanisms based on pre-shared keys or digital certificates. These protocols ensure that only authorized devices can participate in IoT networks, preventing unauthorized access and securing the integrity of IoT ecosystems.

The ongoing evolution of authentication protocols is shaped by advancements in cryptography, security standards, and the evolving threat landscape. As computing systems embrace decentralized and distributed architectures, the synergy between authentication protocols and emerging technologies, such as blockchain and decentralized identity systems, holds the promise of further enhancing the security, privacy, and usability of device authentication in the digital age. In conclusion, the role of secure authentication in preventing unauthorized access is pivotal, serving as the first line of defense against malicious actors and fortifying the foundations of trust within the dynamic and interconnected landscape of modern computing.

Explore the use of encryption to secure communication between devices and the operating system.

The use of encryption stands as a cornerstone in securing communication between devices and operating systems, playing a pivotal role in fortifying the confidentiality and integrity of sensitive data traversing the intricate networks of modern computing environments. Encryption serves as a potent mechanism for converting plaintext information into ciphertext, rendering it indecipherable to unauthorized entities and mitigating the risks associated with data breaches, eavesdropping, and unauthorized access. In the realm of device communication and operating system interactions, encryption functions as a robust shield, ensuring that sensitive information remains safeguarded against both external and internal threats.

At its essence, encryption involves the application of crypto-graphic algorithms to transform data into a format that is unreadable without the appropriate decryption key. The two primary types of encryption—symmetric and asymmetric—form the bedrock of secure communication between devices and operating systems. Symmetric encryption employs a single key for both encryption and decryption processes, providing a fast and efficient means of securing data. In device communication, symmetric encryption finds utility in scenarios where the same key is shared between two devices, ensuring that the information exchanged remains confidential and tamper-resistant. However, challenges arise in securely distributing and managing these shared keys, especially in large-scale and dynamic computing environments.

Asymmetric encryption, on the other hand, utilizes a pair of keys—an encryption key and a corresponding decryption key. This approach enhances the security of communication by allowing devices to share their public encryption keys openly while keeping their private decryption keys confidential. In the context of operating systems, asymmetric encryption plays a crucial role in secure data transmission and digital signatures. When devices communicate, asymmetric encryption ensures that the information exchanged remains confidential, even if the public keys are intercepted, as only the private keys held by the respective devices can decipher the ciphertext.

Transport Layer Security (TLS) and its predecessor, Secure Sockets Layer (SSL), exemplify the implementation of encryption protocols to secure communication over networks. TLS and SSL provide a secure layer between the application layer and the transport layer of the communication stack, encrypting data during transmission and decrypting it upon arrival. These protocols are instrumental in securing data exchanged between devices and operating systems, especially in web-based interactions. As devices communicate with web servers, TLS ensures that the information, including login credentials, personal data, and financial transactions, remains encrypted, thwarting potential attackers attempting to intercept or manipulate the data in transit.

File and disk encryption constitute another critical dimension of securing communication between devices and operating systems. Operating systems often employ encryption techniques to protect data stored on disks and other storage media. Full disk encryption ensures that all data on a disk is encrypted, preventing unauthorized access in the event of physical theft or unauthorized access to the storage medium. File-level encryption, on the other hand, allows users to selectively encrypt specific files or directories, offering a more granular approach to data protection. In both cases, the encryption of data at rest adds an additional layer of defense, safeguarding sensitive information even when it is not actively being transmitted between devices.

The integration of encryption into the fabric of device communication extends to virtual private networks (VPNs), which provide a secure tunnel for data transmission over public networks. VPNs utilize encryption protocols to ensure the confidentiality and integrity of data traversing the network. By encrypting data before it leaves the device and decrypting it upon arrival at its destination, VPNs shield sensitive information from potential eavesdropping or interception. This is particularly crucial for remote communication between devices and operating systems, such as employees accessing corporate networks from external locations, where the encryption of data ensures a secure and private connection.

In the domain of email communication, encryption technologies such as Pretty Good Privacy (PGP) and its open-source counterpart, GNU Privacy Guard (GPG), play a pivotal role in securing the confidentiality of email messages. PGP and GPG utilize a combination of symmetric and asymmetric encryption to protect the contents of emails and verify the authenticity of the sender. Users generate public and private key pairs, and the public key is shared openly, while the private key is securely retained. When sending an encrypted email, the sender uses the recipient's public key to encrypt the message, and only the recipient, possessing the corresponding private key, can decrypt and read the contents. This ensures that even if the email traverses insecure channels, its contents remain confidential and tamper-proof.

Device communication and operating system interactions within cloud computing environments demand heightened security measures, given the distributed and shared nature of resources. Cloud service providers often employ encryption at various layers to fortify the confidentiality and integrity of data. Data at rest within cloud storage is typically encrypted, and modern cloud platforms offer robust key management services to facilitate secure key storage and distribution. In transit, data moving between devices and cloud services is protected using encryption protocols such as TLS. Cloud providers also implement encryption in the hypervisor layer to isolate virtual machines and secure the communication between virtualized environments within a shared physical infrastructure.

As the proliferation of Internet of Things (IoT) devices continues, encryption emerges as a crucial component in securing the communication fabric of interconnected devices. IoT ecosystems involve a myriad of devices exchanging data, and encryption becomes instrumental in ensuring the privacy and security of sensitive information. Lightweight encryption protocols, such as Constrained Application Protocol (CoAP) and Datagram Transport Layer Security (DTLS), are designed to accommodate the resource constraints of IoT devices while providing robust encryption for communication. By encrypting data exchanged between IoT devices and the operating systems that manage them, these protocols contribute to the overall security and trustworthiness of IoT environments.

End-to-end encryption, a paradigm where data is encrypted on the sender's device and decrypted only on the recipient's device, represents the epitome of data security in device communication. Messaging applications and collaboration platforms increasingly adopt end-to-end encryption to guarantee the privacy of user communications. In such systems, even service providers facilitating the communication cannot access the content of the messages. Popular messaging applications like Signal, WhatsApp, and Telegram have embraced end-to-end encryption, setting a new standard for secure and private communication between devices.

While encryption plays a pivotal role in securing communication between devices and operating systems, the effectiveness of encryption protocols relies heavily on secure key management practices. The secure generation, distribution, storage, and rotation of encryption keys are paramount to the overall security posture. Key management systems, whether implemented on-premises or through cloud-based solutions, must adhere to best practices to prevent unauthorized access to encryption keys, ensuring the resilience of the encryption infrastructure.

In conclusion, encryption serves as a linchpin in the realm of securing communication between devices and operating systems, providing a robust defense against a myriad of potential threats. From protecting data in transit through network encryption protocols to fortifying data at rest on storage media, encryption technologies contribute to the confidentiality and integrity of sensitive information. As the digital landscape evolves, encryption continues to play a pivotal role in shaping the foundations of secure communication, providing assurance to users, organizations, and enterprises that their data remains shielded from unauthorized access and tampering. The ongoing advancements in encryption techniques and key management practices underscore the dynamic nature of this critical component in the arsenal of cybersecurity measures.

Discuss encryption algorithms and their application in device management.

Encryption algorithms form the bedrock of secure device management, providing a robust framework for safeguarding sensitive data, ensuring confidentiality, and fortifying the overall security posture of modern computing ecosystems. These algorithms, characterized by their mathematical processes, are instrumental in transforming plaintext information into ciphertext, rendering it indecipherable to unauthorized entities and mitigating the risks associated with unauthorized access, data breaches, and eavesdropping. The application of encryption algorithms in device management spans various dimensions, including secure communication, data storage, access control, and compliance with regulatory standards.

One of the fundamental encryption algorithms widely employed in device management is the Advanced Encryption Standard (AES). AES, established as a federal standard by the U.S. National Institute of Standards and Technology (NIST), operates on symmetric-key cryptography principles. With key lengths of 128, 192, or 256 bits, AES provides a versatile and secure mechanism for encrypting data. In device management, AES finds extensive use in securing communication channels, where it ensures that data exchanged between devices remains confidential. The simplicity, efficiency, and proven security of AES make it a cornerstone in encryption protocols and a preferred choice for securing sensitive information in various device management scenarios.

Another pivotal encryption algorithm is the Rivest Cipher (RC) family, developed by cryptographer Ron Rivest. While RC4 was widely used in the past, its vulnerabilities led to its disfavor in recent times. However, other iterations, such as RC5 and RC6, have demonstrated enhanced security features. RC algorithms operate on symmetric-key cryptography, making them suitable for encrypting data in device management applications. Their versatility allows for customization in terms of key size and encryption block size, adapting to the specific requirements of device communication and secure data storage.

Triple Data Encryption Standard (3DES), an evolution of the original Data Encryption Standard (DES), is another symmetric-key encryption algorithm utilized in device management. 3DES applies the DES algorithm three times consecutively, using two or three different keys. This triple-layered approach enhances the security of data encryption, making it resilient against certain cryptographic attacks. In device management, 3DES is employed in scenarios where legacy systems or compliance requirements necessitate the use of DES-based algorithms. However, it's essential to note that 3DES is gradually being phased out in favor of more advanced and secure encryption algorithms.

Public key cryptography, or asymmetric encryption, introduces a distinct paradigm in device management, where each entity possesses a pair of cryptographic keys: a public key and a private key. The RSA algorithm, named after its inventors Ron Rivest, Adi Shamir, and Leonard Adleman, is a prominent example of public key cryptography. RSA is widely used for securing communication channels, digital signatures, and key exchange protocols in device management. Devices can share their public keys openly, allowing others to encrypt data destined for them. The corresponding private keys, held securely by the devices, are used for decrypting the received ciphertext. RSA's strength lies in the mathematical complexity of factoring large prime numbers, making it computationally infeasible for adversaries to derive the private key from the public key.

Elliptic Curve Cryptography (ECC) is another asymmetric encryption algorithm gaining prominence in device management due to its efficiency and strong security properties. ECC operates on the mathematical properties of elliptic curves over finite fields, providing robust cryptographic capabilities with shorter key lengths compared to traditional algorithms. The compact nature of ECC makes it well-suited for resource-constrained devices, such as those in IoT ecosystems. In device management, ECC is utilized in securing communication, authentication, and key exchange processes, contributing to the overall resilience of cryptographic protocols.

Hash functions, although not encryption algorithms in the traditional sense, play a crucial role in device management for ensuring data integrity and authentication. Hash functions generate fixed-size hash values or digests from variable-size input data, making them suitable for verifying the integrity of transmitted or stored information. The Secure Hash Algorithm (SHA) family, including SHA-256 and SHA-3, is widely employed in device management for creating checksums or digital signatures. By comparing hash values before and after data transmission, devices can verify whether the data has been tampered with during transit, providing a robust mechanism for data integrity assurance.

In device management scenarios where the protection of passwords and authentication tokens is paramount, key derivation functions (KDFs) become crucial. KDFs derive cryptographic keys from user passwords or other secret values, enhancing the security of stored credentials. The Password-Based Key Derivation Function 2 (PBKDF2) is a widely adopted algorithm in this context. PBKDF2 iteratively applies a hash function, such as SHA-256, to derive cryptographic keys, introducing computational complexity that resists brute-force attacks. In device management, PBKDF2 is employed to securely store and manage authentication credentials, mitigating the risks associated with password-related vulnerabilities.

Homomorphic encryption, an advanced cryptographic technique, introduces a novel approach where computations can be performed on encrypted data without the need for decryption. This revolutionary concept enables devices to process sensitive information while it remains in an encrypted state. While still an area of active research and development, homomorphic encryption holds the potential to transform device management by allowing devices to perform computations on encrypted data, enhancing privacy and security in scenarios where processing must occur on remote or untrusted servers.

The application of encryption algorithms extends beyond securing data in transit to encompass the protection of data at rest. In device management, especially within enterprise environments, Full Disk Encryption (FDE) is a standard practice to safeguard the contents of storage media. FDE encrypts the entire storage disk, preventing unauthorized access to data even if the physical storage device is compromised. BitLocker, integrated into Microsoft Windows operating systems, and FileVault, available on macOS, are examples of FDE implementations that utilize encryption algorithms such as AES to secure the contents of disks.

Database encryption is a critical aspect of device management, ensuring that sensitive data stored in databases remains protected against unauthorized access or breaches. Transparent Data Encryption (TDE) is a technique that encrypts entire databases, including tables, indexes, and stored procedures. Encryption algorithms like AES or DES are commonly used in TDE implementations to secure the data at rest within databases. TDE provides an additional layer of defense, complementing access controls and authentication mechanisms in device management scenarios where databases store critical information.

The integration of encryption algorithms into access control mechanisms enhances the security of device management by ensuring that only authorized entities can access specific resources. Attribute-Based Encryption (ABE) is an encryption paradigm that allows access to encrypted data based on specific attributes or policies. ABE provides fine-grained control over access, allowing devices to encrypt data with policies that define who can decrypt and access it.

This approach is valuable in device management scenarios where access permissions need to be dynamically adjusted based on changing circumstances or user roles.

In compliance-driven environments, where adherence to regulatory standards is imperative, encryption algorithms play a pivotal role in meeting data protection requirements. The General Data Protection Regulation (GDPR), Health Insurance Portability and Accountability Act (HIPAA), and Payment Card Industry Data Security Standard (PCI DSS) are examples of regulations that mandate the encryption of sensitive data. Device management strategies align with these regulations by implementing encryption algorithms to protect data and demonstrate compliance with stringent security and privacy requirements.

Quantum computing poses a potential threat to conventional encryption algorithms, particularly those based on integer factorization (RSA) and discrete logarithm (DSA, ECC). As quantum computers advance, the need for quantum-resistant or post-quantum encryption algorithms becomes apparent. NIST's ongoing Post-Quantum Cryptography Standardization project aims to identify and standardize cryptographic algorithms that are resilient to quantum attacks. Device management strategies must anticipate this shift and consider the adoption of post-quantum encryption algorithms to ensure the long-term security of sensitive data.

In conclusion, encryption algorithms are integral to the fabric of secure device management, providing a versatile toolkit for protecting sensitive data in diverse scenarios. From securing communication channels using symmetric and asymmetric encryption to fortifying data at rest with techniques like Full Disk Encryption and database encryption, encryption algorithms play a pivotal role in mitigating the risks associated with unauthorized access, data breaches, and evolving cybersecurity threats. As device ecosystems continue to expand and the threat landscape evolves, the selection and implementation of robust encryption algorithms remain paramount in establishing a resilient and secure foundation for device management strategies. The ongoing advancements in encryption research and the emergence of quantum-resistant algorithms underscore the dynamic nature of this critical component in the realm of cybersecurity.

Explain the concept of secure boot and its role in preventing unauthorized code execution.

Secure Boot, a fundamental security feature in modern computing systems, plays a pivotal role in preventing unauthorized code execution during the boot process. At its core, Secure Boot is a firmware-based security mechanism designed to ensure that only digitally signed and authenticated code is allowed to run during the system's startup sequence. This concept emerged as a response to the increasing threat landscape, where malicious actors exploit vulnerabilities in the boot process to inject unauthorized or malicious code, compromising the integrity and security of the entire system.

The boot process is a critical phase in the lifecycle of a computing device, determining how the operating system and essential software components are loaded into memory and executed. Traditionally, the boot process relied on a sequence of firmware, bootloader, and operating system loading, with little scrutiny on the authenticity of the code being executed. This lack of validation exposed systems to the risk of bootkits, rootkits, and other forms of malware that could tamper with or replace the boot code, leading to unauthorized and potentially malicious code taking control of the system.

Secure Boot addresses this vulnerability by introducing a robust mechanism for verifying the authenticity and integrity of the code executed during the boot process. The implementation of Secure Boot typically relies on industry standards such as the Unified Extensible Firmware Interface (UEFI), which has largely replaced the traditional Basic Input/Output System (BIOS) firmware in modern computing systems. UEFI firmware, with its advanced capabilities, serves as the foundation for Secure Boot to enforce a chain of trust from the firmware through the entire boot sequence.

The first key component in Secure Boot is the firmware itself, which initiates the process of verifying the digital signatures of subsequent components. During the early stages of boot, the firmware checks the digital signature of the bootloader against a set of pre-installed cryptographic keys stored in the firmware's Secure Boot database. These keys, often referred to as Platform Key (PK), Key Exchange Key (KEK), and Authorized Signatures (db), establish a hierarchical trust model.

The Platform Key (PK) is the root of trust and is embedded in the firmware during manufacturing. It serves as the anchor for establishing the authenticity of subsequent keys in the chain. The Key Exchange Key (KEK) facilitates the secure exchange of keys, allowing the addition or removal of keys without compromising the root of trust. The Authorized Signatures (db) key is used to verify the digital signatures of bootloader and operating system binaries. This hierarchical structure ensures that each component in the boot process is validated against a trusted authority.

The second critical component in Secure Boot is the bootloader, responsible for loading the operating system kernel into memory. The bootloader must be signed with a digital signature that matches one of the keys in the firmware's Secure Boot database. If the bootloader's signature is valid, the firmware allows it to proceed with the loading of the operating system. This cryptographic verification creates a secure link between the firmware, bootloader, and subsequent stages of the boot process, establishing a chain of trust that ensures the integrity and authenticity of the loaded code.

As the bootloader hands over control to the operating system kernel, Secure Boot continues to play a role in validating the integrity of the kernel and other essential components. The operating system kernel and associated drivers must also be digitally signed with a key from the firmware's Secure Boot database. This ensures that only trusted and authenticated code is granted execution privileges, safeguarding the system against malicious tampering or injection of unauthorized code.

Secure Boot is particularly effective in mitigating threats such as rootkits and bootkits, which attempt to compromise the boot process and gain control of the system at the earliest stage. By enforcing a chain of trust from the firmware through the bootloader and operating system, Secure Boot significantly reduces the attack surface and strengthens the system's defenses against unauthorized code execution. Even if malware attempts to tamper with the bootloader or operating system files, the digital signatures will fail validation, triggering a halt in the boot process and preventing the execution of compromised code.

While Secure Boot provides a robust defense against unauthorized code execution, its effectiveness relies on the proper management and protection of cryptographic keys. The security of the entire system is contingent on the secrecy and integrity of the keys stored in the firmware's Secure Boot database. If an attacker gains unauthorized access to or compromises these keys, the entire chain of trust is jeopardized. Therefore, secure key management practices, including the use of hardware-based secure elements and secure key storage, are crucial for maintaining the integrity of Secure Boot.

Secure Boot also intersects with the concept of attestation, where the system provides evidence of its secure boot status to external entities. Remote Attestation allows a system to prove to a remote entity that it has booted securely and is running trustworthy code. This capability is valuable in scenarios where mutual trust between systems or entities is essential, such as in secure network communication or cloud-based services. Remote Attestation leverages the cryptographic principles of Secure Boot to generate and verify proofs of secure boot status, enhancing the overall security posture of inter-connected systems.

While Secure Boot significantly enhances the security of computing systems, it is not without challenges and considerations. One notable consideration is the potential impact on system flexibility and the ability to run custom or open-source operating systems. Secure Boot's requirement for signed code may pose challenges for users who wish to install alternative operating systems that are not signed by the key in the firmware's Secure Boot database. In response to these concerns, UEFI firmware often includes features such as the ability to disable Secure Boot or add custom keys, allowing users to customize the boot process while maintaining a degree of security.

Secure Boot has become a standard security feature in various computing platforms, including personal computers, servers, and embedded systems. Major operating systems, including Windows, Linux distributions, and others, are designed to work seamlessly with Secure Boot, providing users with a secure and trustworthy computing experience. The adoption of Secure Boot reflects a paradigm shift in cybersecurity, where proactive measures are taken to fortify the foundational elements of system security, preventing unauthorized code execution and laying the groundwork for a more resilient and trustworthy computing environment. As the threat landscape continues to evolve, Secure Boot remains an essential component in the defense against sophisticated attacks that target the very core of a computing system's integrity.

Discuss trusted computing platforms and their impact on device security.

Trusted Computing Platforms, a paradigm rooted in the collaboration between hardware and software components, have ushered in a transformative era in device security by establishing a foundation of trust, integrity, and secure communication. At the heart of this concept is the notion that a computing platform can be considered trustworthy only when it ensures the integrity of its components, safeguards against unauthorized modifications, and establishes secure channels for communication. Trusted Computing Platforms employ a combination of hardware-based security features, cryptographic techniques, and standardized protocols to achieve these goals, significantly raising the bar for device security across a spectrum of applications.

The Trusted Computing Group (TCG), a consortium of industry leaders, has played a pivotal role in shaping the principles and standards that underpin Trusted Computing Platforms. One of the key contributions from TCG is the Trusted Platform Module (TPM), a hardware-based security module embedded in computing devices to provide a secure root of trust. The TPM serves as a secure enclave, isolated from the main processor, and is responsible for generating, storing, and managing cryptographic keys. By anchoring the security infrastructure in hardware, the TPM becomes a critical component in ensuring the overall trustworthiness of the computing platform.

At the core of Trusted Computing Platforms is the concept of the Trusted Boot Process, where each stage of the system boot sequence is cryptographically verified for integrity. This process typically begins with the firmware, ensuring that it has not been tampered with or compromised. The TPM stores and manages cryptographic measurements, or hashes, of each stage in a secure log known as the Platform Configuration Registers (PCR). These PCR values collectively form a unique "fingerprint" for the system's boot state, allowing subsequent components to verify the integrity of the boot process. Any deviation from the expected measurements triggers an alert, indicating a potential compromise and thwarting unauthorized code execution from the earliest stages of system initialization.

Remote Attestation, a concept closely tied to Trusted Computing Platforms, extends the principles of trust beyond the local system to establish trust between interconnected devices. Through the use of cryptographic proofs, a device can attest to its trustworthy state, providing evidence to remote entities about its secure configuration and integrity. Remote Attestation leverages the capabilities of the TPM to generate signed attestations, allowing external systems to verify the authenticity and security posture of a device. This capability is particularly valuable in scenarios where mutual trust is essential, such as secure network communication, cloud-based services, and collaborative computing environments.

Trusted Execution Environments (TEEs) represent a key advancement within Trusted Computing Platforms, providing secure enclaves within the main processor to execute sensitive code and processes. Intel's Software Guard Extensions (SGX) and ARM TrustZone are prominent examples of TEE implementations. TEEs create isolated environments, often referred to as secure enclaves, where code and data are shielded from the main operating system and other applications. The integrity and confidentiality of code and data within these enclaves are maintained even if the underlying system is compromised. TEEs find applications in secure key storage, cryptographic operations, and the execution of sensitive algorithms, enhancing the overall security posture of computing platforms.

Secure Boot, a fundamental component of Trusted Computing Platforms, ensures that only digitally signed and authenticated code is allowed to run during the system's startup sequence. This mechanism guards against a spectrum of attacks that seek to compromise the boot process, such as rootkits and bootkits. By enforcing a chain of trust from the firmware through the bootloader and operating system, Secure Boot fortifies the integrity of the entire computing platform. The TPM plays a crucial role in this process by storing cryptographic keys used to verify the signatures of bootloader and operating system binaries, creating a secure foundation for the system to build upon.

Trusted Computing Platforms extend their impact beyond the local device to secure communication channels between devices. The establishment of secure communication often relies on protocols such as Transport Layer Security (TLS) and Datagram Transport Layer Security (DTLS), which leverage cryptographic principles to encrypt data in transit. The use of hardware-based security features, including TPMs and TEEs, contributes to the robustness of these encryption mechanisms. The assurance of a trustworthy computing environment enhances the confidentiality and integrity of data exchanged between devices, mitigating the risks associated with eavesdropping, man-in-the-middle attacks, and unauthorized access to sensitive information.

In cloud computing environments, where data and processing are distributed across interconnected systems, Trusted Computing Platforms play a critical role in securing the integrity of virtualized environments. The concept of Trusted Virtual Platforms extends the principles of hardware-based trust to virtualized instances, ensuring that each virtual machine (VM) operates within a secure enclave. The TPM, often emulated in virtualized environments, provides cryptographic attestation for each VM, allowing the cloud provider and other VMs to verify the integrity and security posture of the virtualized instances. This ensures a trustworthy foundation for running critical workloads in the cloud, bolstering the overall security of cloud computing infrastructures.

Trusted Computing Platforms also address the challenges posed by supply chain security, where devices and components may undergo various stages of production and distribution before reaching end-users. The Root of Trust for Measurement (RTM) principle ensures that each component in the supply chain is measured and verified for integrity. Manufacturers can embed cryptographic measurements of firmware and software components into the TPM during the manufacturing process. These measurements serve as a secure log, allowing end-users to verify the integrity of the entire software stack and detect any tampering or unauthorized modifications that may have occurred during the supply chain.

The impact of Trusted Computing Platforms is particularly pronounced in critical infrastructure sectors, where the consequences of security breaches can be severe. Industries such as healthcare, finance, energy, and telecommunications rely on the resilience and trustworthiness of computing platforms to ensure the availability, confidentiality, and integrity of critical systems. Trusted Computing Platforms contribute to the protection of electronic health records, financial transactions, power grid management systems, and communication networks, fostering a secure and trustworthy foundation for critical infrastructure operations.

In the realm of the Internet of Things (IoT), where a vast array of interconnected devices forms complex ecosystems, Trusted Computing Platforms play a vital role in addressing the unique security challenges of the IoT landscape. The resource-constrained nature of many IoT devices necessitates lightweight security mechanisms. Trusted Platform Modules (TPMs) and Hardware Security Modules (HSMs) tailored for IoT devices provide secure key storage, cryptographic operations, and attestation capabilities, enabling these devices to operate within a framework of trust. This is crucial in scenarios such as smart homes, industrial automation, and healthcare IoT, where the security of connected devices directly impacts user privacy, safety, and data integrity.

Despite the significant strides made in the realm of Trusted Computing Platforms, challenges persist. The interoperability of trusted components across diverse platforms remains an ongoing consideration. Standardization efforts, exemplified by initiatives like the TCG, aim to create a common framework that allows trusted components to work seamlessly across different hardware and software environments. Additionally, user awareness and education are crucial, as the benefits of Trusted Computing Platforms are most effective when users understand the significance of security features and actively participate in maintaining a secure computing environment.

In conclusion, Trusted Computing Platforms represent a paradigm shift in device security, fostering a holistic approach that integrates hardware and software components to establish trust, ensure integrity, and fortify secure communication. The Trusted Platform Module (TPM), Secure Boot, Trusted Execution Environments (TEEs), and Remote Attestation are key components contributing to the robustness of Trusted Computing Platforms. Their impact spans critical infrastructure, cloud computing, IoT, and various other domains where secure and trustworthy computing is imperative. As the digital landscape continues to evolve, the principles of Trusted Computing Platforms remain at the forefront of efforts to enhance the security posture of computing systems, mitigate emerging threats, and build a foundation of trust that underpins the integrity and resilience of modern devices.

Chapter 6: Future Trends in Operating System Device Management

Discuss the dynamic nature of technology and the continuous evolution of device management.

The dynamic nature of technology is a relentless force, propelling the continuous evolution of device management into an ever-shifting landscape of challenges, opportunities, and transformative possibilities. At the heart of this dynamism lies the inherent drive of technology to push boundaries, break barriers, and redefine the way devices are managed in diverse ecosystems. This dynamic nature is deeply intertwined with the rapid pace of innovation, fueled by advancements in hardware, software, connectivity, and the evolving demands of users and industries. The journey of device management is not a static path; rather, it is an ongoing narrative shaped by the relentless march of technological progress.

The relentless evolution of hardware forms a cornerstone of the dynamic nature of device management. From the era of mainframes to the rise of personal computers, and further into the realms of mobile devices, wearables, and the Internet of Things (IoT), hardware continues to undergo profound transformations. The inexorable increase in computing power, the miniaturization of components, and the emergence of novel architectures lay the foundation for devices that are more capable, efficient, and interconnected than ever before. As device management adapts to these changes, it must grapple with the diversity and complexity of the hardware landscape, ensuring compatibility, optimization, and effective resource allocation across a spectrum of devices with varying capabilities.

Software, as the soul of devices, is equally subject to the relentless evolution driven by technological dynamics. Operating systems evolve from one generation to the next, introducing new features, security enhancements, and performance optimizations. The rise of cloud computing brings about a paradigm shift, where software functionalities extend beyond the confines of local devices to distributed and interconnected systems. The advent of containerization and microservices further reshapes software architecture, offering flexibility, scalability, and agility in deploying and managing applications. Device management, in this context, becomes a dynamic orchestration of software components, necessitating adaptive strategies to accommodate the evolving software landscape and harness its potential for enhanced functionality and user experiences.

Connectivity is a pivotal dimension that amplifies the dynamism of device management. The evolution from traditional wired connections to wireless technologies like Wi-Fi and Bluetooth has revolutionized how devices communicate with each other and the broader network. The advent of 5G technology promises unprecedented speed and reliability, unlocking new possibilities for real-time communication, low-latency applications, and widespread connectivity for IoT devices. This evolution in connectivity reshapes the expectations for device management, demanding strategies that accommodate the intricacies of diverse network infrastructures, ensure seamless handovers between different connectivity modes, and leverage the potential of low-latency communication for mission-critical applications.

The dynamic nature of device management is also intimately linked to the evolving needs and expectations of users. As technology becomes more integrated into daily life, users demand a seamless, intuitive, and personalized experience across a myriad of devices. The concept of user-centric device management emerges as a crucial consideration, emphasizing user-friendly interfaces, adaptive settings, and the ability to seamlessly transition between devices without sacrificing continuity. The rise of Bring Your Own Device (BYOD) trends in workplaces further underscores the need for device management strategies that strike a balance between user autonomy and organizational security, accommodating the diverse array of devices users bring into professional environments.

Security, a perennial concern, undergoes constant evolution in response to emerging threats, vulnerabilities, and the expanding attack surface presented by interconnected devices. The dynamic nature of cyber threats necessitates continuous adaptation of security protocols, threat detection mechanisms, and encryption standards. Device management becomes a cybersecurity battleground, implementing measures such as secure boot processes, encryption algorithms, and authentication protocols to fortify devices against evolving threats. The integration of artificial intelligence and machine learning into security frameworks introduces a dynamic element, allowing devices to adapt and respond to emerging threats in real-time, transforming device management into a proactive defense mechanism.

The advent of edge computing introduces a paradigm shift in device management, decentralizing computing resources and pushing computational capabilities closer to the data source. This evolution addresses the limitations of centralized cloud computing, particularly in scenarios where low-latency processing and real-time decision-making are critical. Device management strategies must now grapple with the complexities of managing distributed edge devices, ensuring synchronization, coordination, and efficient resource utilization in a decentralized computing landscape.

The Internet of Things (IoT), an embodiment of interconnected devices, amplifies the dynamic nature of device management to unprecedented levels. The sheer scale, heterogeneity, and distributed nature of IoT ecosystems present unique challenges in terms of device discovery, provisioning, monitoring, and maintenance. As the number of IoT devices proliferates, device management strategies evolve to incorporate edge computing, advanced analytics, and automation to cope with the massive influx of data generated by interconnected devices. The dynamic nature of IoT extends beyond traditional computing devices to include a diverse array of sensors, actuators, and embedded systems, requiring adaptive and scalable device management solutions.

Automation, driven by advancements in artificial intelligence and machine learning, emerges as a transformative force in device management. Autonomic computing, where devices possess self-management capabilities, becomes a reality. Automated provisioning, configuration, monitoring, and troubleshooting redefine the role of device management, enabling systems to adapt to changing conditions, predict failures, and optimize performance without constant human intervention. This automation not only enhances efficiency but also allows device management strategies to scale in response to the growing complexity and diversity of devices in modern ecosystems.

The concept of zero-trust security architectures challenges traditional notions of perimeter-based security and assumes that no device, user, or system can be inherently trusted. This approach aligns with the dynamic nature of modern device management, emphasizing continuous verification, real-time monitoring, and adaptive access controls. The zero-trust model reflects an acknowledgment of the evolving threat landscape, where threats can emerge from within as well as external to the traditional security perimeter. Device management, in adopting a zero-trust mindset, becomes a dynamic guardian, constantly assessing the trustworthiness of devices and users throughout their lifecycle.

The dynamic nature of technology and device management is further exemplified by the emergence of decentralized identity systems and blockchain technologies. Decentralized identity solutions enable users to have greater control over their personal information, enhancing privacy and security. Blockchain, with its immutable and transparent ledger, finds applications in device management, providing a tamper-resistant record of device configurations, updates, and transactions. These innovations contribute to the evolving landscape of device management, introducing decentralized and secure models for identity verification, access control, and device authentication.

Standardization efforts, represented by organizations such as the Internet Engineering Task Force (IETF), Institute of Electrical and Electronics Engineers (IEEE), and the Trusted Computing Group (TCG), play a vital role in shaping the dynamic landscape of device management. Standards provide a common framework, ensuring interoperability, compatibility, and a shared language for device management protocols. The dynamic evolution of technology necessitates agile and adaptive standards that can accommodate emerging trends, such as the proliferation of IoT devices, the rise of edge computing, and the integration of artificial intelligence into device management frameworks.

The dynamic nature of device management extends its influence into industries ranging from healthcare and finance to manufacturing and transportation. In healthcare, for instance, the advent of wearable devices, remote patient monitoring, and IoT-enabled medical equipment introduces novel challenges in managing diverse and interconnected devices while ensuring patient privacy and data security. Similarly, in finance, the dynamic landscape of mobile banking, digital transactions, and the integration of fintech solutions demands robust device management strategies to secure financial data, prevent fraud, and ensure regulatory compliance.

In conclusion, the dynamic nature of technology continuously propels the evolution of device management into uncharted territories, reshaping its foundations, expanding its capabilities, and presenting novel challenges. From the relentless evolution of hardware and software to the transformative impact of connectivity, security, and user expectations, device management remains at the forefront of technological innovation. The convergence of emerging trends such as edge computing, IoT, automation, zero-trust security, and decentralized technologies further underscores the dynamic nature of device management. As technology continues to advance at an unprecedented pace, device management must embrace agility, adaptability, and continuous innovation to navigate the intricate landscapes of modern computing ecosystems and ensure the seamless integration, security, and optimal performance of devices in this dynamic and ever-evolving technological era.

Introduce the importance of staying abreast of emerging trends in operating systems.

Staying abreast of emerging trends in operating systems is of paramount importance in today's rapidly evolving technological landscape. Operating systems serve as the foundational software that facilitates communication between hardware and user applications, shaping the overall computing experience. As technology continues to advance, new trends in operating systems emerge, offering enhanced features, improved security measures, and increased efficiency. One key aspect of staying informed about these trends is the ability to harness the latest technological advancements, ensuring that computing systems can leverage cutting-edge capabilities for optimal performance.

The evolution of operating systems is driven by a multitude of factors, including advancements in hardware, changes in user needs, and innovations in software development. Keeping abreast of these trends enables IT professionals, developers, and system administrators to make informed decisions about adopting and implementing the most suitable operating systems for their specific requirements. For instance, the transition from traditional monolithic architectures to microservices and containerization has become a prominent trend. Understanding and incorporating these changes into the operational framework can lead to more scalable, flexible, and resilient systems, aligning with the demands of modern computing environments.

Security is another critical aspect that underscores the significance of staying informed about emerging operating system trends. As cyber threats continue to evolve in sophistication and frequency, operating systems must adapt to fortify their defenses. The integration of advanced security features, such as secure boot, encryption, and enhanced access controls, reflects a prevailing trend in contemporary operating systems. By staying abreast of these developments, organizations can better safeguard their data, systems, and user privacy, mitigating the risks associated with cyber threats.

Furthermore, staying informed about emerging operating system trends is essential for ensuring compatibility with the latest hardware innovations. As new processors, storage technologies, and input devices enter the market, operating systems must evolve to support and capitalize on these advancements. This compatibility ensures that users can take full advantage of the latest hardware capabilities, optimizing system performance and enabling a seamless user experience.

The rise of cloud computing and virtualization is another transformative trend influencing operating systems. Modern OS architectures are increasingly designed to seamlessly integrate with cloud services and virtualized environments. This adaptability is crucial for businesses seeking to leverage the scalability, flexibility, and cost-effectiveness of cloud solutions. Staying abreast of these trends allows organizations to align their IT infrastructure with evolving paradigms, fostering agility and innovation in their operations.

Moreover, the user experience is a pivotal consideration in the development and evolution of operating systems. With the proliferation of mobile devices, IoT (Internet of Things) devices, and diverse computing platforms, operating systems must be versatile and user-friendly. Emerging trends in user interface design, gesture controls, and voice recognition are shaping the next generation of operating systems. By staying informed about these developments, developers can create interfaces that resonate with users, enhancing accessibility and usability across a spectrum of devices.

In the context of software development, staying abreast of emerging operating system trends is crucial for ensuring that applications remain compatible and optimized. New APIs (Application Programming Interfaces), programming languages, and development frameworks often align with the latest features and capabilities of operating systems. Developers who stay informed can leverage these tools to create more efficient and feature-rich applications, enhancing the overall software ecosystem.

Furthermore, the evolving landscape of open-source software plays a significant role in shaping operating system trends. Open-source operating systems, such as Linux distributions, continue to gain popularity due to their collaborative development model, community support, and cost-effectiveness. Staying informed about the latest developments in open-source communities allows organizations to harness the power of community-driven innovation, contributing to and benefiting from a vast pool of collective knowledge.

In conclusion, staying abreast of emerging trends in operating systems is imperative in the dynamic realm of technology. The ability to adapt to new paradigms, security measures, hardware innovations, and user experience enhancements is essential for organizations and individuals alike. Operating systems serve as the backbone of computing infrastructure, and their evolution directly impacts the efficiency, security, and functionality of digital systems. By remaining informed, stakeholders can navigate the ever-changing landscape of operating systems, making informed decisions that optimize performance, security, and user satisfaction in an increasingly interconnected and technologically advanced world.

Explore how machine learning algorithms are being applied to optimize device management.

Machine learning algorithms have emerged as powerful tools in the realm of device management, offering innovative solutions to optimize the deployment, monitoring, and maintenance of a diverse range of devices. One significant application of machine learning in device management is predictive maintenance. By leveraging historical data and real-time sensor information, machine learning algorithms can analyze patterns and predict potential device failures before they occur. This proactive approach enables organizations to schedule maintenance activities more efficiently, reducing downtime, and minimizing the impact on operations. Predictive maintenance not only enhances device reliability but also contributes to cost savings by preventing catastrophic failures and extending the overall lifespan of devices.

Another crucial aspect of device management that benefits from machine learning is fault detection and troubleshooting. Machine learning algorithms can be trained on datasets containing information about known issues and their resolutions. As devices operate, these algorithms continuously analyze incoming data, quickly identifying patterns indicative of faults or anomalies. By automating the detection process, organizations can streamline troubleshooting procedures, identify root causes more rapidly, and implement corrective measures in a timely manner. This not only enhances the efficiency of device management but also improves the overall reliability of the deployed infrastructure.

Machine learning's impact on device configuration and optimization is also noteworthy. Traditionally, configuring and optimizing devices required manual adjustments based on predefined rules. Machine learning algorithms, however, can analyze vast datasets to identify optimal configurations dynamically. Through continuous learning and adaptation, these algorithms can fine-tune device settings to maximize performance, energy efficiency, and resource utilization. This dynamic optimization capability is particularly valuable in large-scale deployments where manual configuration would be time-consuming and impractical.

In the context of security, machine learning plays a pivotal role in threat detection and mitigation within device management. As the threat landscape evolves, traditional rule-based security systems may struggle to keep pace. Machine learning algorithms, on the other hand, excel at recognizing patterns indicative of security threats, even in complex and dynamic environments. By analyzing network traffic, user behavior, and system logs, machine learning can detect anomalies that may signify a security breach. This proactive threat detection allows organizations to respond swiftly, preventing or minimizing the impact of security incidents on their device infrastructure.

Machine learning also enhances device management through intelligent resource allocation. In dynamic computing environments, allocating resources optimally is a complex task. Machine learning algorithms can analyze historical usage patterns, workload characteristics, and performance metrics to predict resource needs accurately. This predictive capability enables automated resource allocation, ensuring that devices receive the necessary computing power, storage, and network resources in real-time. This not only optimizes device performance but also contributes to overall energy efficiency by preventing unnecessary resource over-provisioning.

Furthermore, machine learning facilitates contextual awareness in device management. By integrating data from various sources, including sensors, user interactions, and environmental factors, machine learning algorithms can develop a comprehensive understanding of the context in which devices operate. This contextual awareness enables more intelligent decision-making, such as adapting device behavior based on user preferences, environmental conditions, or operational requirements. For example, in a smart building system, machine learning algorithms can optimize lighting and HVAC systems based on occupancy patterns, leading to energy savings without compromising comfort.

In the realm of Internet of Things (IoT), where a multitude of interconnected devices generate vast amounts of data, machine learning is instrumental in extracting meaningful insights. These insights can be used to enhance device management strategies by identifying usage patterns, predicting maintenance needs, and optimizing communication between devices. In industrial IoT applications, for instance, machine learning algorithms can analyze sensor data from machinery to predict equipment failures, schedule maintenance, and optimize production processes for increased efficiency.

Machine learning also plays a crucial role in automating routine tasks associated with device management. Tasks such as software updates, patch management, and configuration changes can be time-consuming when performed manually. Machine learning algorithms can automate these processes by learning from historical data and user preferences. This automation not only reduces the workload on IT personnel but also minimizes the risk of human errors that can occur during manual interventions. As a result, organizations can ensure that devices are consistently and securely managed, adhering to best practices and compliance requirements.

Moreover, machine learning contributes to adaptive and personalized user experiences within device management. By analyzing user behavior, preferences, and usage patterns, machine learning algorithms can tailor device settings and functionalities to individual users. This personalization enhances user satisfaction and productivity, as devices adapt to the specific needs and workflows of each user. Whether in a corporate IT environment or in consumer-oriented devices, this adaptive approach to device management contributes to a more seamless and user-friendly experience.

In conclusion, the application of machine learning algorithms to optimize device management represents a transformative paradigm in the field of information technology. From predictive maintenance and fault detection to resource allocation, security, and automation, machine learning brings a wealth of capabilities that enhance the efficiency, reliability, and adaptability of device management processes. As technology continues to advance and devices become increasingly interconnected and complex, the role of machine learning in device management is poised to grow, shaping the future of how organizations deploy, monitor, and maintain their digital infrastructure.

Discuss predictive analytics for anticipating and addressing device-related issues.

Predictive analytics has emerged as a transformative approach in anticipating and addressing device-related issues, offering organizations a proactive and data-driven strategy for managing their digital infrastructure. At its core, predictive analytics leverages historical data, real-time information, and advanced algorithms to forecast potential issues before they manifest, enabling timely interventions and strategic decision-making. One key application of predictive analytics in the realm of device management is predictive maintenance. By analyzing historical performance data, failure patterns, and environmental conditions, organizations can develop models that predict when a device is likely to experience a failure or require maintenance. This proactive approach not only minimizes unplanned downtime but also optimizes maintenance schedules, ensuring that resources are deployed efficiently.

The foundation of predictive analytics lies in data collection and analysis. Devices generate vast amounts of data during their operation, encompassing performance metrics, error logs, usage patterns, and environmental factors. Predictive analytics algorithms sift through this data to identify patterns and correlations that may indicate potential issues. The integration of sensors and IoT devices further enhances the data available for analysis, providing a comprehensive view of the device's operational context. This rich dataset serves as the input for machine learning models that learn from historical data, enabling them to make predictions about future events, such as device failures or performance degradation.

In the context of predictive maintenance, organizations can implement condition-based monitoring, where sensors continuously collect data on the device's health and performance. Predictive analytics models then analyze this data in real-time, identifying anomalies or patterns indicative of impending issues. For example, in manufacturing environments, sensors on machinery can monitor factors like temperature, vibration, and energy consumption. Predictive analytics can detect deviations from normal operating conditions, signaling potential equipment failures. By acting on these predictions, organizations can schedule maintenance activities during planned downtime, avoiding costly disruptions to operations.

Moreover, predictive analytics contributes to the optimization of device-related workflows by forecasting demand and usage patterns. In scenarios where devices experience varying workloads, such as servers in a data center or network devices handling fluctuating traffic, predictive analytics can analyze historical usage data to anticipate peak periods. This foresight allows organizations to dynamically allocate resources, scale capacity, and optimize configurations to accommodate expected demand. By aligning resources with anticipated workloads, organizations can enhance performance, minimize response times, and ensure a seamless user experience.

Predictive analytics also plays a pivotal role in identifying potential security threats and vulnerabilities within device ecosystems. By analyzing network traffic, user behavior, and system logs, predictive analytics algorithms can detect anomalies that may signify a security breach. Unusual patterns, such as unauthorized access attempts or anomalous data transfers, can trigger alerts, prompting security teams to investigate and mitigate potential threats. This proactive approach to security enhances the organization's ability to prevent and respond to cyber threats, safeguarding sensitive data and ensuring the integrity of the device infrastructure.

Furthermore, predictive analytics contributes to the optimization of energy consumption and resource utilization in device management. In environments where energy efficiency is a priority, such as smart buildings or data centers, predictive analytics models can analyze historical data to identify patterns of energy usage. By forecasting future energy demands based on usage patterns and external factors like weather conditions, organizations can implement strategies to optimize energy consumption. For instance, heating, ventilation, and air conditioning (HVAC) systems can be adjusted in anticipation of temperature changes, leading to energy savings without compromising comfort or operational efficiency.

In the realm of Internet of Things (IoT), where a multitude of interconnected devices generate vast amounts of data, predictive analytics is instrumental in extracting actionable insights. Predictive models can analyze sensor data to anticipate device failures, optimize maintenance schedules, and enhance overall system efficiency. In healthcare, for instance, predictive analytics applied to medical devices can help forecast equipment malfunctions, enabling timely maintenance to ensure the reliability of critical healthcare infrastructure.

The integration of predictive analytics into device management workflows also facilitates cost savings by preventing unnecessary replacements and optimizing resource allocation. Rather than adhering to rigid maintenance schedules or replacing devices based on predetermined lifecycles, organizations can use predictive analytics to identify devices that genuinely require attention or replacement. This targeted approach reduces the costs associated with premature replacements and allows organizations to maximize the useful life of their devices.

Moreover, predictive analytics contributes to a more efficient and adaptive user experience by personalizing device interactions based on historical usage patterns. By analyzing user behavior, preferences, and application usage, predictive analytics models can tailor device settings and functionalities to individual users. This personalization enhances user satisfaction and productivity, as devices adapt to the specific needs and workflows of each user. For instance, predictive analytics can anticipate the applications a user is likely to use at a particular time of day, pre-loading them for quicker access and a more seamless user experience.

In conclusion, predictive analytics stands at the forefront of transforming device management by providing organizations with the tools to anticipate and address issues before they impact operations. From predictive maintenance and fault detection to resource optimization, security, and personalized user experiences, predictive analytics empowers organizations to harness the potential of data for strategic decision-making. As the volume and complexity of data generated by devices continue to grow, the role of predictive analytics in device management is poised to expand, shaping a future where organizations can proactively manage their digital infrastructure for enhanced efficiency, reliability, and user satisfaction.

Discuss the impact of edge computing on device management strategies.

The advent of edge computing has ushered in a paradigm shift in device management strategies, reshaping the way organizations deploy, monitor, and maintain their digital infrastructure. Edge computing involves processing data closer to the source of generation, at the edge of the network, rather than relying solely on centralized cloud servers. This decentralized approach has profound implications for device management, impacting various aspects of the ecosystem.

One notable impact of edge computing on device management is the reduction in latency. By processing data closer to where it is generated, edge computing minimizes the round-trip time for data to travel to a centralized cloud server and back. This low-latency environment is particularly critical for applications that demand real-time responsiveness, such as autonomous vehicles, augmented reality, and industrial automation. In the context of device management, reduced latency enables faster decision-making and response times, enhancing the overall efficiency of monitoring, troubleshooting, and maintenance activities.

Moreover, the distributed nature of edge computing decentralizes the device management infrastructure. Instead of relying solely on a central cloud server, device management functions can be distributed across edge nodes, allowing for more localized and autonomous decision-making. This distribution of management functions is especially advantageous in scenarios where connectivity to the central cloud may be intermittent or unreliable. Edge computing enables devices to continue operating and managing themselves even when disconnected from the central infrastructure, contributing to increased robustness and resilience in device management strategies.

The scalability of edge computing is another factor influencing device management strategies. Edge nodes can be deployed in a scalable manner to accommodate varying workloads and device densities. This scalability is particularly beneficial in scenarios where a large number of devices need to be managed, such as in smart cities, industrial IoT deployments, or large-scale sensor networks. By distributing management functions across edge nodes, organizations can effectively scale their device management infrastructure to meet the demands of diverse and dynamic environments.

Furthermore, edge computing facilitates localized data processing and storage, reducing the need for transmitting large volumes of data to centralized cloud servers. This has significant implications for bandwidth usage and network efficiency. In device management, the ability to process and store data locally at the edge means that only relevant information needs to be transmitted to the central management system. This not only conserves network bandwidth but also reduces the dependency on a continuous and high-speed internet connection, making device management more feasible in resource-constrained or remote environments.

Security considerations in device management are also influenced by the adoption of edge computing. The distributed nature of edge computing allows organizations to implement security measures closer to the source of data generation. Localized security protocols and encryption mechanisms can be applied at the edge, providing a more granular and adaptive approach to safeguarding devices and data. This distributed security model helps mitigate risks associated with transmitting sensitive data over long distances and minimizes the potential attack surface for malicious actors, enhancing the overall security posture of device management strategies.

Moreover, edge computing enables organizations to adhere to data privacy and regulatory requirements more effectively. By processing and storing data locally, organizations can maintain greater control over the privacy and security of sensitive information. This is particularly crucial in industries such as healthcare, finance, and government, where strict regulatory frameworks govern the handling of data. Edge computing empowers organizations to implement privacy-preserving strategies in device management, ensuring compliance with regional and industry-specific data protection regulations.

The dynamic nature of edge computing aligns well with the requirements of emerging applications, such as the Internet of Things (IoT) and Industry 4.0. In these scenarios, a multitude of devices with diverse capabilities and functions are interconnected, generating vast amounts of data. Edge computing allows organizations to manage this complexity by distributing computing and management tasks across the network, closer to the devices. This adaptability is particularly valuable in industries like manufacturing, where edge computing can optimize production processes, monitor equipment health, and facilitate predictive maintenance, all within a localized and responsive framework.

In addition, edge computing enhances device autonomy by enabling more intelligent and context-aware decision-making at the edge. Devices equipped with edge computing capabilities can process and analyze data locally, making decisions based on real-time insights without relying on continuous communication with a central server. This autonomy is beneficial in scenarios where immediate responses are crucial, such as in autonomous vehicles or critical infrastructure monitoring. In the context of device management, autonomous edge devices can perform self-configuration, self-healing, and other management tasks without constant reliance on a centralized system.

The integration of artificial intelligence (AI) and machine learning (ML) at the edge further amplifies the impact on device management strategies. Edge devices can leverage on-device AI/ML models for tasks such as anomaly detection, predictive maintenance, and intelligent resource allocation. This capability enables devices to learn from local data patterns, adapt to changing conditions, and optimize their own operations. In device management, AI and ML at the edge empower organizations to implement more sophisticated and adaptive strategies, enhancing the overall efficiency and effectiveness of monitoring and maintenance activities.

Furthermore, edge computing contributes to energy efficiency in device management. By processing and analyzing data locally, devices can reduce the need for frequent communication with centralized servers, minimizing the energy consumption associated with data transmission. This is particularly relevant for battery-powered or energy-constrained devices, such as IoT sensors or mobile devices. Edge computing allows organizations to optimize energy usage, extending the battery life of devices and reducing the environmental impact of continuous data transmission to centralized cloud servers.

In conclusion, the impact of edge computing on device management strategies is multifaceted and transformative. From reducing latency and decentralizing management infrastructure to enhancing scalability, security, and device autonomy, edge computing presents a paradigm that aligns with the evolving demands of modern digital ecosystems. As organizations continue to adopt edge computing in diverse industries and applications, the role of edge-centric device management strategies is poised to become increasingly pivotal, shaping a future where devices operate autonomously, adaptively, and efficiently within decentralized and distributed computing environments.

Explore how edge devices are changing the landscape of operating system architectures.

The proliferation of edge devices is fundamentally reshaping the landscape of operating system architectures, ushering in a new era where computing capabilities are distributed, decentralized, and optimized for the unique challenges posed by edge computing environments. Traditional operating system architectures, designed primarily for centralized computing models, are being augmented and, in some cases, replaced by innovative approaches that address the demands of edge computing. At the core of this transformation is the need for operating systems that can efficiently manage the diverse and dynamic nature of edge devices, ranging from IoT sensors and edge servers to embedded systems and mobile devices.

One of the key characteristics of edge devices is their heterogeneity. Unlike the relatively homogenous environments of traditional data centers, edge computing encompasses a vast array of devices with varying processing power, memory, and storage capacities. Operating systems for edge devices must, therefore, be adaptable and lightweight, capable of running on resource-constrained devices without compromising performance. This shift has led to the emergence of lightweight and specialized operating systems designed specifically for the constraints of edge computing. These operating systems prioritize minimal resource usage, efficient task scheduling, and quick startup times to accommodate the diverse range of devices at the edge.

The decentralized nature of edge computing, with processing distributed across a multitude of devices, necessitates a shift from monolithic operating system architectures to more modular and containerized approaches. Traditional monolithic operating systems were designed for centralized servers with ample resources, but they may be ill-suited for the resource constraints and dynamic workloads of edge devices. Containerization and microservices architectures have gained prominence in the context of edge computing, allowing for the encapsulation of individual application components into lightweight, isolated containers. This modular approach enables better resource utilization, scalability, and flexibility in deploying applications across diverse edge devices.

Security is a paramount concern in the landscape of edge devices, where the attack surface is broader, and devices may operate in less secure environments. Operating systems for edge devices must prioritize security features that address the unique challenges of edge computing, including physical vulnerabilities, limited communication bandwidth, and diverse communication protocols. Secure boot mechanisms, encrypted file systems, and enhanced access controls become integral components of edge operating systems, providing robust defenses against potential threats. Additionally, the adoption of containerization allows for the isolation of application components, limiting the impact of security breaches and facilitating secure deployment and updates.

The real-time nature of many edge applications, such as industrial automation, autonomous vehicles, and healthcare monitoring, demands operating systems that can provide predictable and low-latency responses. Traditional operating systems may struggle to meet the stringent latency requirements of these applications. Consequently, real-time operating systems (RTOS) and lightweight kernels are gaining prominence in the edge computing landscape. RTOS, with their deterministic scheduling and minimal overhead, are well-suited for applications that require precise control over task execution timing, ensuring that critical operations occur within specified time frames.

Furthermore, edge devices are often deployed in environments with intermittent or limited connectivity to central infrastructure. Operating systems for edge devices must be designed to operate effectively in disconnected or low-bandwidth scenarios, allowing devices to function autonomously and seamlessly reconnect when connectivity is restored. Edge operating systems incorporate features such as local caching, edge-based processing, and optimized communication protocols to ensure that devices can operate efficiently even in challenging network conditions. This adaptability is crucial for applications ranging from remote monitoring in agriculture to edge-based processing in industrial settings.

The rise of edge computing has also led to a paradigm shift in how software updates and maintenance are handled. Traditional operating systems often rely on centralized update mechanisms, where updates are pushed from a central server to all connected devices.

In edge computing, this approach may be impractical due to limited bandwidth, diverse device architectures, and the need for continuous operation. Edge operating systems are embracing decentralized update strategies, where updates are distributed efficiently, possibly leveraging peer-to-peer communication or edge gateways. This ensures that devices can receive updates autonomously, minimizing disruption to operations and reducing the strain on network resources.

Moreover, edge computing introduces new considerations for power efficiency and energy consumption. Many edge devices operate on battery power or have strict energy constraints. Operating systems for edge devices must optimize power usage, incorporating features such as dynamic power management, efficient sleep modes, and fine-grained control over hardware resources. This focus on energy efficiency is essential for extending the battery life of mobile devices, minimizing the environmental impact, and ensuring the viability of edge deployments in remote or off-grid locations.

The integration of artificial intelligence (AI) and machine learning (ML) at the edge further complicates the operating system landscape. Edge devices increasingly require the capability to run inference models locally for tasks such as image recognition, natural language processing, and anomaly detection. Operating systems must support the deployment and execution of AI/ML workloads efficiently, potentially leveraging hardware accelerators and specialized processing units. This introduces a new layer of complexity to edge operating systems, requiring them to seamlessly integrate with AI frameworks and libraries while maintaining a balance between performance and resource utilization.

As edge computing evolves, the concept of "edge-native" operating systems is gaining traction. These operating systems are purpose-built for the unique characteristics and requirements of edge devices, offering a holistic solution that encompasses the challenges of heterogeneity, security, real-time processing, and energy efficiency. Edge-native operating systems prioritize modularity, flexibility, and adaptability to ensure compatibility with the diverse ecosystem of edge devices and applications.

In conclusion, the landscape of operating system architectures is undergoing a profound transformation driven by the proliferation of edge devices. The shift towards lightweight, modular, and security-focused operating systems reflects the need to address the unique challenges posed by edge computing environments. From real-time operating systems to containerized approaches, edge-native operating systems are redefining how devices are managed, applications are deployed, and computing resources are distributed in the era of edge computing. As the edge ecosystem continues to expand, the evolution of operating systems will play a crucial role in shaping the efficiency, security, and adaptability of edge devices across diverse industries and applications.

Explore the challenges and opportunities presented by the increasing number of IoT devices.

The proliferation of Internet of Things (IoT) devices has ushered in a new era of connectivity and data-driven capabilities, presenting both challenges and opportunities across various domains. One of the foremost challenges is the sheer magnitude of devices entering the network landscape. As IoT devices become ubiquitous in homes, industries, and cities, the strain on existing infrastructure becomes palpable. Network congestion, bandwidth limitations, and potential security vulnerabilities are exacerbated as billions of devices transmit and receive data simultaneously. Moreover, the diversity of IoT devices, each with unique communication protocols and data formats, complicates the seamless integration of these technologies, hindering interoperability and creating siloed ecosystems.

Security emerges as a paramount concern in the IoT landscape. The sheer volume of connected devices offers a vast attack surface for malicious actors seeking to exploit vulnerabilities. Inadequate security measures, such as default passwords and insufficient encryption protocols, expose IoT devices to cyber threats, potentially leading to data breaches, unauthorized access, and even compromise of critical infrastructure. As the number of IoT devices continues to surge, the need for robust security frameworks, regular updates, and standardized protocols becomes imperative to mitigate risks and safeguard sensitive information.

Interoperability, or the lack thereof, is another significant hurdle. The heterogeneity in device manufacturers, communication protocols, and data formats impedes seamless communication and collaboration among IoT devices. This lack of interoperability not only hinders the development of comprehensive IoT solutions but also limits the potential for innovation and scalability. Standardization efforts are essential to establish a common framework that enables different devices to communicate effectively, fostering a cohesive IoT ecosystem that transcends the current fragmented landscape.

Amidst these challenges, there exist vast opportunities for innovation, efficiency, and improved quality of life. In the realm of healthcare, for instance, IoT devices facilitate remote patient monitoring, enabling healthcare professionals to gather real-time data and enhance diagnostic accuracy. Wearable devices, connected to the Internet, provide individuals with personalized health insights, fostering proactive healthcare management. The industrial sector benefits from IoT-enabled smart manufacturing, where sensors and actuators optimize production processes, reduce downtime, and enhance overall operational efficiency.

The agricultural sector experiences a transformative shift through precision farming enabled by IoT devices. Smart sensors gather data on soil conditions, weather patterns, and crop health, empowering farmers to make informed decisions, optimize resource utilization, and increase yields. In smart cities, IoT technologies offer solutions to urban challenges, such as traffic congestion, energy consumption, and waste management. Smart traffic lights, connected vehicles, and environmental sensors contribute to the development of intelligent urban infrastructures that enhance sustainability and improve residents' quality of life.

The vast amounts of data generated by IoT devices fuel the rise of big data analytics and artificial intelligence (AI) applications. This data-driven paradigm allows businesses and organizations to glean valuable insights, optimize operations, and enhance decision-making processes. Predictive maintenance in the industrial sector, for example, utilizes data from IoT-enabled sensors to anticipate equipment failures, reducing downtime and maintenance costs. In retail, IoT devices enhance customer experiences through personalized recommendations and streamlined purchasing processes, revolutionizing the way businesses engage with consumers.

As the IoT landscape continues to evolve, the scalability and resilience of existing networks come under scrutiny. The transition to 5G networks holds promise in addressing some of the connectivity challenges posed by the growing number of IoT devices. The increased bandwidth and low-latency capabilities of 5G enable faster and more reliable communication, facilitating the seamless integration of a multitude of devices. However, the widespread adoption of 5G also brings forth concerns related to infrastructure investments, spectrum allocation, and potential health implications, necessitating a balanced approach to its implementation.

Ethical considerations surrounding privacy and data ownership become increasingly pertinent in the era of IoT. The extensive collection of personal data by interconnected devices raises questions about consent, transparency, and the responsible use of information. Striking a balance between leveraging the benefits of IoT for societal advancement and safeguarding individual privacy requires robust regulatory frameworks, industry standards, and public awareness initiatives. The development of ethical guidelines and privacy-by-design principles is crucial to ensure that the deployment of IoT technologies aligns with ethical standards and respects individuals' rights.

In conclusion, the proliferation of IoT devices presents a multifaceted landscape of challenges and opportunities. The scale and complexity of IoT ecosystems necessitate concerted efforts to address issues such as security vulnerabilities, interoperability, and ethical considerations. However, the potential for transformative innovation, enhanced efficiency, and improved quality of life is vast. Striking a balance between addressing challenges and capitalizing on opportunities requires collaborative efforts from stakeholders across industries, governments, and academia. As the IoT ecosystem matures, the resilience of networks, the development of robust regulatory frameworks, and a commitment to ethical practices will be pivotal in shaping a connected future that is secure, interoperable, and beneficial for society as a whole.

Discuss strategies for managing diverse devices in an IoT-centric ecosystem.

Managing the diversity of devices within an Internet of Things (IoT)-centric ecosystem poses a multifaceted challenge that necessitates the development and implementation of comprehensive strategies. One key aspect of effective device management involves establishing standardized communication protocols. Given the heterogeneous nature of IoT devices, each often designed by different manufacturers and utilizing varied communication technologies, the establishment of common protocols becomes imperative for seamless interaction. Standardization fosters interoperability, enabling devices from different vendors to communicate effectively and ensuring a cohesive ecosystem that transcends the current fragmentation. Industry-wide collaboration and the development of open standards are crucial in this regard, encouraging a more integrated and interoperable IoT landscape.

Furthermore, device management strategies should prioritize robust security measures to mitigate the inherent vulnerabilities in interconnected environments. Security considerations should be embedded throughout the entire device lifecycle, encompassing design, manufacturing, deployment, and decommissioning phases. Encryption, secure authentication mechanisms, and regular security updates are essential components of a comprehensive security strategy. As the number of IoT devices continues to proliferate, adopting a proactive approach to cybersecurity becomes crucial to safeguard against potential threats, unauthorized access, and data breaches. Collaborative efforts between industry stakeholders, regulatory bodies, and cybersecurity experts are pivotal in developing and enforcing security standards that fortify the resilience of IoT ecosystems.

Interoperability, or the ability of diverse devices to work seamlessly together, remains a cornerstone in effective device management. Establishing a framework that enables interoperability requires not only standardized communication protocols but also a commitment to creating an open and inclusive ecosystem. Industry consortia, alliances, and collaborative initiatives play a significant role in driving interoperability by fostering a shared vision and common goals among diverse stakeholders. By promoting the development and adoption of interoperable solutions, these collaborative efforts contribute to a more cohesive and user-friendly IoT environment.

An integral aspect of device management in IoT ecosystems involves the implementation of comprehensive device lifecycle management practices. This encompasses the provisioning, monitoring, maintenance, and decommissioning of devices throughout their operational lifespan. Automated provisioning mechanisms streamline the onboarding process, ensuring that devices are configured securely and efficiently. Continuous monitoring enables real-time visibility into device performance, allowing for the detection of anomalies, potential security threats, or performance issues. Routine maintenance, including software updates and patches, is critical to addressing vulnerabilities and ensuring devices operate optimally. When devices reach the end of their lifecycle, secure decommissioning processes must be in place to prevent data exposure and environmental impact.

Scalability is a fundamental consideration in managing diverse devices within IoT ecosystems, particularly as the number of connected devices continues to escalate. Implementing scalable solutions involves designing architectures and frameworks that can accommodate the growing influx of devices without compromising performance or security. Cloud-based solutions and edge computing play pivotal roles in facilitating scalability, allowing organizations to efficiently manage and process vast amounts of data generated by diverse IoT devices. Scalability also extends to the management platforms themselves, ensuring that they can adapt to the evolving needs of the IoT ecosystem as it expands and matures.

Data management is intricately linked to device management in IoT ecosystems, as the vast amounts of data generated by diverse devices require efficient handling and processing. Edge computing, where data is processed closer to the source of generation, alleviates the strain on centralized cloud servers and reduces latency. Implementing data governance policies helps organizations manage and derive value from the data while ensuring compliance with privacy regulations. Advanced analytics and machine learning algorithms further contribute to intelligent data processing, offering insights that can inform decision-making and optimize device performance.

To enhance device management in IoT ecosystems, organizations should embrace a user-centric approach. User experience considerations are crucial in ensuring that end-users can easily interact with and derive value from connected devices. Intuitive interfaces, clear documentation, and user-friendly applications contribute to a positive user experience. Additionally, proactive customer support, responsive troubleshooting mechanisms, and educational initiatives help users navigate the complexities of managing diverse IoT devices, fostering greater user adoption and satisfaction.

Governance and regulatory frameworks play a pivotal role in shaping effective device management strategies within IoT ecosystems. Governments and regulatory bodies should collaborate with industry stakeholders to establish guidelines, standards, and policies that address security, privacy, and ethical considerations. These frameworks provide a regulatory foundation that encourages responsible practices among device manufacturers, service providers, and end-users. International cooperation is crucial to harmonize regulations and create a cohesive global approach to IoT device management, considering the cross-border nature of IoT deployments.

In conclusion, managing the diverse array of devices within an IoT-centric ecosystem requires a holistic and multidimensional approach. Standardized communication protocols, robust security measures, interoperability initiatives, comprehensive lifecycle management practices, scalability considerations, effective data management, user-centric design, and regulatory frameworks collectively contribute to a resilient and well-managed IoT landscape. As the IoT ecosystem continues to evolve, the collaboration of industry stakeholders, regulatory bodies, and technology innovators will be essential in navigating the challenges and realizing the full potential of the interconnected world.

Introduce containerization and microservices as trends influencing device management.

Containerization and microservices represent transformative trends in the realm of software development and deployment, exerting a profound influence on device management practices within the broader landscape of information technology. Containerization, epitomized by technologies such as Docker and Kubernetes, introduces a lightweight and portable paradigm for packaging and deploying applications. In this context, a container encapsulates an application and its dependencies, enabling consistent deployment across diverse environments. The encapsulation of applications into containers streamlines the deployment process, fostering consistency and reproducibility across different stages of development, testing, and production. This approach significantly impacts device management by providing a standardized and modular framework for deploying applications on diverse devices within an Internet of Things (IoT) ecosystem.

Complementary to containerization, the adoption of microservices architecture represents a paradigm shift in how software is designed and organized. Microservices entail the decomposition of monolithic applications into small, independent services, each responsible for specific functionalities. This modular approach enhances flexibility, scalability, and maintainability of software systems. In the context of device management, microservices offer a decentralized and distributed model that aligns with the diverse and dynamic nature of IoT ecosystems. Each microservice can be tailored to manage specific aspects of device functionality, such as provisioning, monitoring, or security, allowing for more granular control and targeted improvements.

The integration of containerization and microservices in device management introduces several advantages. Firstly, the encapsulation of device management functionalities into containers enhances portability, allowing for consistent deployment across various devices and environments. This is particularly valuable in IoT scenarios where devices may have different hardware specifications, operating systems, and configurations. The containerized approach facilitates seamless scaling of device management services, ensuring efficient utilization of resources and accommodating the dynamic nature of IoT ecosystems.

Moreover, the modular nature of microservices aligns well with the heterogeneity of IoT devices and the diverse requirements associated with managing them. Each microservice can be designed to address a specific device management task, such as firmware updates, configuration management, or diagnostics. This granularity enables organizations to tailor their device management strategies to the unique characteristics and needs of different devices within the ecosystem. Additionally, microservices architecture enhances fault isolation, as issues in one microservice do not necessarily impact the entire device management system, contributing to increased resilience and reliability.

Container orchestration platforms, exemplified by Kubernetes, play a pivotal role in managing the deployment and scaling of containerized microservices. These platforms automate the process of deploying, scaling, and managing containers, providing a centralized and efficient means of overseeing complex IoT device environments. Kubernetes, in particular, excels in orchestrating containers across clusters of devices, ensuring high availability, load balancing, and seamless updates. This centralized control facilitates device management at scale, addressing the challenges posed by the increasing number and diversity of IoT devices in large deployments.

Security considerations are paramount in device management, especially in the context of IoT, where a breach can have far-reaching consequences. Containerization and microservices, when implemented with a security-first mindset, can enhance the overall security posture of device management systems. The isolation provided by containerization ensures that each microservice operates within its own environment, reducing the attack surface and mitigating the impact of potential security vulnerabilities. Furthermore, the modular nature of microservices allows for the application of security measures tailored to specific functionalities, enabling a more targeted and effective security strategy.

The evolution towards containerized microservices in device management also aligns with the broader industry trend of DevOps, emphasizing collaboration and automation between development and operations teams. DevOps practices promote continuous integration, continuous delivery, and continuous deployment, fostering a more agile and responsive development cycle. In the context of device management, this translates to the ability to rapidly iterate on and deploy updates, patches, and new functionalities, ensuring that device management systems remain adaptive to evolving requirements and emerging threats.

While the adoption of containerization and microservices in device management introduces numerous benefits, challenges and considerations must also be addressed. The dynamic and distributed nature of microservices introduces complexities in monitoring, debugging, and tracing, necessitating the implementation of robust observability solutions. Effective management of containerized microservices also requires skillsets in container orchestration tools, necessitating training and upskilling of personnel. Additionally, organizations must carefully plan and implement their container security strategies to mitigate potential risks associated with container vulnerabilities and misconfigurations.

In conclusion, containerization and microservices are pivotal trends shaping the landscape of device management, especially in the context of the Internet of Things. These approaches offer a flexible, scalable, and modular framework that aligns with the diverse and dynamic nature of IoT ecosystems. The combination of containerization and microservices enhances portability, scalability, security, and agility in managing devices, providing organizations with the tools needed to navigate the complexities of modern IoT environments. As the adoption of IoT devices continues to rise, the integration of these trends in device management will likely become increasingly central to the development and deployment of robust, scalable, and secure IoT solutions.

Discuss their role in enhancing scalability and flexibility in operating systems.

The evolution of containerization and microservices has played a pivotal role in reshaping the landscape of operating systems, ushering in a new era marked by heightened scalability and flexibility. Containerization, represented prominently by technologies such as Docker, has emerged as a transformative force by encapsulating applications and their dependencies within lightweight, portable units known as containers. These containers operate in an isolated environment, ensuring consistency across various stages of the development lifecycle and providing a standardized approach to software deployment. This approach, in turn, enhances scalability by enabling applications to be seamlessly moved between different computing environments, from development and testing to production, without encountering compatibility issues. The ability of containers to encapsulate an application's dependencies, libraries, and configurations ensures a consistent environment, eliminating the notorious "it works on my machine" problem that has plagued software development and system administration for years.

Furthermore, the integration of containerization with microservices architecture amplifies the scalability and flexibility of operating systems. Microservices, as a paradigm, advocates for the decomposition of monolithic applications into small, independently deployable services, each focused on a specific business capability. This modular approach to software design allows for the development, deployment, and scaling of individual components independently. Operating systems, when equipped to support microservices, gain the capability to manage a diverse and dynamic set of services seamlessly. The scalability benefits of microservices are particularly pronounced as each service can be scaled independently based on demand, optimizing resource utilization and ensuring efficient performance even in the face of varying workloads.

The combination of containerization and microservices is particularly instrumental in enhancing scalability across distributed systems. Container orchestration platforms, exemplified by Kubernetes, provide a robust framework for managing the deployment, scaling, and operation of containerized microservices. Kubernetes, in particular, excels in orchestrating containers across clusters of machines, offering automated load balancing, self-healing capabilities, and seamless rollouts of updates. This orchestration layer significantly contributes to the scalability of both applications and underlying operating systems by automating the distribution of workloads, ensuring high availability, and facilitating the efficient allocation of resources based on demand.

Scalability, however, is not solely about handling increased workloads; it also encompasses the ability to accommodate diverse environments and architectures. Containerization fosters portability by encapsulating applications and their dependencies, allowing them to run consistently across various operating systems and cloud platforms. This portability not only enhances scalability by facilitating the movement of applications between different environments but also provides flexibility in choosing the most suitable operating system for specific workloads. Containers abstract away the underlying infrastructure, allowing developers and operators to focus on the application logic rather than dealing with the intricacies of different operating systems.

Flexibility in operating systems is further accentuated by the dynamic nature of microservices. Traditional monolithic applications often required substantial effort and downtime to introduce changes or updates. In contrast, microservices can be updated, deployed, or scaled independently, allowing for more agile development and operational practices. This flexibility is particularly beneficial in scenarios where certain components of an application need to be modified or enhanced without affecting the entire system. Microservices enable a modular approach to development and deployment, empowering organizations to adapt to changing requirements swiftly and efficiently.

Moreover, the introduction of containerization and microservices has profound implications for cloud-native computing. Cloud-native applications, designed to leverage the scalability and flexibility of cloud environments, often rely on containerized microservices. Operating systems that support these containerized workloads play a critical role in the seamless execution and management of cloud-native applications. The cloud-native paradigm not only enhances scalability by leveraging the dynamic nature of containers but also provides flexibility in terms of deployment options, allowing organizations to choose between public, private, or hybrid cloud environments based on their specific needs.

Security considerations remain paramount in the pursuit of scalability and flexibility. Containerization, while introducing encapsulation and isolation, requires robust security measures to mitigate potential risks associated with container vulnerabilities. Likewise, the distributed nature of microservices demands a comprehensive security strategy that addresses the challenges posed by inter-service communication and data exchange. The flexibility gained through containerization and microservices should be coupled with stringent security practices, including regular vulnerability assessments, secure configuration management, and the implementation of least privilege principles.

In conclusion, the symbiotic relationship between containerization and microservices has redefined the landscape of operating systems, fostering scalability and flexibility in ways previously unattainable. Containers provide a consistent and portable unit for deploying applications, eliminating compatibility issues and enabling seamless movement across diverse environments. Microservices, with their modular and independently deployable nature, enhance the scalability of applications and operating systems by allowing individual components to scale autonomously based on demand. The orchestration of containerized microservices, facilitated by platforms like Kubernetes, further contributes to scalability and efficiency. This paradigm shift towards containerization and microservices not only addresses the challenges of modern computing but also empowers organizations to build and operate systems that are agile, adaptable, and capable of meeting the evolving demands of the digital era.

Chapter 7: Troubleshooting and Problem Resolution

Define the importance of effective troubleshooting in device management.

Effective troubleshooting in device management stands as a cornerstone in ensuring the optimal performance, reliability, and security of diverse and interconnected systems. In the intricate landscape of modern technology, where a myriad of devices collaborates within ecosystems ranging from personal devices to complex industrial networks, the ability to diagnose and resolve issues efficiently becomes paramount. The importance of effective troubleshooting is multifaceted, encompassing aspects of user satisfaction, system stability, operational efficiency, and overall organizational success.

First and foremost, effective troubleshooting is essential for maintaining a positive user experience. Users interact with a vast array of devices daily, ranging from smartphones and tablets to smart home appliances and industrial machinery. When devices encounter issues, whether it's a software glitch, connectivity problem, or hardware malfunction, users may face disruptions in their tasks, leading to frustration and a decline in productivity. Timely and accurate troubleshooting mitigates these challenges, restoring functionality swiftly and minimizing downtime. In the realm of customer-facing services and products, a positive user experience is not only critical for customer satisfaction but also for the reputation and competitiveness of the organization.

In the context of enterprise-level device management, where the stakes are higher due to the interconnected nature of systems and the potential impact on business operations, effective troubleshooting becomes even more crucial. In business environments, any disruption to devices, servers, or networks can have cascading effects on productivity, revenue, and customer service. An organization's ability to promptly identify and resolve issues directly correlates with its operational efficiency and, ultimately, its bottom line. Efficient troubleshooting practices contribute to maintaining a stable and reliable IT infrastructure, ensuring that devices operate optimally to support business processes.

Moreover, effective troubleshooting is indispensable for ensuring the security of devices and the data they handle. In an era where cyber threats are prevalent, the identification and resolution of security vulnerabilities or breaches are of utmost importance. Timely response to security incidents, whether it involves malware infections, unauthorized access attempts, or data breaches, is a critical aspect of device management. A robust troubleshooting process helps security teams investigate, contain, and mitigate the impact of security incidents, safeguarding sensitive information and preventing potential reputational damage.

Scalability is another dimension where the importance of effective troubleshooting becomes evident. As the number of devices within an ecosystem grows, so does the complexity of potential issues. In large-scale deployments, such as those in industrial IoT or smart city initiatives, the ability to troubleshoot efficiently at scale is imperative. Automated troubleshooting tools and practices, coupled with a well-defined incident response strategy, enable organizations to manage a vast number of devices without compromising on the speed and accuracy of issue resolution. This scalability is crucial for maintaining the integrity and functionality of systems in the face of evolving technological landscapes.

Furthermore, effective troubleshooting is integral to the lifecycle management of devices. As devices evolve, undergo updates, or encounter new challenges, the ability to diagnose and resolve issues ensures their longevity and continued relevance. Whether it involves addressing compatibility issues, updating firmware, or resolving software bugs, the troubleshooting process is intertwined with the ongoing maintenance and improvement of devices. In industries where devices have long lifecycles, such as manufacturing or critical infrastructure, proactive troubleshooting contributes to extending the useful life of assets and optimizing the return on investment.

The advent of the Internet of Things (IoT) further amplifies the significance of effective troubleshooting. In IoT ecosystems, where a multitude of interconnected devices collaborates to deliver intelligent and automated functionalities, the ability to troubleshoot across diverse endpoints becomes a complex yet essential endeavor. Issues in one device can have cascading effects on others, and identifying the root cause amidst the intricate network of sensors, actuators, and communication protocols requires advanced troubleshooting capabilities. The success of IoT deployments hinges on the ability to address issues swiftly, ensuring that the interconnected devices operate seamlessly to deliver the intended benefits.

Education and continuous improvement are fundamental components of effective troubleshooting. A well-trained and skilled workforce equipped with the knowledge of troubleshooting methodologies, tools, and best practices is crucial for success. This involves not only technical proficiency but also the ability to collaborate across teams, communicate effectively, and adapt to the evolving landscape of technology. Organizations that invest in ongoing training and skill development for their IT and device management teams are better positioned to navigate the complexities of modern technology and address issues in a proactive and efficient manner.

In conclusion, effective troubleshooting in device management is a linchpin in ensuring the smooth functioning, security, and longevity of interconnected systems. It is not merely a reactive process but a proactive and strategic endeavor that requires a combination of technical expertise, collaboration, and continuous learning. From enhancing user satisfaction to safeguarding critical infrastructure, the importance of troubleshooting transcends individual devices to shape the overall success and resilience of organizations in the dynamic and interconnected digital era.

Explore the role of troubleshooting in maintaining system stability and performance.

Troubleshooting plays a pivotal role in maintaining system stability and performance, serving as the linchpin in the ongoing effort to ensure the seamless operation of complex and interconnected technologies. The stability of a system is contingent upon its ability to operate reliably under various conditions, and when disruptions occur, effective troubleshooting becomes the catalyst for identifying and resolving issues. A stable system is characterized by its resilience to unforeseen challenges, minimal downtime, and the consistent delivery of services. Troubleshooting, in this context, acts as the proactive and reactive mechanism that safeguards system stability, preventing and addressing issues that may compromise the overall functionality of the system.

One of the fundamental contributions of troubleshooting to system stability lies in its capacity to identify and rectify issues that might lead to disruptions. Whether caused by hardware malfunctions, software bugs, or external factors, disruptions can destabilize a system and impede its ability to deliver services effectively. The troubleshooting process involves a systematic approach to diagnosing problems, determining their root causes, and implementing corrective measures. This approach ensures that issues are not merely addressed on a superficial level but are thoroughly investigated, leading to comprehensive and sustainable solutions that contribute to the overall stability of the system.

Moreover, troubleshooting is instrumental in mitigating the impact of system failures and minimizing downtime. In the dynamic landscape of modern technology, where businesses and organizations rely heavily on the continuous availability of systems and services, any interruption can have cascading effects on productivity, customer satisfaction, and revenue. Effective troubleshooting practices involve not only identifying the root cause of an issue but also implementing rapid and accurate solutions. This responsiveness is particularly crucial in mission-critical environments where even short periods of downtime can lead to significant financial losses or reputational damage. By swiftly addressing issues and restoring normal operations, troubleshooting becomes a key factor in maintaining system stability and minimizing disruptions.

System performance, closely intertwined with stability, is another domain significantly influenced by troubleshooting. Performance issues can manifest in various forms, ranging from slow response times and bottlenecks to inefficient resource utilization. Troubleshooting, in this context, is essential for diagnosing the factors contributing to performance degradation and implementing optimizations to enhance overall efficiency. Performance tuning, a subset of troubleshooting, involves iterative processes of measurement, analysis, and adjustment to optimize system behavior. Effective troubleshooting practices enable organizations to identify and rectify performance bottlenecks, ensuring that systems operate at their peak efficiency and deliver optimal responsiveness to end-users.

In the quest for system stability and performance, troubleshooting extends beyond merely addressing issues as they arise. It encompasses a proactive approach to identifying potential points of failure and implementing preventive measures to avert future disruptions. Regular monitoring and analysis of system metrics, coupled with predictive analytics, enable organizations to anticipate issues before they escalate into critical problems. This preventative troubleshooting not only safeguards system stability but also contributes to a more resilient and reliable infrastructure that can adapt to evolving challenges. By identifying and addressing underlying issues proactively, organizations can maintain a stable and high-performance computing environment.

The evolving landscape of technology introduces new challenges to system stability and performance, and troubleshooting adapts to address these challenges. With the rise of cloud computing, virtualization, and distributed architectures, troubleshooting becomes more complex as systems become more interconnected and dynamic. Cloud-based environments, for instance, introduce additional layers of abstraction and dependencies, requiring specialized troubleshooting techniques to navigate the intricacies of virtualized infrastructure. Troubleshooting in distributed systems involves addressing issues related to network communication, data consistency, and fault tolerance. The ability to troubleshoot effectively in these evolving environments is crucial for organizations looking to harness the benefits of emerging technologies while maintaining stability and performance.

The intricacies of troubleshooting are further amplified when considering the diverse range of devices and platforms within modern computing ecosystems. From traditional desktops and servers to mobile devices, IoT sensors, and edge computing nodes, troubleshooting encompasses a broad spectrum of hardware and software configurations. The heterogeneity of devices introduces challenges related to compatibility, interoperability, and varying performance characteristics. A holistic approach to troubleshooting acknowledges this diversity and leverages tools and methodologies that cater to the specificities of different devices. In multi-device and multi-platform environments, troubleshooting becomes a unifying practice that ensures the cohesive operation of the entire ecosystem.

Security, an integral aspect of system stability, is closely linked to troubleshooting. Security incidents, whether resulting from external attacks or internal vulnerabilities, can compromise the stability and performance of a system. Effective troubleshooting in the realm of cybersecurity involves the rapid detection and containment of security breaches, followed by comprehensive analysis to understand the root causes and prevent future occurrences. The integration of troubleshooting with security practices creates a robust defense mechanism that not only addresses immediate threats but also contributes to the overall resilience of the system against potential security vulnerabilities.

In conclusion, troubleshooting is a linchpin in the maintenance of system stability and performance, offering a multifaceted approach to identifying, addressing, and preventing issues across diverse computing environments. It serves as the frontline defense against disruptions, minimizing downtime, and ensuring the continuous delivery of services. Beyond its reactive role, troubleshooting encompasses proactive practices that anticipate and prevent issues, contributing to a more resilient and adaptive computing infrastructure. In the ever-evolving landscape of technology, effective troubleshooting remains an indispensable practice for organizations striving to maintain stable, high-performance systems that can withstand the challenges of the digital era.

Discuss various diagnostic tools and utilities for identifying device-related issues.

A plethora of diagnostic tools and utilities exist to facilitate the identification and resolution of device-related issues across diverse computing environments. These tools play a critical role in troubleshooting by providing insights into the performance, health, and functionality of hardware and software components. One of the foundational diagnostic tools is the System Information utility, commonly found in operating systems such as Windows. This tool offers an overview of the system's hardware configuration, software environment, and driver status, providing a comprehensive snapshot that aids in diagnosing potential issues. System Information can reveal crucial details, including the device's manufacturer, model, installed RAM, and current device drivers, assisting users and technicians in pinpointing hardware or software-related anomalies.

For more in-depth insights into system components and their real-time behavior, Performance Monitor, or its counterpart Activity Monitor in macOS, is a valuable diagnostic tool. These utilities offer a detailed view of system resource utilization, displaying information on CPU usage, memory consumption, disk activity, and network performance. By monitoring these metrics, users and administrators can identify bottlenecks, resource-hungry processes, or irregularities that may indicate underlying device-related issues impacting overall system performance.

In the realm of network diagnostics, utilities like Ping and Traceroute are indispensable for identifying connectivity issues. Ping sends small packets to a target device and measures the round-trip time, helping to assess network latency and packet loss. Traceroute, on the other hand, maps the route that data takes from the source to the destination, providing insights into the network path and identifying potential points of failure. These tools are fundamental in troubleshooting network-related device issues, enabling administrators to pinpoint connectivity problems, locate network congestion, or identify problematic routers or switches.

To delve deeper into network diagnostics, Wireshark stands out as a powerful packet analysis tool. Wireshark captures and analyzes network traffic, allowing users to inspect individual packets, identify communication patterns, and detect anomalies. This tool is instrumental in diagnosing network-related issues, such as packet loss, latency, or unusual traffic patterns, by providing a granular view of the data flowing through the network. Wireshark is widely used in scenarios where a nuanced understanding of network behavior is crucial for resolving connectivity or performance issues.

In the context of storage devices, diagnostic utilities like CHKDSK (Check Disk) on Windows and Disk Utility on macOS offer functionality for identifying and repairing file system and disk errors. CHKDSK scans and corrects issues on hard drives, detecting bad sectors, file system corruption, or other disk-related problems. Disk Utility provides similar capabilities on macOS, enabling users to verify and repair disk permissions, check SMART status, and format storage devices. These utilities are vital for maintaining the health and reliability of storage devices, preventing data loss and ensuring the optimal functioning of the file system.

Device Manager in Windows and its equivalent System Profiler in macOS serve as centralized hubs for managing and diagnosing hardware-related issues. Device Manager provides a comprehensive view of installed hardware components, allowing users to inspect device properties, update drivers, and troubleshoot driver-related problems. In macOS, System Profiler offers a detailed overview of hardware and software configurations, aiding in the identification of incompatible or malfunctioning devices. These utilities are essential for maintaining the integrity of hardware components, ensuring that drivers are up to date, and addressing issues related to device recognition and compatibility.

For diagnosing software-related issues and conflicts, the Event Viewer on Windows and Console on macOS serve as powerful diagnostic tools. Event Viewer compiles logs and event records generated by the operating system and applications, offering insights into system events, errors, and warnings. By analyzing these logs, users and administrators can identify patterns that may indicate software-related issues, conflicts, or application failures. Console on macOS provides a similar functionality, aggregating system logs and offering a centralized view of events. These diagnostic tools are indispensable for uncovering the root causes of software-related device issues and streamlining the troubleshooting process.

In scenarios where device issues are intertwined with the configuration of network settings, IPCONFIG on Windows and ifconfig on Unix-based systems provide essential diagnostic capabilities. IPCONFIG reveals information about network interfaces, IP addresses, subnet masks, and DNS configurations. On Unix-based systems, ifconfig offers similar insights into network interfaces and their configurations. By using these commands, users and administrators can troubleshoot connectivity issues, verify network configurations, and renew or release IP addresses, addressing a broad spectrum of network-related device issues.

In the realm of hardware diagnostics, manufacturers often provide specialized tools for diagnosing and testing their devices. For instance, the Windows Memory Diagnostic tool facilitates the identification of memory-related issues by running thorough tests on RAM modules, detecting memory corruption, and providing diagnostic reports. Similarly, hard drive manufacturers offer diagnostic utilities, such as Western Digital's Data Lifeguard Diagnostics or Seagate SeaTools, which assess the health of hard drives, perform SMART tests, and identify potential failures. These manufacturer-specific tools are tailored to the intricacies of particular devices, offering specialized diagnostic capabilities that enhance the accuracy of issue identification and resolution.

In the evolving landscape of virtualization and containerization, diagnostic tools tailored for these environments have become essential. Docker, a widely used containerization platform, provides diagnostic commands like "docker inspect" and "docker stats" that offer insights into container configurations, resource usage, and running processes. Kubernetes, a popular container orchestration platform, includes tools like kubectl that facilitate the diagnosis of issues within containerized environments. These tools enable administrators to examine the status of containers, troubleshoot networking problems, and identify performance bottlenecks in dynamic and scalable containerized systems.

The advent of cloud computing introduces new challenges and opportunities for diagnostic tools. Cloud service providers offer comprehensive monitoring and diagnostic services, such as Amazon CloudWatch, Azure Monitor, and Google Cloud Operations Suite. These services provide real-time insights into the performance and health of cloud-based infrastructure, offering metrics, logs, and alerts that aid in diagnosing issues related to virtual machines, storage, networking, and other cloud resources. Cloud-native diagnostic tools are essential for organizations leveraging the scalability and flexibility of cloud environments, providing visibility into the operation of devices deployed in the cloud.

In conclusion, a diverse array of diagnostic tools and utilities plays a pivotal role in identifying and resolving device-related issues across various computing environments. From system information tools and performance monitors to network diagnostics, storage utilities, and specialized manufacturer-specific diagnostics, these tools offer a comprehensive toolkit for users, administrators, and technicians. As technology continues to evolve, diagnostic tools will adapt to address the challenges posed by emerging paradigms such as virtualization, containerization, and cloud computing. The effective use of diagnostic tools not only streamlines the troubleshooting process but also contributes to the overall stability, reliability, and performance of devices in the dynamic and interconnected landscape of modern computing.

Explore the functionalities of tools such as system logs, diagnostic software, and built-in OS utilities.

System logs, diagnostic software, and built-in operating system (OS) utilities are integral components of the toolset that facilitates the identification, analysis, and resolution of issues across diverse computing environments. System logs serve as a rich source of information, capturing events, errors, and warnings generated by the operating system and applications. These logs, often accessible through tools like the Event Viewer on Windows or Console on macOS, provide a chronological record of system activities. Analyzing system logs aids in diagnosing a range of issues, from hardware failures and software conflicts to security incidents. By examining the entries in system logs, users and administrators can gain insights into the root causes of problems, track system behavior over time, and identify patterns that may indicate potential issues impacting system stability.

Diagnostic software constitutes a broad category of tools designed to assess the health, performance, and functionality of various system components. Examples of diagnostic software include hardware diagnostic tools, network analyzers, and system monitoring applications. For instance, hardware diagnostic tools, such as Windows Memory Diagnostic or manufacturer-specific utilities for hard drives, conduct thorough tests to identify faults in memory modules or storage devices. These tools contribute to the early detection of hardware failures, enabling users to address issues before they escalate. Network analyzers, like Wireshark, facilitate in-depth packet analysis, helping diagnose network-related problems such as packet loss, latency, or unusual traffic patterns. System monitoring applications, including Performance Monitor on Windows or Activity Monitor on macOS, offer real-time insights into resource utilization, aiding in the identification of performance bottlenecks or resource-hungry processes. Diagnostic software provides a proactive means of assessing system health and functionality, allowing for preventive measures and rapid issue resolution.

Built-in OS utilities represent a diverse set of tools embedded within operating systems to perform essential functions related to system management, configuration, and troubleshooting. These utilities are integral to the day-to-day operation of the operating system and provide users with a range of capabilities. For example, IPCONFIG on Windows and ifconfig on Unix-based systems are utilities for configuring and displaying network interface information, enabling users to troubleshoot connectivity issues, renew IP addresses, or check network configurations. The System Information utility, found in Windows, offers a comprehensive overview of hardware and software configurations, aiding in the diagnosis of device-related issues. Disk Utility on macOS provides functionalities for formatting, partitioning, and repairing storage devices, contributing to the maintenance of healthy file systems. Device Manager on Windows and System Profiler on macOS serve as centralized hubs for managing and troubleshooting hardware components, offering insights into driver status, device properties, and hardware configurations. These built-in OS utilities empower users and administrators with essential tools for system maintenance, configuration, and issue resolution, reducing the dependency on external diagnostic software.

An integral aspect of system logs is their role in security diagnostics. Security-related events, such as failed login attempts, access violations, or malware detection, are often recorded in system logs. Security Information and Event Management (SIEM) solutions, which aggregate and analyze log data, play a crucial role in security diagnostics. SIEM tools like Splunk, ELK Stack, or the built-in Windows Security and Audit logs enable organizations to detect and respond to security incidents. By correlating log entries and identifying patterns indicative of malicious activities, security professionals can swiftly respond to potential threats. Security diagnostics, facilitated by system logs and SIEM tools, contribute to the overall cybersecurity posture of an organization, ensuring the timely identification and mitigation of security vulnerabilities or breaches.

In the realm of diagnostic software, specialized tools address specific aspects of system health and performance. Antivirus and anti-malware software, for instance, focus on diagnosing and mitigating threats posed by malicious software. These tools scan the system for viruses, Trojans, and other forms of malware, aiming to detect and remove potential security risks. Examples of antivirus software include Windows Defender, Norton AntiVirus, or Bitdefender. Additionally, diagnostic tools like CPU stress tests or benchmarking applications evaluate the performance and stability of the central processing unit (CPU) and other hardware components. Tools like Prime95 or AIDA64 stress test the CPU, revealing potential issues such as overheating or hardware instability. By subjecting the system to intensive workloads, these tools help identify weaknesses and ensure that the hardware operates within expected parameters. The diagnostic software landscape is diverse, catering to specific aspects of system health, security, and performance.

Built-in OS utilities also play a crucial role in system performance diagnostics. Performance Monitor on Windows and Activity Monitor on macOS offer real-time insights into resource utilization, aiding in the identification of performance bottlenecks and resource-hungry processes. These utilities provide detailed metrics related to CPU usage, memory consumption, disk activity, and network performance. By monitoring these metrics, users and administrators can assess system performance, identify potential issues, and optimize resource allocation. Performance tuning utilities, such as the Windows Registry Editor or macOS Terminal commands, enable users to customize system settings, enhancing performance based on specific requirements. Built-in utilities like the Task Manager on Windows or Force Quit on macOS allow users to terminate unresponsive processes, contributing to the overall stability and responsiveness of the system. System performance diagnostics, facilitated by built-in OS utilities, are integral to maintaining a high-performing computing environment.

Moreover, system logs are instrumental in troubleshooting application-specific issues. Application logs, which record events and errors generated by software applications, provide a detailed account of application behavior. Analyzing application logs is crucial for diagnosing crashes, identifying software bugs, and resolving compatibility issues. Developers and support teams often rely on application logs to trace the execution flow, understand error messages, and pinpoint issues that may impact the user experience. In web development, tools like browser developer consoles or network inspection tools aid in diagnosing issues related to web applications. These tools provide real-time insights into network requests, JavaScript errors, and rendering performance, facilitating the identification and resolution of web application issues. The synergy between system logs and application-specific diagnostic tools contributes to a holistic approach to troubleshooting, ensuring that both system-wide and application-specific issues are addressed comprehensively.

Diagnostic software extends its functionality to address issues related to device drivers, which serve as crucial intermediaries between hardware and the operating system. Driver-related problems, such as outdated or incompatible drivers, can lead to malfunctions, crashes, or performance issues. Driver diagnostic tools, like Driver Verifier on Windows, verify the integrity and stability of device drivers by subjecting them to controlled stress tests. These tools help identify driver-related issues before they impact system stability. Windows Device Manager, a built-in utility, allows users to update, roll back, or uninstall drivers, providing a centralized hub for managing and troubleshooting driver-related problems. The integration of diagnostic software and built-in OS utilities in driver management ensures the seamless operation of hardware components within the system.

Furthermore, diagnostic software plays a critical role in addressing issues related to data integrity and file systems. Disk diagnostic tools, such as CHKDSK on Windows or Disk Utility on macOS, conduct thorough scans of storage devices, identifying and repairing file system errors and bad sectors. These tools contribute to the overall health and reliability of storage devices, preventing data corruption and ensuring the integrity of stored data. In scenarios where data recovery is required, specialized tools like Recuva or PhotoRec facilitate the retrieval of lost or deleted files, contributing to data preservation and mitigating the impact of data loss events. The integration of diagnostic software and built-in OS utilities in storage management ensures the availability and integrity of critical data within the system.

The evolution of diagnostic software extends to virtualization and containerization environments. Tools tailored for virtualization platforms, such as VMware vSphere or Microsoft Hyper-V Manager, offer diagnostics capabilities for virtual machines and their underlying infrastructure. These tools provide insights into resource allocation, performance metrics, and the overall health of virtualized environments. Container orchestration platforms, like Kubernetes, include diagnostic commands and tools, such as kubectl, that facilitate the monitoring and troubleshooting of containerized applications. These tools offer visibility into the status of containers, pod health, and resource utilization, enabling administrators to address issues within dynamic and scalable containerized systems. The integration of diagnostic software with virtualization and containerization platforms ensures the efficient operation of these technologies in modern computing landscapes.

In conclusion, system logs, diagnostic software, and built-in OS utilities collectively form a robust toolkit for identifying, analyzing, and resolving issues across diverse computing environments. System logs, enriched with security information, provide a chronological record of system activities and play a crucial role in security diagnostics. Diagnostic software, ranging from antivirus tools to CPU stress tests, addresses specific aspects of system health, security, and performance. Built-in OS utilities, such as Performance Monitor and Disk Utility, offer essential functionalities for system management, configuration, and troubleshooting. The synergy between these tools facilitates a comprehensive approach to diagnostics, ensuring the stability, reliability, and optimal performance of devices within the dynamic and interconnected landscape of modern computing.

Identify and discuss common issues encountered in device management.

Device management, a critical facet of modern IT infrastructure, is riddled with a myriad of common issues that organizations and users regularly encounter. One prominent challenge lies in the realm of compatibility and interoperability. With the diverse range of devices and operating systems prevalent in today's computing landscape, ensuring seamless compatibility between different hardware components and software platforms becomes a complex undertaking. Device drivers, serving as crucial intermediaries between hardware and operating systems, often pose compatibility challenges. Device management systems must grapple with the need to support an extensive array of devices while navigating the intricacies of driver compatibility, versioning, and updates. The issue is particularly pronounced in environments where legacy hardware coexists with cutting-edge devices, necessitating a delicate balance between modernization efforts and the support for existing infrastructure.

Security concerns loom large in device management, with cybersecurity threats evolving in sophistication and frequency. The proliferation of connected devices within the Internet of Things (IoT) exacerbates the attack surface, exposing devices to potential vulnerabilities. Security breaches, ranging from unauthorized access to data breaches, pose significant risks. Inadequately secured devices may become entry points for malicious actors seeking to compromise networks or launch distributed denial-of-service (DDoS) attacks. Device management must grapple with implementing robust security measures, including regular security updates, encryption protocols, and access controls, to mitigate the risk of unauthorized access and protect sensitive data. Balancing security with usability is an ongoing challenge, as stringent security measures may hinder user convenience and device functionality.

A perennial issue in device management is the sheer scale and diversity of devices that organizations must oversee. This challenge becomes particularly acute in large enterprises with sprawling IT infrastructures encompassing a multitude of endpoints – from traditional desktops and laptops to smartphones, tablets, and IoT devices. The management of such a diverse fleet involves dealing with varying configurations, operating systems, and usage patterns. Ensuring uniform policies, updates, and security measures across this heterogeneous landscape requires robust device management solutions. Furthermore, the proliferation of remote work has intensified this challenge, necessitating the management of devices distributed across geographically dispersed locations, each with its unique set of considerations.

The lifecycle management of devices introduces another layer of complexity. Devices have finite lifespans, and as they age, maintaining optimal performance, security, and compatibility becomes increasingly challenging. Legacy devices may lack support for modern security protocols or fail to meet evolving performance expectations. Upgrading or replacing devices at the right time requires strategic planning and budget considerations. Conversely, premature obsolescence may lead to unnecessary costs. Balancing the need for technological innovation with prudent device lifecycle management practices is crucial for organizations seeking to optimize performance while managing costs effectively.

Interconnected devices often give rise to issues related to network connectivity and bandwidth management. In environments with a multitude of devices competing for network resources, congestion and bandwidth limitations can result in degraded performance. Network-related issues may manifest as slow data transfer, latency in communication between devices, or even complete network outages. Effective device management entails optimizing network configurations, implementing Quality of Service (QoS) policies, and employing traffic monitoring tools to identify and resolve bandwidth-related issues. The growing prevalence of bandwidth-intensive applications and data-intensive workloads further underscores the importance of proactive network management in device ecosystems.

Maintaining compliance with regulatory requirements and industry standards represents a persistent challenge in device management. Industries such as healthcare, finance, and government must adhere to stringent regulations governing data protection, privacy, and security. Device management systems must navigate the complex landscape of compliance requirements, ensuring that devices and data meet the stipulated standards. Non-compliance can result in legal repercussions, financial penalties, and reputational damage. Staying abreast of evolving regulatory landscapes and adapting device management practices accordingly is an ongoing endeavor for organizations operating in regulated industries.

Another common issue in device management is the need for effective troubleshooting and issue resolution. Devices, by their nature, are prone to malfunctions, software bugs, and user errors. Rapidly diagnosing and resolving issues is crucial to minimizing downtime, ensuring user productivity, and maintaining overall system stability. Device management must encompass robust troubleshooting processes, leveraging diagnostic tools, logs, and remote management capabilities. The complexity of issues varies from simple software glitches to more intricate hardware failures, requiring a versatile set of skills and tools to address the diverse array of problems that may arise.

The proliferation of mobile devices introduces a unique set of challenges in device management. Smartphones and tablets, often used for both personal and professional purposes, blur the lines between personal and corporate data. Device management systems must grapple with the need to secure corporate data on personal devices while respecting user privacy. Implementing Bring Your Own Device (BYOD) policies adds complexity, requiring organizations to strike a delicate balance between empowering employees with device flexibility and ensuring the security and compliance of corporate data. Mobile device management (MDM) solutions have emerged to address these challenges, offering capabilities such as remote wipe, encryption, and application management for mobile endpoints.

Data protection and privacy concerns are paramount in device management, especially as devices increasingly store and process sensitive information. Organizations must contend with the challenge of safeguarding data against unauthorized access, loss, or theft. Encryption, access controls, and secure authentication mechanisms are critical components of a robust data protection strategy. Device management systems must ensure that data privacy regulations are adhered to, with a focus on transparent data handling practices and user consent. As data breaches become more sophisticated, device management practices must evolve to mitigate the risks associated with data exposure and maintain user trust.

Energy efficiency and sustainable device management have gained prominence as organizations strive to minimize their environmental footprint. The extensive use of computing devices contributes to energy consumption, and inefficient management practices can lead to unnecessary waste. Implementing power management policies, optimizing device configurations for energy efficiency, and employing hardware that adheres to eco-friendly standards are essential considerations in sustainable device management. Balancing operational requirements with environmental responsibility requires organizations to adopt a holistic approach to device lifecycle management and energy-efficient computing practices.

In conclusion, common issues encountered in device management span a wide spectrum, reflecting the intricate challenges posed by the diverse, interconnected, and ever-evolving landscape of modern technology. From compatibility and security concerns to the management of diverse device fleets, network complexities, and regulatory compliance, organizations must navigate these challenges to ensure the seamless functioning, security, and compliance of their device ecosystems. Proactive and strategic device management practices, informed by evolving technologies and industry best practices, are essential for organizations seeking to harness the benefits of technological innovation while mitigating the complexities inherent in device management.

Provide detailed solutions and troubleshooting steps for each identified problem.

Addressing the multitude of issues encountered in device management involves a comprehensive approach that encompasses solutions tailored to each challenge. Compatibility and interoperability concerns, often arising from the diverse range of devices and operating systems, demand proactive measures. Employing comprehensive device management solutions that support a wide array of devices and operating systems is crucial. Implementing compatibility testing during device procurement and regularly updating drivers and firmware ensure seamless interoperability. Additionally, adopting standardized protocols and communication interfaces helps mitigate compatibility issues. Collaborating with vendors and leveraging standardized frameworks contribute to creating a more unified and interoperable device ecosystem.

Security challenges in device management necessitate multifaceted solutions. Implementing robust security measures, such as regular software updates, encryption protocols, and access controls, is imperative. Employing endpoint security solutions, including firewalls, antivirus software, and intrusion detection systems, fortifies defenses against malware and unauthorized access. Educating users about cybersecurity best practices, including password hygiene and recognizing phishing attempts, strengthens the human element of security. Implementing multifactor authentication further enhances the security posture. Additionally, conducting regular security audits and penetration testing aids in identifying vulnerabilities and fortifying defenses against potential threats.

Managing the diverse fleet of devices in large enterprises involves deploying efficient device management solutions. Employing centralized device management platforms capable of handling multiple device types, operating systems, and configurations streamlines management processes. Adopting mobile device management (MDM) or unified endpoint management (UEM) solutions allows for centralized control, enabling tasks like software deployment, configuration management, and security enforcement across various devices. Utilizing automation and remote management capabilities minimizes manual intervention, improving operational efficiency. Collaborative efforts among IT teams ensure consistent policies and updates across the diverse device landscape.

Device lifecycle management demands strategic planning to optimize device performance and cost-effectiveness. Adopting proactive strategies involves establishing clear lifecycle policies and schedules for device procurement, maintenance, and retirement. Implementing regular hardware and software updates extends device lifespan and ensures compatibility with evolving technologies. Leveraging predictive analytics and monitoring tools aids in identifying devices approaching end-of-life or potential failures, allowing for timely upgrades or replacements. Recycling and responsible disposal of outdated devices contribute to sustainability efforts while ensuring compliance with environmental regulations.

Network connectivity and bandwidth management challenges necessitate effective network optimization strategies. Implementing Quality of Service (QoS) policies prioritizes critical traffic, minimizing network congestion and ensuring optimal performance for essential applications. Employing bandwidth monitoring tools helps identify bottlenecks and bandwidth-intensive processes, facilitating informed network optimization decisions. Utilizing load balancing techniques and optimizing network configurations improve bandwidth utilization and reduce latency. Regular network audits aid in identifying and resolving connectivity issues, ensuring efficient network operation.

Maintaining compliance with regulatory requirements and industry standards demands meticulous adherence to established protocols. Organizations must continuously monitor regulatory changes and adapt device management practices accordingly. Employing compliance management solutions that automate compliance checks and ensure adherence to industry standards simplifies the compliance process. Conducting regular audits and documentation of compliance efforts ensures transparency and readiness for regulatory assessments. Collaborating with legal and compliance teams helps align device management practices with prevailing regulations and standards.

Effective troubleshooting and issue resolution require a structured approach. Developing comprehensive troubleshooting guides and protocols aids in systematically diagnosing and resolving issues. Leveraging diagnostic tools, such as system logs, performance monitors, and remote management utilities, assists in identifying root causes efficiently. Encouraging user reporting of issues and providing training on basic troubleshooting steps empowers users to resolve minor issues independently. Establishing tiered support systems within IT departments ensures efficient escalation and resolution of complex problems.

Managing mobile devices necessitates a balance between security and user flexibility. Implementing robust mobile device management (MDM) or unified endpoint management (UEM) solutions enables organizations to enforce security policies, such as remote wipe, encryption, and containerization, without compromising user privacy. Implementing Bring Your Own Device (BYOD) policies involves clear delineation of corporate and personal data on devices, employing containerization or virtualization technologies to segregate work and personal profiles. Educating users on BYOD policies and security best practices fosters a culture of responsible device usage while safeguarding corporate data.

Data protection and privacy concerns in device management require stringent measures. Implementing encryption protocols, access controls, and secure authentication mechanisms fortify data protection. Employing data loss prevention (DLP) solutions aids in monitoring and preventing unauthorized access or data leakage. Conducting regular security awareness training educates users about data handling practices, reinforcing the importance of data privacy. Ensuring compliance with data protection regulations, such as GDPR or HIPAA, involves implementing stringent data handling policies and transparency in data processing practices.

Promoting energy efficiency and sustainable device management involves adopting eco-friendly practices. Employing power management policies that optimize device energy consumption reduces environmental impact. Utilizing energy-efficient hardware and components and adhering to eco-label certifications ensure sustainability. Implementing e-waste management programs facilitates responsible disposal and recycling of outdated devices, minimizing environmental pollution. Educating users about energy-saving practices and environmental impact fosters a culture of sustainability within organizations.

In conclusion, addressing the diverse array of issues encountered in device management demands a multifaceted approach tailored to each challenge. From compatibility and security concerns to network optimization, compliance, troubleshooting, and sustainability, organizations must employ a combination of strategic planning, technology adoption, user education, and regulatory compliance to navigate the complexities inherent in device management. Proactive and holistic solutions fortify device ecosystems, ensuring optimal performance, security, compliance, and sustainability in the dynamic landscape of modern technology.

Explore strategies for troubleshooting devices remotely.

Troubleshooting devices remotely has become a critical aspect of modern IT support, especially with the rise of remote work and the prevalence of distributed computing environments. Remote troubleshooting involves diagnosing and resolving issues on devices without the need for physical presence. Successful remote troubleshooting strategies encompass a combination of advanced technologies, effective communication, and a systematic approach to problem-solving.

One fundamental element of remote troubleshooting is the utilization of remote access tools. These tools enable IT support personnel to connect to a user's device over the internet, providing them with real-time access to the system. Remote desktop software, such as TeamViewer, AnyDesk, or Microsoft Remote Desktop, allows support professionals to view the user's screen, control the mouse and keyboard, and perform troubleshooting tasks as if they were physically present. These tools facilitate quick and efficient issue resolution by eliminating the need for users to attempt complex tasks on their own and enabling IT support to directly interact with the system.

In addition to remote access tools, remote diagnostic utilities play a crucial role in troubleshooting devices. These utilities provide insights into system performance, hardware health, and software configurations without requiring direct access. System monitoring tools, like SolarWinds, Nagios, or PRTG Network Monitor, allow IT professionals to remotely monitor resource utilization, network activity, and system health. By analyzing these metrics, support teams can identify patterns, anomalies, or potential issues that may require attention. Diagnostic utilities also include remote scripting and command-line tools that enable the execution of commands on remote devices, providing a means to gather information or perform actions without direct interaction.

Implementing robust endpoint management solutions is another key strategy for remote troubleshooting. Endpoint management platforms, such as Microsoft Endpoint Manager, VMware Workspace ONE, or Jamf Pro for macOS environments, offer centralized control over devices, allowing IT administrators to push updates, enforce security policies, and deploy software remotely. These solutions streamline device management tasks and facilitate troubleshooting by providing a unified interface for monitoring and controlling devices across the organization. Endpoint management platforms also often include remote wipe and lockdown capabilities, enhancing security measures and enabling IT teams to take proactive measures in response to security incidents.

Effective communication is a cornerstone of successful remote troubleshooting. Establishing clear channels of communication between IT support and end-users is vital. Remote support tools often include chat or messaging features that enable real-time communication. Clear and concise communication helps in understanding the nature of the problem, gathering relevant information, and providing instructions to users for specific troubleshooting steps. Additionally, utilizing video conferencing tools, such as Zoom or Microsoft

Teams, allows for face-to-face communication, fostering a more personal and collaborative troubleshooting experience. Video conferencing can be especially beneficial for visual diagnostics, where observing the user's physical setup or device behavior provides valuable insights.

Creating detailed documentation and knowledge bases is essential for remote troubleshooting efficiency. Knowledge bases can serve as repositories of common issues, known solutions, and step-by-step guides for troubleshooting specific problems. Providing users with access to self-help documentation empowers them to address straightforward issues independently. For more complex problems, IT support can refer to these resources to quickly access relevant information and solutions. Regularly updating and expanding the knowledge base ensures that it remains a reliable reference for both support teams and end-users, contributing to a more efficient remote troubleshooting process.

Implementing automated diagnostic scripts and remote monitoring agents enhances the proactive aspect of remote troubleshooting. Automated scripts can perform predefined diagnostic tests or gather specific information on a remote device without user intervention. For example, scripting languages like PowerShell or Bash can be used to retrieve system logs, check network configurations, or verify the status of critical services. Remote monitoring agents, embedded in devices, continuously collect and transmit data about the system's health, performance, and security. Solutions like ConnectWise Automate or ManageEngine Desktop Central leverage automation to preemptively detect and address issues before they impact users, contributing to a more proactive and responsive remote troubleshooting approach.

Machine learning and artificial intelligence (AI) technologies are increasingly being integrated into remote troubleshooting strategies. AI-powered algorithms can analyze large datasets to identify patterns, predict potential issues, and recommend solutions. Chatbots equipped with natural language processing capabilities can interact with users, gather information about issues, and provide automated troubleshooting guidance. Predictive analytics tools can anticipate hardware failures or performance degradation, allowing IT support teams to take preemptive actions. Integrating AI into remote troubleshooting not only improves the efficiency of issue resolution but also augments the capabilities of support teams by providing intelligent insights and recommendations.

Remote collaboration tools are indispensable for troubleshooting complex issues that require the collaboration of multiple team members. Platforms like Slack, Microsoft Teams, or Atlassian Jira facilitate real-time collaboration, enabling support teams to share information, exchange ideas, and collectively work on resolving issues. Collaborative documentation tools, such as Confluence or Google Docs, provide a centralized space for documenting troubleshooting processes, solutions, and relevant information. The seamless integration of these tools into the remote troubleshooting workflow enhances collaboration and knowledge-sharing among support professionals.

Security considerations are paramount in remote troubleshooting, particularly when accessing sensitive systems or corporate networks. Implementing secure remote access protocols, such as Virtual Private Network (VPN) connections or Secure Shell (SSH) tunnels, ensures that data transmitted during remote sessions is encrypted and secure. Multi-factor authentication adds an additional layer of security, requiring users to verify their identity through multiple authentication methods. Endpoint security solutions, including antivirus software and intrusion detection systems, play a crucial role in preventing security breaches during remote troubleshooting sessions. Regularly auditing and updating security measures help mitigate potential risks associated with remote access.

Training and skill development for IT support teams are essential components of effective remote troubleshooting. Providing comprehensive training on remote troubleshooting tools, techniques, and best practices equips support professionals with the skills needed to navigate the unique challenges of remote support. Training should cover not only technical aspects but also effective communication strategies, customer service skills, and problem-solving methodologies. Encouraging continuous learning and staying abreast of emerging technologies ensures that support teams remain proficient in addressing evolving challenges in the remote troubleshooting landscape.

In conclusion, remote troubleshooting strategies encompass a multifaceted approach that leverages advanced technologies, effective communication, and proactive methodologies. From the use of remote access tools and diagnostic utilities to the implementation of endpoint management solutions and collaboration platforms, organizations must integrate a diverse set of tools and practices to ensure efficient and secure remote troubleshooting. As technology continues to evolve, embracing emerging technologies like AI, automation, and predictive analytics further enhances the capabilities of remote support teams. Continuous training, documentation, and a focus on security considerations are integral elements of a successful remote troubleshooting strategy in the dynamic and interconnected world of IT support.

Discuss the use of remote access tools and technologies for problem resolution.

The use of remote access tools and technologies has become integral to problem resolution in the dynamic landscape of IT support and technical assistance. Remote access tools empower support professionals to connect to and interact with end-users' devices or systems over the internet, facilitating real-time troubleshooting and issue resolution without the need for physical presence. These tools have evolved to offer a range of functionalities, from screen sharing and remote control to file transfer and diagnostic capabilities, creating a seamless bridge between IT support teams and end-users.

One of the primary functions of remote access tools is to enable remote desktop control. These tools, such as TeamViewer, AnyDesk, or Microsoft Remote Desktop, provide support professionals with the ability to view the user's desktop in real-time, take control of the mouse and keyboard, and perform troubleshooting tasks as if they were physically present. This functionality is invaluable for resolving complex issues that require direct interaction with the user's system. It allows IT support to navigate through menus, configure settings, and execute commands, providing a hands-on approach to problem resolution.

Screen sharing is another crucial feature of remote access tools. In situations where end-users need guidance or demonstration of specific processes, support professionals can share their own screens or view the user's screen. This real-time collaboration enhances communication and understanding, enabling support teams to visually identify issues, guide users through troubleshooting steps, and demonstrate solutions. Screen sharing fosters a collaborative troubleshooting experience, bridging the geographical gap between support teams and end-users.

File transfer capabilities provided by remote access tools facilitate the exchange of files between support professionals and end-users. This is particularly useful when troubleshooting involves the deployment of software updates, configuration files, or diagnostic tools. By securely transferring files over the remote connection, support teams can ensure that the necessary resources are available on the user's system, streamlining the troubleshooting process and expediting issue resolution. It eliminates the need for separate file-sharing platforms and simplifies the transfer of relevant files directly within the remote access session.

Diagnostic functionalities embedded in some remote access tools enhance the troubleshooting process by providing support professionals with insights into system information, hardware configurations, and performance metrics. These tools allow support teams to gather valuable data about the user's device, aiding in the identification of potential issues or areas requiring attention. Diagnostic capabilities may include system information reports, hardware health checks, and network diagnostics, offering a comprehensive view of the user's environment and contributing to a more informed approach to problem resolution.

Security is a paramount concern in the use of remote access tools, given the sensitive nature of the information and systems being accessed. Secure remote access protocols, such as Virtual Private Network (VPN) connections, Transport Layer Security (TLS), or Secure Shell (SSH) tunnels, are commonly employed to encrypt the communication between the support professional's system and the end-user's device. Encryption ensures that data transmitted during the remote session remains confidential and secure, mitigating the risk of interception or unauthorized access. Multi-factor authentication adds an extra layer of security, requiring users to verify their identity through multiple authentication methods before granting access.

The deployment of remote access tools for problem resolution aligns with the growing trend of remote work and the need for agile support solutions. Remote access technologies enable support teams to assist end-users regardless of their geographical location, fostering a more flexible and responsive IT support model. In scenarios where physical presence is impractical or time-sensitive, remote access tools offer a timely and efficient means of addressing issues, minimizing downtime, and ensuring continuous productivity.

Moreover, remote access tools contribute to the efficiency of IT support by reducing the need for on-site visits. Traditionally, support professionals had to physically travel to the location of an issue, resulting in increased response times and operational costs. Remote access tools eliminate these constraints, allowing support teams to address problems promptly from their own workstations. This efficiency gains significance in organizations with geographically dispersed teams or a large number of endpoints, where remote troubleshooting becomes a crucial component of IT service delivery.

Collaborative troubleshooting is facilitated through the use of remote access tools, fostering better communication and understanding between support professionals and end-users. The ability to visually share information, demonstrate processes, and work collaboratively on issue resolution enhances the overall support experience. Collaboration features, such as chat functionalities or the ability to annotate on shared screens, enable real-time communication during remote sessions. This collaborative approach not only expedites problem resolution but also empowers end-users by involving them in the troubleshooting process, contributing to their knowledge and confidence in dealing with technical issues.

Remote access tools cater to the diverse needs of support professionals by offering compatibility with various operating systems and devices. Cross-platform support ensures that IT teams can connect to and troubleshoot devices running different operating systems, whether it be Windows, macOS, Linux, or mobile operating systems. This flexibility is especially crucial in environments with heterogeneous IT infrastructures, where a diverse range of devices and platforms coexist. The universality of remote access tools ensures that support professionals can provide assistance across the entire spectrum of devices within an organization.

As organizations increasingly adopt cloud-based services and virtualized environments, remote access tools play a pivotal role in managing and troubleshooting these infrastructures. Cloud-based remote access solutions offer the flexibility to connect to devices and systems hosted in cloud environments, providing support teams with the ability to troubleshoot virtual machines, servers, or applications. This adaptability is essential in the context of modern IT architectures, where cloud services and virtualization have become integral components of organizational infrastructure.

However, while remote access tools offer numerous benefits, their deployment necessitates a careful consideration of potential challenges and security risks. Unauthorized access poses a significant threat, emphasizing the importance of implementing robust authentication mechanisms, access controls, and monitoring procedures. Security best practices, such as regularly updating and patching remote access tools, ensuring secure configurations, and conducting periodic security audits, are imperative to mitigate risks and safeguard against potential vulnerabilities.

In conclusion, the use of remote access tools and technologies has revolutionized the landscape of problem resolution in IT support. These tools empower support professionals to overcome geographical barriers, collaborate effectively with end-users, and provide timely assistance in diverse computing environments. From remote desktop control and screen sharing to file transfer and diagnostic capabilities, remote access tools offer a versatile toolkit for troubleshooting. Their deployment aligns with the evolving trends of remote work, virtualization, and cloud computing, providing organizations with agile and efficient solutions for maintaining the functionality and security of their IT ecosystems.

Highlight the importance of collaboration in complex troubleshooting scenarios.

Collaboration stands as a cornerstone in the realm of complex troubleshooting scenarios, playing a pivotal role in navigating the intricacies of modern IT challenges. In the dynamic landscape of technology, where systems are increasingly interconnected and dependencies abound, the complexity of troubleshooting has grown exponentially. In this context, collaboration emerges as a force multiplier, fostering a collective and multidimensional approach to problem-solving. The importance of collaboration becomes particularly pronounced when confronted with issues that transcend the boundaries of individual expertise or organizational silos.

One fundamental aspect of collaboration in complex troubleshooting scenarios is the pooling of diverse skills and knowledge. IT environments are multifaceted, encompassing a myriad of technologies, platforms, and applications. In the face of complex issues, each contributing element may require a specialized set of skills for analysis and resolution. Collaboration allows teams to bring together individuals with varied expertise, ranging from network specialists and system administrators to security experts and application developers. This diverse skill set forms a collective intelligence, enabling a more comprehensive understanding of the issue at hand and a richer pool of potential solutions.

Moreover, collaboration thrives on effective communication, which is essential for dissecting complex troubleshooting scenarios. In intricate technical environments, where the interplay of different components can lead to cascading effects, understanding the nuances of the problem requires clear and transparent communication. Collaborative troubleshooting encourages open dialogue, knowledge-sharing, and the articulation of technical details in a way that is comprehensible to team members with diverse backgrounds. This shared understanding is vital for aligning efforts, coordinating actions, and collectively working towards the resolution of complex issues.

Complex troubleshooting scenarios often demand interdisciplinary collaboration, where teams with varied specializations come together to address multifaceted challenges. For instance, a network issue might impact application performance, requiring collaboration between network engineers and application developers to identify the root cause. Similarly, security incidents may necessitate collaboration between cybersecurity experts and system administrators to contain and mitigate the impact. Interdisciplinary collaboration breaks down organizational silos, fostering a holistic perspective that recognizes the interconnected nature of IT systems.

In the context of complex troubleshooting, collaboration extends beyond the confines of a single team or department. It involves the convergence of efforts across organizational boundaries, bringing together different departments, external vendors, and, in some cases, even end-users. For instance, resolving an issue related to a third-party application may require collaboration with the application vendor's support team. End-user involvement is also crucial, especially in scenarios where issues are user-specific or where their insights into system behavior are invaluable. The synergy between internal teams, external partners, and end-users forms a collaborative ecosystem that collectively contributes to effective troubleshooting.

Furthermore, collaboration is essential for knowledge transfer and skill development within an organization. In the realm of complex troubleshooting, where solutions may require a combination of expertise from different domains, collaborative efforts become invaluable learning opportunities. Junior team members can benefit from the experience and insights of more seasoned professionals, contributing to their skill development and fostering a culture of continuous learning. Knowledge transfer within a collaborative troubleshooting environment ensures that the organization builds a reservoir of expertise that can be tapped into for future challenges.

The importance of collaboration is accentuated in scenarios where time is of the essence. Complex issues often translate into extended downtime, affecting productivity and potentially impacting the bottom line. Collaborative troubleshooting, by harnessing the collective brainpower of a team, accelerates the identification of root causes and the formulation of effective solutions. Rapid information exchange, real-time coordination, and parallelized efforts enabled by collaboration contribute to swift and efficient problem resolution, minimizing the impact of issues on business operations.

In the era of remote work and distributed teams, collaboration tools and platforms have become integral to the collaborative troubleshooting process. Technologies such as video conferencing, instant messaging, and collaborative documentation platforms bridge the geographical gap between team members, enabling real-time communication and information sharing. Collaborative troubleshooting, facilitated by these tools, ensures that teams can effectively collaborate irrespective of their physical location. This is particularly pertinent in scenarios where the expertise required for troubleshooting may be distributed across different offices or regions.

Collaborative troubleshooting not only addresses the immediate challenges posed by complex issues but also lays the foundation for continuous improvement. Post-resolution debriefings and retrospective analyses, conducted collaboratively, provide opportunities to reflect on the troubleshooting process, identify areas for improvement, and establish best practices. These collaborative reviews contribute to the development of a knowledge base that captures the lessons learned from each troubleshooting scenario. Over time, this knowledge base becomes a valuable resource, empowering teams to anticipate, prevent, or swiftly resolve similar issues in the future.

Effective collaboration in troubleshooting scenarios also involves the use of collaborative tools for documentation and information sharing. Platforms like Confluence, SharePoint, or even shared Google Docs serve as repositories for storing troubleshooting procedures, solutions, and relevant information. Collaborative documentation ensures that the insights gained during the troubleshooting process are captured, organized, and made accessible to team members. This documentation not only aids in current problem resolution but also becomes a valuable resource for onboarding new team members and maintaining institutional knowledge.

Despite its myriad benefits, collaborative troubleshooting is not without challenges. It requires a culture that fosters openness, trust, and effective communication. Teams must be willing to share information, admit uncertainty, and engage in constructive discussions. Cultural barriers, such as hierarchical structures that hinder open communication, can impede collaborative efforts. Overcoming these challenges requires a concerted effort to cultivate a collaborative mindset, where individuals value the collective success over individual recognition.

In conclusion, the importance of collaboration in complex troubleshooting scenarios cannot be overstated. As IT environments become increasingly complex and interconnected, the ability to bring together diverse skills, foster interdisciplinary collaboration, and facilitate effective communication becomes a strategic imperative. Collaboration accelerates the identification and resolution of complex issues, minimizes downtime, and contributes to continuous learning and improvement. Whether addressing interdisciplinary challenges, coordinating efforts across organizational boundaries, or leveraging collaborative tools for remote troubleshooting, the essence of collaboration lies in its power to transform individual efforts into a collective force capable of tackling the most intricate IT problems.

Discuss communication strategies among IT teams and support personnel.

Effective communication strategies among IT teams and support personnel are paramount in navigating the complex and ever-evolving landscape of technology. In the dynamic world of IT, where collaboration is essential, communication serves as the linchpin that binds teams together, facilitates the exchange of knowledge, and ensures a seamless flow of information. The multifaceted nature of IT operations demands a variety of communication strategies, encompassing both interpersonal interactions and the utilization of diverse communication tools, to address the challenges posed by diverse technologies, distributed teams, and the need for agile problem-solving.

One fundamental aspect of communication within IT teams revolves around fostering an environment of openness and transparency. Creating a culture where team members feel comfortable sharing information, insights, and concerns is crucial. Open communication cultivates a sense of trust, enabling team members to collaborate more effectively and ensuring that critical information is not siloed within individual departments or among specific team members. This transparency extends to both successes and challenges, encouraging a culture of shared responsibility where team members collectively celebrate achievements and collaborate to address obstacles.

In complex IT environments, effective documentation serves as a linchpin for communication. Documenting processes, configurations, troubleshooting steps, and solutions is essential for knowledge management and transfer. Well-organized and accessible documentation ensures that team members can easily access the information they need, reducing reliance on tribal knowledge and facilitating continuity in operations. Collaborative documentation platforms, such as Confluence or SharePoint, enhance the accessibility and collaborative creation of documentation, allowing teams to contribute to a collective knowledge base.

Furthermore, the importance of interpersonal communication cannot be overstated. Regular team meetings, whether in-person or virtual, provide a forum for team members to discuss ongoing projects, share updates, and address challenges. These meetings foster a sense of camaraderie and help ensure that everyone is aligned with the team's goals and priorities. Additionally, team members can use these forums to voice concerns, seek input from colleagues, and provide updates on their respective areas of expertise.

In distributed or remote work environments, where physical proximity is not a given, leveraging virtual communication tools becomes imperative. Video conferencing platforms, such as Zoom or Microsoft Teams, offer a virtual space for face-to-face meetings, enhancing the personal connection among team members. These platforms facilitate not only formal meetings but also informal interactions, fostering a sense of camaraderie and teamwork that transcends geographical boundaries. Instant messaging and collaboration tools, such as Slack or Microsoft Teams chat, provide channels for real-time communication, enabling quick exchanges, clarifications, and coordination among team members.

In the realm of support personnel, communication strategies become even more critical. Support teams often serve as the bridge between end-users and technical solutions, requiring effective communication skills to understand and articulate technical issues in a way that is comprehensible to non-technical users. Active listening, a foundational element of effective communication, is crucial for support personnel to understand the nuances of reported issues, gather relevant information, and empathize with end-users' challenges.

Moreover, support personnel must be adept at adapting their communication style to the technical proficiency of end-users. Clear and jargon-free explanations, coupled with the ability to ask probing questions, enable support teams to elicit detailed information from end-users and guide them through troubleshooting steps. In situations where remote troubleshooting is necessary, support personnel must communicate instructions in a concise and understandable manner, leveraging remote access tools to directly assist end-users and address technical issues.

Service desks and ticketing systems play a central role in managing and coordinating communication within support teams. These platforms provide a structured and organized way to log, track, and prioritize reported issues. Effective ticket management involves clear documentation of the issue, steps taken for troubleshooting, and resolutions provided. Collaborative ticketing systems, integrated with communication tools, facilitate the exchange of information among support personnel, enabling them to collaborate on issue resolution, share insights, and provide a seamless support experience for end-users.

Additionally, the use of Knowledge Base (KB) articles contributes to efficient communication within support teams. KB articles document known issues, common troubleshooting steps, and solutions, providing a valuable resource for support personnel. Regularly updating and expanding the KB ensures that support teams have access to a comprehensive repository of information, streamlining the troubleshooting process and empowering them to address issues more efficiently. This collective knowledge base becomes a crucial tool for onboarding new support personnel and fostering continuous learning within the team.

In situations where escalated issues or major incidents require the involvement of specialized teams, effective communication becomes paramount. Incident management processes, guided by frameworks such as ITIL (Information Technology Infrastructure Library), emphasize clear communication channels, defined roles and responsibilities, and regular updates to stakeholders. Communication plans, detailing how information will be disseminated during incidents, help manage expectations, reduce uncertainty, and ensure that stakeholders are informed throughout the resolution process.

Collaboration tools, including shared dashboards and notification systems, enhance communication during incident response. These tools provide real-time visibility into the status of ongoing incidents, key metrics, and updates, allowing teams to coordinate their efforts more effectively. Automated alerts and notifications ensure that relevant stakeholders are promptly informed of critical developments, enabling a swift and coordinated response to incidents. Post-incident communication, including root cause analyses and lessons learned, contributes to continuous improvement and strengthens the resilience of IT systems.

Furthermore, communication plays a crucial role in change management processes within IT teams. Changes to systems, configurations, or software implementations have implications for the entire organization, and effective communication is essential to mitigate potential disruptions. Change management communication strategies involve notifying stakeholders, including end-users, about upcoming changes, outlining the reasons for the changes, and providing clear instructions on any actions they may need to take. Transparent and proactive communication ensures that everyone is on the same page, reducing resistance to change and enhancing the overall success of the change management process.

In conclusion, communication strategies among IT teams and support personnel are foundational to the success of modern IT operations. Openness, transparency, and effective documentation create a collaborative environment where knowledge is shared, and teams work cohesively towards common goals. Leveraging a combination of interpersonal communication, virtual collaboration tools, documentation platforms, and incident management processes ensures that IT teams can navigate the complexities of technology, address challenges efficiently, and provide seamless support to end-users. The dynamic nature of IT demands an adaptive and proactive approach to communication, making it a linchpin for success in the ever-evolving world of technology.

Chapter 8: Case Studies - Successful Device Management Implementations

Define the purpose of case studies in showcasing successful device management implementations.

Case studies serve as powerful tools in showcasing successful device management implementations by providing detailed narratives that delve into the intricacies, challenges, strategies, and triumphs of real-world scenarios. The primary purpose of these case studies is to offer a comprehensive and contextualized understanding of how organizations have effectively implemented device management solutions to achieve their objectives. By presenting a detailed account of the journey from problem identification to successful implementation and outcomes, case studies serve multiple essential roles in illustrating the value and impact of device management initiatives.

Firstly, case studies offer a tangible demonstration of the practical application of device management strategies in addressing specific challenges faced by organizations. Whether the focus is on enhancing security, streamlining operations, or optimizing device performance, case studies provide a narrative structure that allows readers to immerse themselves in the intricacies of the implementation process. These narratives bring to life the unique contexts, constraints, and decision points encountered by organizations, making the information more relatable and actionable for readers contemplating similar device management endeavors.

Moreover, case studies offer valuable insights into the decision-making processes associated with device management implementations. They provide a detailed examination of the considerations, evaluations, and trade-offs made by organizations when selecting and deploying device management solutions. Decision-makers and IT professionals can glean insights into the factors that influenced technology choices, the rationale behind specific configurations, and the strategic thinking that guided the implementation process. This depth of information is instrumental for others seeking guidance in navigating the complexities of device management decisions within their own organizational contexts.

Case studies play a crucial role in highlighting the challenges and obstacles encountered during device management implementations. They offer a candid exploration of the hurdles faced by organizations, ranging from compatibility issues and security concerns to organizational resistance and unforeseen technical complexities. By shedding light on these challenges, case studies provide a realistic portrayal of the complexities inherent in device management initiatives, helping readers anticipate potential pitfalls and formulate proactive strategies to mitigate risks.

Additionally, case studies emphasize the importance of collaboration and stakeholder engagement in successful device management implementations. They often showcase how cross-functional teams, involving IT personnel, management, end-users, and, at times, external vendors, collaboratively work towards common goals. The narratives detail the communication strategies, change management approaches, and collaborative efforts that contribute to the success of device management initiatives. This emphasis on collaboration provides valuable lessons for organizations seeking to foster a holistic and cooperative environment within their teams.

One of the critical purposes of case studies is to highlight the measurable outcomes and benefits derived from successful device management implementations. Whether the focus is on cost savings, increased operational efficiency, enhanced security posture, or improved user satisfaction, case studies offer a quantitative and qualitative analysis of the impact achieved. These outcomes serve as tangible proof points, allowing organizations contemplating similar device management strategies to gauge potential returns on investment and understand the broader business implications of their decisions.

Furthermore, case studies contribute to the knowledge-sharing ecosystem within the technology and device management domains. They serve as repositories of best practices, innovative approaches, and valuable lessons learned from successful implementations. By documenting and disseminating this knowledge, case studies foster a culture of continuous learning and improvement within the industry. Organizations and professionals can draw upon the experiences of others to inform their own strategies, ultimately contributing to the evolution and advancement of device management practices.

In showcasing successful device management implementations, case studies also underscore the adaptability and scalability of solutions across diverse organizational contexts. They illustrate how device management strategies can be tailored to meet the unique needs of different industries, organizational sizes, and technological landscapes. This adaptability ensures that the insights gleaned from case studies remain relevant and applicable across a broad spectrum of scenarios, allowing organizations to derive inspiration and guidance irrespective of their specific circumstances.

Moreover, case studies serve as persuasive and compelling advocacy tools for technology vendors and solution providers. By featuring successful implementations of their products or services, vendors can demonstrate the practical value and impact of their offerings in real-world scenarios. These case studies become persuasive narratives that showcase the efficacy of specific device management solutions, influencing the decision-making processes of potential customers and partners. They provide a tangible demonstration of the capabilities and benefits that organizations can realize by adopting the showcased device management technologies.

In conclusion, the purpose of case studies in showcasing successful device management implementations is multifaceted and impactful. Through detailed narratives, these case studies offer a tangible and contextualized understanding of device management initiatives, providing insights into decision-making processes, highlighting challenges and solutions, emphasizing collaboration, showcasing measurable outcomes, contributing to knowledge-sharing, and serving as persuasive tools for technology vendors. As organizations navigate the complexities of device management in an ever-evolving technological landscape, case studies stand as invaluable resources that illuminate the path towards successful implementations and transformative outcomes.

Highlight the practical application of concepts discussed throughout the book.

Throughout this comprehensive exploration, the practical application of the concepts discussed in this book emerges as a guiding thread, weaving together theoretical foundations and actionable insights. The concepts elucidated, ranging from device management strategies to troubleshooting methodologies, are not merely abstract principles but pragmatic tools that organizations can wield to navigate the challenges and harness the opportunities in the dynamic landscape of information technology.

The foundational concepts of device management come to life in their application within organizations. As discussed, device management is not a one-size-fits-all endeavor but a nuanced orchestration of strategies tailored to the specific needs and goals of each organization. Practical application involves the strategic selection of device management solutions that align with the organizational structure, technological ecosystem, and overarching business objectives. The nuanced understanding of device lifecycle management, security protocols, and configuration strategies provides organizations with a blueprint for creating resilient and efficient IT environments.

In the realm of Internet of Things (IoT), the practical application of concepts becomes particularly evident as organizations embrace the transformative potential of connected devices. The discussion on challenges and opportunities in IoT underscores the importance of robust device management frameworks to address the complexities introduced by the proliferation of IoT devices. Practical considerations, such as interoperability, security protocols, and data governance, become pivotal in the deployment and management of diverse IoT ecosystems. Organizations can leverage the insights from this discourse to craft effective strategies for deploying, monitoring, and maintaining their IoT infrastructures.

The integration of containerization and microservices into device management strategies exemplifies the practical evolution of IT architectures. As organizations strive for agility, scalability, and flexibility, the adoption of containerization technologies, such as Docker and Kubernetes, becomes a tangible manifestation of these concepts. The ability to encapsulate applications and dependencies into portable containers facilitates seamless deployment across diverse environments. The practical application of microservices architecture enables organizations to decouple complex systems into modular and independently deployable units, enhancing flexibility and facilitating more granular control over device management processes.

The importance of effective troubleshooting in device management finds practical resonance in its application across various scenarios. Troubleshooting is not merely a reactive measure but a proactive and iterative process that organizations employ to maintain system stability and performance. The practicality lies in the systematic approach to problem-solving, leveraging diagnostic tools, logs, and automation to identify and resolve issues efficiently. The emphasis on remote troubleshooting strategies aligns with the contemporary shift towards remote work and distributed computing environments, highlighting the practical need for solutions that transcend physical boundaries.

Diagnostic tools and utilities, explored in detail, find practical utility in the day-to-day operations of IT professionals. The discussion on system logs, diagnostic software, and built-in OS utilities underscores their role in providing actionable insights into system health, performance, and potential issues. The practical application involves the integration of these tools into routine monitoring and maintenance practices, enabling organizations to preemptively address issues before they escalate. The in-depth exploration of diagnostic tools serves as a practical guide for IT teams seeking to enhance their troubleshooting capabilities and maintain robust device management practices.

Common issues encountered in device management, as identified and discussed, find their practical resolution through the implementation of detailed solutions and troubleshooting steps. From connectivity issues and software conflicts to security vulnerabilities, organizations can draw upon the practical insights provided to develop comprehensive mitigation strategies. The emphasis on proactive measures, such as regular updates, security patches, and user training, aligns with the practical imperative of creating resilient and secure device management practices that stand up to the ever-evolving threat landscape.

Remote troubleshooting strategies, a focal point of the discourse, find immediate and practical relevance in the contemporary landscape of distributed workforces and globalized operations. The practical application of remote access tools, automated scripts, and collaborative platforms enables IT teams to overcome geographical constraints and provide swift support to end-users. The importance of effective communication in remote troubleshooting aligns with practical strategies for establishing clear channels of communication, leveraging video conferencing, and creating comprehensive documentation to facilitate seamless interactions between support teams and end-users.

The integration of artificial intelligence (AI) and machine learning (ML) into troubleshooting strategies signals a practical shift towards intelligent and predictive device management practices. Practical applications of AI and ML range from automated analysis of system logs to the deployment of chatbots for interactive troubleshooting. The potential to predict and preemptively address issues based on historical data and patterns introduces a practical dimension to troubleshooting that transcends traditional reactive approaches.

In the context of collaborative troubleshooting, the practical application lies in the establishment of communication strategies and collaborative tools that foster effective teamwork. The emphasis on knowledge sharing, interdisciplinary collaboration, and the use of collaborative documentation platforms speaks directly to the practical need for cohesive and cooperative troubleshooting efforts. Organizations can practically implement these strategies to create a culture of shared responsibility, continuous learning, and collective problem-solving.

Security considerations throughout the book underscore the practical imperative of safeguarding device management processes and infrastructures. The integration of security measures, such as multi-factor authentication, secure remote access protocols, and regular security audits, aligns with practical strategies for mitigating risks and ensuring the confidentiality and integrity of sensitive data. The practical application of security measures becomes paramount in an era where cybersecurity threats are increasingly sophisticated and pervasive.

Training and skill development, discussed as essential components of effective device management, find practical application in the continuous learning initiatives of organizations. The practicality lies in providing comprehensive training on device management tools, troubleshooting techniques, and security best practices to equip IT professionals with the skills needed to navigate the complexities of modern IT environments. The emphasis on staying abreast of emerging technologies underscores the practical need for ongoing skill development to keep pace with the evolving landscape.

The purpose of case studies, explored towards the end of the book, becomes inherently practical in showcasing successful device management implementations. These narratives serve as practical blueprints, offering tangible insights into how organizations have applied the concepts discussed throughout the book to address real-world challenges. By presenting detailed accounts of decision-making processes, challenges faced, and measurable outcomes achieved, case studies provide practical guidance for organizations contemplating similar device management initiatives.

In conclusion, the practical application of concepts discussed throughout this book emerges as the linchpin that transforms theoretical frameworks into actionable strategies. From device management strategies and IoT implementations to troubleshooting methodologies and security considerations, the practicality lies in how organizations can leverage these insights to enhance their operations, optimize their infrastructures, and navigate the complexities of the digital age. The discourse transcends theoretical abstraction, offering a practical roadmap for organizations to not only understand these concepts but to apply them in ways that foster resilience, innovation, and success in the ever-evolving landscape of information technology.

Explore a case where a large enterprise successfully optimized device management for improved efficiency.

In the dynamic landscape of enterprise IT, optimization of device management is a critical imperative for large organizations seeking to enhance efficiency, streamline operations, and ensure the seamless functionality of their technological ecosystems. One illustrative case of a large enterprise successfully navigating this complex terrain is the transformational journey undertaken by XYZ Corporation, a multinational conglomerate with diverse business units and a sprawling technological infrastructure.

XYZ Corporation, with its extensive network of offices, subsidiaries, and remote teams, faced the multifaceted challenges inherent in managing a diverse array of devices, ranging from traditional desktops and laptops to mobile devices and Internet of Things (IoT) endpoints. The sheer scale and complexity of the organization's technological landscape necessitated a holistic and strategic approach to device management. The enterprise embarked on a comprehensive optimization initiative aimed at maximizing operational efficiency, ensuring security compliance, and aligning device management strategies with overarching business objectives.

The first phase of XYZ Corporation's optimization journey involved a meticulous assessment of the existing device management ecosystem. This encompassed an inventory of all devices across the organization, an evaluation of current configurations, and an in-depth analysis of device performance metrics. The organization recognized the need for a unified device management solution that could cater to the diverse range of devices while providing centralized control and visibility. This realization marked the inception of a strategic shift towards adopting a unified endpoint management (UEM) framework.

The UEM framework became the linchpin of XYZ Corporation's device management optimization strategy. It allowed the organization to consolidate the management of diverse devices under a single, cohesive platform. The UEM solution provided granular control over device configurations, enabling centralized policy enforcement, software deployment, and security updates. This centralization not only simplified the management process but also fostered consistency and standardization across the enterprise's device landscape, mitigating the challenges associated with device heterogeneity.

Security, a paramount concern for a large enterprise operating across various industries, was a focal point in XYZ Corporation's optimization efforts. The UEM framework facilitated robust security measures, including the enforcement of encryption policies, application whitelisting, and the implementation of multi-factor authentication. The organization leveraged advanced threat detection capabilities within the UEM solution to proactively identify and respond to potential security risks. This proactive security stance not only fortified the organization against evolving cyber threats but also ensured compliance with stringent industry regulations.

Furthermore, XYZ Corporation recognized the significance of real-time monitoring and reporting in optimizing device management. The UEM solution provided comprehensive insights into device performance, user behavior, and compliance status through a centralized dashboard. This data-driven approach empowered IT administrators with the visibility needed to make informed decisions, identify performance bottlenecks, and proactively address emerging issues. The organization implemented automated reporting mechanisms to generate regular updates on key performance indicators, enabling continuous optimization and informed decision-making.

The optimization initiative extended beyond traditional endpoint devices to encompass the burgeoning landscape of IoT devices deployed by XYZ Corporation. With a multitude of sensors, connected machinery, and IoT-enabled devices spread across manufacturing facilities and logistics operations, managing this diverse IoT ecosystem posed unique challenges. The organization implemented specialized IoT device management tools that integrated seamlessly with the UEM framework. This integration allowed XYZ Corporation to monitor, configure, and update IoT devices efficiently, ensuring optimal performance, compliance, and security across the entire spectrum of connected devices.

The practical application of containerization and microservices architecture played a pivotal role in XYZ Corporation's device management optimization. Recognizing the need for agile and scalable solutions, the organization embraced containerization technologies such as Docker and Kubernetes. Containerized applications facilitated seamless deployment, scalability, and resource efficiency. Microservices architecture further enhanced flexibility, enabling XYZ Corporation to decouple device management functionalities into modular and independently deployable components. This architectural shift streamlined updates, reduced downtime, and provided the agility needed to adapt to evolving device management requirements.

The troubleshooting aspect of device management received dedicated attention in XYZ Corporation's optimization journey. The organization implemented advanced diagnostic tools and automated scripts that could identify and resolve issues proactively. Machine learning algorithms were integrated into troubleshooting processes, enabling predictive analytics to anticipate potential device failures based on historical data patterns. The organization also prioritized user-centric troubleshooting by leveraging remote support tools that allowed IT teams to assist end-users directly, reducing resolution times and enhancing the overall user experience.

Collaboration emerged as a cornerstone in XYZ Corporation's device management optimization, recognizing that success in such a multifaceted endeavor necessitated a concerted effort from cross-functional teams. Interdisciplinary collaboration became ingrained in the organization's culture, with IT professionals, security experts, and business units working collaboratively towards common device management goals. Regular team meetings, training sessions, and knowledge-sharing forums facilitated a collective understanding of device management strategies, ensuring that all stakeholders were aligned with the overarching optimization objectives.

The organization also invested in continuous training and skill development programs for its IT teams. Recognizing the dynamic nature of technology, XYZ Corporation prioritized keeping its workforce abreast of emerging trends, new technologies, and evolving best practices in device management. This commitment to skill development not only empowered IT professionals with the expertise needed for successful optimization but also contributed to a culture of innovation and adaptability within the organization.

The practical application of AI in troubleshooting and predictive analytics significantly enhanced XYZ Corporation's device management optimization. The organization implemented AI-driven algorithms that could analyze historical data, identify patterns, and predict potential issues before they manifested. This proactive approach minimized disruptions, reduced downtime, and optimized resource utilization. AI-powered chatbots were deployed to assist end-users with common issues, providing instant support and freeing up IT teams to focus on more complex problem-solving tasks.

The optimization journey of XYZ Corporation culminated in measurable outcomes that underscored the practical success of their device management strategies. Operational efficiency saw a marked improvement, with streamlined processes, reduced downtime, and faster issue resolution contributing to overall productivity gains. Security compliance metrics demonstrated a significant enhancement, with a robust security posture and adherence to industry regulations. The organization witnessed cost savings through optimized resource utilization, reduced support ticket volumes, and efficient use of containerized applications.

In conclusion, the case of XYZ Corporation exemplifies the practical application of device management concepts to achieve transformative outcomes in a large enterprise setting. From the strategic adoption of UEM and IoT device management to the implementation of containerization, microservices architecture, and AI-driven troubleshooting, the organization's optimization journey reflects a holistic and adaptive approach to device management. The success of XYZ Corporation's initiatives underscores the importance of aligning device management strategies with organizational objectives, embracing innovation, and fostering a collaborative and continuously learning culture within the enterprise.

Discuss the challenges faced and the strategies implemented for success.

Embarking on the journey to optimize device management for improved efficiency, XYZ Corporation encountered a myriad of challenges reflective of the complexities inherent in large-scale enterprises. One of the foremost challenges was the sheer diversity of devices spread across the organization. From traditional desktops and laptops to a multitude of mobile devices and an ever-expanding landscape of Internet of Things (IoT) endpoints, managing this heterogeneous device ecosystem posed a significant hurdle. The challenge was not merely technical but extended to the operational and logistical complexities of coordinating device management strategies across different business units, geographic locations, and technology stacks.

In response to this challenge, XYZ Corporation strategically opted for a unified endpoint management (UEM) framework. The UEM solution emerged as a centralizing force, providing a consolidated platform to manage the diverse range of devices under a cohesive umbrella. This strategic decision aimed to simplify the management process, enhance consistency, and standardize configurations across the organization. By doing so, XYZ Corporation sought to mitigate the challenges associated with device heterogeneity and create a unified approach to device management that could be seamlessly applied across the entirety of its technological landscape.

Security emerged as another formidable challenge in the optimization journey. With the ever-evolving threat landscape and the increasing sophistication of cyber attacks, XYZ Corporation faced the critical task of fortifying its device management practices to ensure the confidentiality, integrity, and availability of sensitive data. The diverse nature of the devices in use, coupled with the global footprint of the organization, added layers of complexity to the security challenge. Addressing this issue required not only robust technical solutions but also a comprehensive strategy that encompassed policy enforcement, employee training, and proactive threat detection.

In response to the security challenge, XYZ Corporation implemented a multifaceted approach within the UEM framework. Encryption policies were enforced across devices to safeguard sensitive data, and application whitelisting measures were put in place to control software execution. Multi-factor authentication was implemented to add an extra layer of security, particularly for remote access scenarios. Additionally, the organization leveraged advanced threat detection capabilities inherent in the UEM solution. These measures collectively aimed to create a security posture that not only complied with industry regulations but also proactively addressed emerging threats, laying the foundation for a resilient and secure device management ecosystem.

The intricacies of real-time monitoring and reporting constituted another set of challenges for XYZ Corporation. The sheer scale of its operations necessitated a granular understanding of device performance, user behavior, and compliance status across the organization. Traditional approaches to monitoring and reporting, such as manual data collection and analysis, were deemed impractical given the vastness of the enterprise. The challenge was to establish a system that provided actionable insights, enabling IT administrators to make informed decisions, identify performance bottlenecks, and proactively address emerging issues in real-time.

To overcome this challenge, XYZ Corporation leveraged the reporting and monitoring capabilities inherent in the UEM solution. The centralized dashboard provided comprehensive insights into device performance metrics, compliance status, and security postures. Automated reporting mechanisms were implemented to generate regular updates on key performance indicators, ensuring that IT administrators had a continuous stream of relevant data. This data-driven approach not only facilitated informed decision-making but also enabled XYZ Corporation to establish a proactive stance, addressing potential issues before they could escalate and impact operations.

The integration of IoT devices into the optimization initiative introduced a unique set of challenges. With a diverse range of sensors, connected machinery, and IoT-enabled devices deployed across manufacturing facilities and logistics operations, managing this expansive and varied IoT ecosystem required specialized considerations. The challenges included interoperability issues, diverse communication protocols, and the need for tailored management strategies that could cater to the specific requirements of IoT devices.

XYZ Corporation responded to these challenges by implementing specialized IoT device management tools that seamlessly integrated with the broader UEM framework. These tools facilitated the monitoring, configuration, and update processes for IoT devices, ensuring that they were managed efficiently and adhered to the same standards of security and compliance as other endpoints. The integration of IoT device management into the overarching strategy aimed not only to overcome the technical challenges posed by IoT diversity but also to ensure that the organization could leverage the transformative potential of IoT technologies without compromising on manageability.

The adoption of containerization and microservices architecture introduced a paradigm shift in device management strategies but also presented its own set of challenges. Containerization technologies, such as Docker and Kubernetes, offered unparalleled benefits in terms of deployment flexibility, resource efficiency, and scalability. However, the challenge lay in the implementation of these technologies across an organization as vast and complex as XYZ Corporation. This involved overcoming resistance to change, ensuring compatibility with existing systems, and navigating the learning curve associated with these emerging technologies.

XYZ Corporation addressed these challenges by prioritizing a phased and well-communicated adoption strategy. The organization initiated pilot projects to test the feasibility and benefits of containerization and microservices in controlled environments. This approach allowed IT teams to gain hands-on experience, identify potential challenges, and refine deployment strategies before scaling up. The emphasis on comprehensive training and skill development played a crucial role, ensuring that the workforce was equipped with the knowledge and expertise needed to navigate the intricacies of containerization technologies. This phased approach, coupled with transparent communication and robust training initiatives, allowed XYZ Corporation to overcome the challenges associated with the adoption of containerization and microservices, paving the way for enhanced agility and scalability in device management.

Troubleshooting, an integral aspect of device management, posed challenges in terms of the increasing complexity of issues and the need for swift and efficient resolution. With a diverse range of devices, each with its own unique configurations and potential points of failure, the challenge for XYZ Corporation was to develop a systematic and proactive troubleshooting approach that could address issues before they impacted operations. The organization also needed to account for the shift towards remote work, requiring remote troubleshooting capabilities to support a geographically dispersed workforce.

In response to these challenges, XYZ Corporation implemented advanced diagnostic tools and automated scripts within the UEM framework. These tools enabled IT teams to identify and resolve issues proactively, often before end-users were aware of them. Machine learning algorithms were integrated into troubleshooting processes, allowing for predictive analytics that anticipated potential device failures based on historical data patterns. Remote support tools were deployed to assist end-users directly, reducing resolution times and minimizing disruptions. The combination of these strategies aimed not only to address the challenges of increasing complexity but also to align troubleshooting practices with the evolving landscape of remote work and distributed computing environments.

Collaboration emerged as a critical success factor in overcoming the challenges inherent in large-scale device management optimization. Interdisciplinary collaboration was essential, given the multifaceted nature of device management challenges. IT professionals, security experts, and representatives from various business units needed to work collaboratively to align device management strategies with overarching organizational goals. Additionally, collaboration was crucial in the context of knowledge-sharing, training initiatives, and troubleshooting efforts.

To foster collaboration, XYZ Corporation implemented regular team meetings, training sessions, and knowledge-sharing forums. These forums provided a platform for IT professionals to share insights, discuss challenges, and collectively develop strategies for optimizing device management. Cross-functional collaboration was encouraged, breaking down silos and creating a shared understanding of device management goals and challenges. The emphasis on collaboration extended to external partnerships with vendors and service providers, leveraging external expertise to enhance the organization's device management capabilities.

Training and skill development emerged as an ongoing challenge and a strategy for success. The dynamic nature of technology required XYZ Corporation to invest continuously in the development of its workforce. The challenges included staying abreast of emerging technologies, overcoming resistance to skill acquisition, and ensuring that IT professionals were equipped with the expertise needed to navigate the evolving device management landscape. This challenge was particularly pronounced in the context of emerging technologies such as containerization and microservices.

XYZ Corporation addressed this challenge through a commitment to continuous training and skill development programs. The organization provided comprehensive training on device management tools, troubleshooting techniques, and emerging technologies. Training initiatives were tailored to the specific needs of different teams, ensuring that each role within the organization had the skills necessary for success. This commitment to ongoing skill development not only addressed immediate challenges but also contributed to creating a culture of innovation, adaptability, and continuous learning within the organization.

The practical application of artificial intelligence (AI) in troubleshooting and predictive analytics introduced challenges related to the integration of AI-driven processes into existing workflows. The organization needed to navigate concerns related to data privacy, algorithmic transparency, and user acceptance of AI-powered solutions. Additionally, the challenge lay in ensuring that AI-driven approaches complemented human expertise rather than replacing it entirely, fostering a collaborative and symbiotic relationship between AI and human IT professionals.

XYZ Corporation addressed these challenges by implementing AI-driven algorithms that seamlessly integrated into existing troubleshooting processes. The organization prioritized transparent communication with end-users, clearly explaining the role of AI in issue resolution and emphasizing the collaborative nature of the troubleshooting approach. Data privacy considerations were paramount, with XYZ Corporation implementing robust security measures to protect sensitive information. Furthermore, the organization emphasized that AI was a tool to enhance, not replace, human expertise. This approach aimed to build trust among IT professionals and end-users, ensuring a positive reception to the integration of AI in troubleshooting practices.

The optimization journey of XYZ Corporation culminated in measurable outcomes that underscored the success of the implemented strategies. Operational efficiency witnessed a substantial improvement, with streamlined processes, reduced downtime, and faster issue resolution contributing to overall productivity gains. Security compliance metrics demonstrated a significant enhancement, with a robust security posture and adherence to industry regulations. Cost savings were realized through optimized resource utilization, reduced support ticket volumes, and efficient use of containerized applications.

In conclusion, the challenges faced by XYZ Corporation in optimizing device management for improved efficiency were multifaceted and reflective of the intricacies inherent in large-scale enterprises. The success of the organization's strategies lay in the holistic and adaptive approach taken to address these challenges. From embracing a UEM framework to fortifying security measures, navigating the complexities of IoT device management, adopting containerization and microservices, and leveraging AI in troubleshooting, XYZ Corporation exemplified a strategic and proactive response to the challenges posed by diverse devices and the evolving technological landscape. The organization's commitment to collaboration, ongoing training, and a data-driven approach contributed to the overall success of its device management optimization initiative, illustrating a transformative journey that others can draw inspiration from in their pursuit of operational excellence.

Examine a case study from the healthcare industry focusing on secure device management.

In the intricate realm of healthcare, where the convergence of technology and patient care is paramount, the case study of MedTech Health Systems provides a compelling narrative of how secure device management plays a pivotal role in safeguarding sensitive patient data, ensuring regulatory compliance, and optimizing operational efficiency. As a leading healthcare provider, MedTech faced the dual challenge of managing an extensive array of medical devices while upholding the highest standards of security and compliance with healthcare regulations, notably the Health Insurance Portability and Accountability Act (HIPAA).

One of the primary challenges confronting MedTech was the diverse landscape of medical devices deployed across its facilities, ranging from bedside monitors and infusion pumps to diagnostic imaging equipment. The management of this heterogeneous device ecosystem demanded a nuanced approach that considered not only the operational intricacies of each device but also the criticality of protecting patient information. The challenge extended beyond traditional endpoint devices to encompass the specialized medical equipment integral to patient care. Failure to effectively manage these devices not only posed operational risks but also threatened the confidentiality and integrity of patient health records.

In response to these challenges, MedTech embarked on a comprehensive device management strategy anchored in the principles of security, compliance, and operational efficiency. The organization implemented a Unified Endpoint Management (UEM) system designed explicitly for the healthcare industry, offering a centralized platform to manage the entire spectrum of medical devices. This UEM solution provided granular control over device configurations, facilitating the enforcement of security policies, software updates, and compliance checks. MedTech recognized that a one-size-fits-all approach was insufficient; hence, the UEM system was tailored to accommodate the diverse requirements of medical devices, each with its own set of functionalities and connectivity specifications.

Security, a paramount concern in healthcare, assumed a central role in MedTech's device management strategy. The organization understood that medical devices, often interconnected through the Internet of Things (IoT), presented an expanded attack surface that required robust protective measures. MedTech deployed encryption protocols to secure data transmitted between devices and backend systems, ensuring that patient information remained confidential and protected from unauthorized access. Multi-factor authentication was enforced across devices, bolstering access controls and adding an additional layer of security to prevent unauthorized entry.

The UEM solution played a crucial role in fortifying MedTech's security posture. It facilitated real-time monitoring of device activities, enabling prompt identification of any anomalies or potential security breaches. Automated alerts were integrated to notify IT administrators of suspicious activities, allowing for swift response and mitigation. MedTech also implemented regular security audits and vulnerability assessments to proactively identify and address potential weaknesses in its device management infrastructure. This proactive security stance not only aligned with HIPAA requirements but also demonstrated MedTech's commitment to maintaining the highest standards of patient data protection.

Furthermore, the challenges of maintaining compliance with healthcare regulations, particularly HIPAA, were at the forefront of MedTech's considerations. The organization recognized that non-compliance not only carried legal implications but also jeopardized patient trust. The UEM solution became a linchpin in ensuring compliance by providing a centralized framework for implementing and enforcing policies in alignment with regulatory requirements. Automated compliance checks were integrated to assess and validate adherence to security protocols, ensuring that devices met the stringent standards mandated by HIPAA.

In the context of secure device management, MedTech faced the additional challenge of addressing the potential risks posed by legacy medical devices with outdated software or operating systems. Recognizing that these devices might lack the robust security features of newer counterparts, the organization implemented a phased approach to upgrade or replace obsolete devices. The UEM solution facilitated this process by allowing IT administrators to prioritize and schedule updates, ensuring minimal disruption to patient care while mitigating security risks associated with outdated systems.

The challenges associated with remote patient monitoring and telehealth services introduced new dimensions to MedTech's device management strategy. The increased reliance on connected devices for remote healthcare delivery demanded a secure and scalable infrastructure. MedTech implemented secure communication protocols and virtual private network (VPN) solutions to safeguard data transmitted between remote devices and centralized healthcare systems. The UEM system played a pivotal role in configuring and managing remote devices, ensuring that they adhered to the same security standards as on-premises medical devices.

Collaboration emerged as a critical success factor in MedTech's secure device management strategy. The organization recognized that effective device management required seamless coordination between IT teams, healthcare providers, and medical device manufacturers. Interdisciplinary collaboration became ingrained in the organization's culture, with regular communication channels established to facilitate dialogue between technical experts, healthcare professionals, and device vendors. This collaborative approach ensured that device management strategies were not only technically sound but also aligned with the clinical workflows and patient care priorities of healthcare professionals.

To address the challenge of secure data exchange between medical devices and Electronic Health Record (EHR) systems, MedTech implemented interoperability standards and secure application programming interfaces (APIs). This allowed for seamless integration of device data into the EHR, enhancing the continuity of care and providing healthcare providers with comprehensive patient information. The UEM system played a key role in managing the configurations and security settings required for interoperability, ensuring a standardized yet secure exchange of health information.

The secure disposal of end-of-life medical devices presented another challenge for MedTech. Recognizing the potential risks associated with data remnants on decommissioned devices, the organization implemented stringent decommissioning procedures. The UEM solution facilitated the secure wiping of data on retired devices, ensuring that no patient information remained on the devices before their disposal or repurposing. This meticulous approach aligned with both environmental sustainability practices and the organization's commitment to patient privacy.

The practical application of artificial intelligence (AI) and machine learning (ML) in MedTech's secure device management strategy ushered in a new era of predictive analytics and proactive issue resolution. AI-driven algorithms were integrated into the UEM system to analyze historical data patterns, identify potential security vulnerabilities, and predict device malfunctions before they could impact patient care. Machine learning models were trained to recognize normal device behavior, enabling the system to detect deviations indicative of security breaches or performance issues. This proactive approach to device management aligned with MedTech's commitment to providing uninterrupted and secure healthcare services.

The optimization journey of MedTech culminated in tangible outcomes that underscored the success of its secure device management strategy. Operational efficiency saw a notable improvement, with streamlined device management processes, reduced downtime, and enhanced interoperability contributing to the overall effectiveness of patient care. Security compliance metrics demonstrated a robust adherence to HIPAA regulations, instilling confidence in both patients and regulatory authorities. The organization achieved cost savings through optimized device utilization, reduced security incidents, and a proactive approach to issue resolution.

In conclusion, the case study of MedTech Health Systems in the healthcare industry exemplifies the critical importance of secure device management in ensuring the seamless and secure delivery of patient care. The organization navigated multifaceted challenges by implementing a comprehensive device management strategy anchored in security, compliance, and operational efficiency. The strategic deployment of a UEM system, integration of advanced security measures, collaborative interdisciplinary approaches, and the infusion of AI-driven predictive analytics collectively contributed to the success of MedTech's secure device management initiative. As healthcare continues to evolve, the lessons learned from MedTech's case study serve as a valuable guide for organizations seeking to optimize device management in a secure and healthcare-compliant manner.

Discuss how stringent security measures were implemented to safeguard patient data.

In the realm of healthcare, where the sanctity of patient data is paramount, the implementation of stringent security measures becomes a critical imperative. This is especially true for organizations like MedTech Health Systems, where the convergence of medical devices, electronic health records (EHR), and interconnected systems creates a complex landscape with heightened privacy concerns. The organization recognized the need to fortify its security posture to safeguard patient data against unauthorized access, cyber threats, and compliance risks. The multifaceted approach to stringent security measures implemented by MedTech illustrates a commitment to maintaining the highest standards of confidentiality, integrity, and availability of sensitive healthcare information.

One of the foundational pillars of MedTech's security strategy was the adoption of encryption protocols to secure data in transit and at rest. Recognizing that medical devices often communicate patient information over networks, the organization implemented robust encryption algorithms to ensure the confidentiality of this data. This measure not only protected patient information from interception during transmission but also added an extra layer of security to safeguard stored data on medical devices and backend systems. By encrypting sensitive data, MedTech aimed to mitigate the risk of unauthorized access, even in the event of a security breach.

Multi-factor authentication emerged as a fundamental component of MedTech's security infrastructure. Acknowledging the inherent vulnerabilities associated with relying solely on passwords for user authentication, the organization implemented multi-factor authentication mechanisms across its device management ecosystem. This required users to authenticate their identity through a combination of something they know (password), something they have (security token or mobile device), or something they are (biometric data). This layered approach significantly bolstered access controls, reducing the risk of unauthorized entry and enhancing the overall security posture of the organization.

The adoption of a Unified Endpoint Management (UEM) system played a pivotal role in implementing stringent security measures across MedTech's diverse device landscape. The UEM system provided a centralized platform for managing the entire spectrum of medical devices, enabling uniform security policies and configurations. Within this framework, MedTech implemented device-level security policies, such as access controls, password complexity requirements, and screen lock settings. These policies were enforced consistently across all managed devices, ensuring a standardized and secure baseline for device security.

Real-time monitoring and automated alerts constituted essential elements of MedTech's security strategy. The organization implemented continuous monitoring of device activities, network traffic, and system logs through the UEM system. Automated alerts were configured to notify IT administrators of any suspicious activities, potential security breaches, or deviations from established security baselines. This real-time visibility empowered the security team to respond swiftly to emerging threats, reducing the time between detection and mitigation. The proactive stance towards monitoring contributed to a dynamic and adaptive security posture, crucial in the face of evolving cyber threats.

Regular security audits and vulnerability assessments became integral components of MedTech's security measures. Recognizing that cybersecurity is an ever-evolving landscape, the organization conducted periodic assessments to identify and address potential weaknesses in its device management infrastructure. Penetration testing, software vulnerability scans, and compliance checks were conducted to ensure that devices met the stringent security standards mandated by healthcare regulations, particularly the Health Insurance Portability and Accountability Act (HIPAA). By proactively identifying and remedying vulnerabilities, MedTech sought to fortify its defenses against potential cyber threats.

In the context of medical devices connected to the Internet of Things (IoT), MedTech faced the challenge of securing an expanded attack surface. IoT devices, ranging from connected infusion pumps to bedside monitors, presented unique security considerations. To address this challenge, MedTech implemented network segmentation to isolate IoT devices from critical backend systems. This segmentation strategy prevented unauthorized lateral movement within the network, limiting the potential impact of a security breach. Additionally, the organization deployed intrusion detection and prevention systems specifically tailored for IoT environments, enhancing its ability to detect and respond to anomalous activities in real-time.

The secure disposal of end-of-life medical devices introduced a distinct facet to MedTech's security measures. Recognizing that decommissioned devices might still contain residual patient data, the organization implemented stringent decommissioning procedures within the UEM system. Before disposal or repurposing, the UEM system facilitated the secure wiping of data on retired devices, ensuring that no patient information remained on the devices. This meticulous approach aligned with both environmental sustainability practices and the organization's commitment to patient privacy, mitigating the risk of data breaches stemming from improperly discarded devices.

The integration of artificial intelligence (AI) and machine learning (ML) into MedTech's security strategy ushered in a new era of proactive threat detection and predictive analytics. AI-driven algorithms were embedded within the UEM system to analyze historical data patterns, identify potential security vulnerabilities, and predict anomalous device behavior. Machine learning models were trained to recognize normal device activities, enabling the system to detect deviations indicative of security breaches or performance issues. This predictive approach to security positioned MedTech to address potential threats before they manifested, reducing the risk of data breaches and enhancing overall cybersecurity resilience.

To address the challenges associated with remote patient monitoring and telehealth services, MedTech implemented secure communication protocols and virtual private network (VPN) solutions. The organization recognized that the increased reliance on connected devices for remote healthcare delivery demanded a secure and scalable infrastructure. Secure VPN connections ensured encrypted communication between remote devices and centralized healthcare systems, safeguarding patient data from interception during transmission. Additionally, the UEM system played a pivotal role in configuring and managing remote devices, ensuring that they adhered to the same security standards as on-premises medical devices.

Interoperability standards and secure application programming interfaces (APIs) were crucial components of MedTech's strategy to secure data exchange between medical devices and Electronic Health Record (EHR) systems. Recognizing the importance of seamless integration of device data into the EHR, MedTech implemented standardized communication protocols and secure APIs. This allowed for the secure exchange of health information, enhancing the continuity of care and providing healthcare providers with comprehensive patient data. The UEM system played a key role in managing the configurations and security settings required for interoperability, ensuring a standardized yet secure exchange of health information.

Collaboration emerged as a cornerstone in implementing stringent security measures at MedTech. The organization recognized that effective security required collaboration not only within its internal teams but also with external stakeholders, including medical device manufacturers and regulatory bodies. Collaborative engagement with device vendors ensured that security patches and updates were promptly implemented, addressing potential vulnerabilities in a timely manner. MedTech actively participated in information-sharing forums, threat intelligence networks, and industry collaborations to stay abreast of emerging cyber threats and best practices in healthcare cybersecurity.

The commitment to ongoing training and awareness programs further reinforced MedTech's security measures. The organization understood that human factors played a crucial role in maintaining a secure environment. Regular training sessions were conducted to educate staff on security best practices, the importance of safeguarding patient data, and the evolving nature of cyber threats. This proactive approach aimed to create a security-aware culture within the organization, empowering staff to be vigilant against social engineering attacks, phishing attempts, and other cybersecurity risks.

In conclusion, the stringent security measures implemented by MedTech Health Systems underscore the organization's commitment to safeguarding patient data in the complex landscape of healthcare technology. From encryption protocols and multi-factor authentication to real-time monitoring, AI-driven threat detection, and collaborative engagement with external stakeholders, MedTech's approach to cybersecurity exemplifies a comprehensive and adaptive strategy. The integration of security measures within the UEM system showcases the importance of a centralized and standardized approach to device management security. As healthcare continues to evolve, MedTech's experience serves as a valuable case study for organizations seeking to fortify their security postures and uphold the highest standards of patient data protection.

Explore a case where a smart city successfully integrated and managed a diverse range of IoT devices.

In the dynamic landscape of urban development, the case of MetroTech City stands out as a testament to the successful integration and management of a diverse range of Internet of Things (IoT) devices within the framework of a smart city. Embracing the vision of a connected and efficient urban environment, MetroTech City embarked on a transformative journey to leverage IoT technologies across various sectors, ranging from transportation and energy management to public safety and citizen services.

The foundational challenge confronting MetroTech City was the sheer diversity of IoT devices dispersed across the urban landscape. From intelligent traffic lights and smart parking meters to environmental sensors and public safety cameras, the city faced the intricate task of orchestrating a multitude of devices with varying functionalities and communication protocols. Recognizing the potential for these devices to enhance the quality of life for residents and streamline city operations, MetroTech City prioritized the development of a robust and unified IoT ecosystem.

Central to MetroTech City's success was the establishment of an integrated IoT platform designed to serve as the nerve center of the smart city's operations. This platform, built upon open standards and interoperability principles, allowed for seamless communication and data exchange among diverse IoT devices. The integration was not merely technological but extended to collaborative partnerships with device manufacturers, service providers, and the local community to ensure a holistic and inclusive approach to smart city development.

In the realm of urban mobility, MetroTech City revolutionized transportation systems through the deployment of IoT-enabled solutions. Smart traffic management systems, equipped with sensors and adaptive algorithms, dynamically regulated traffic flow based on real-time conditions. Connected public transportation, including smart buses and light rail systems, provided residents with accurate arrival times and route information through mobile applications. The integration of IoT devices in transportation not only alleviated traffic congestion but also contributed to environmental sustainability by optimizing fuel efficiency and reducing emissions.

The energy sector witnessed a paradigm shift in MetroTech City with the implementation of IoT devices for smart grid management and energy conservation. IoT-enabled sensors and meters facilitated real-time monitoring of energy consumption, allowing the city to optimize energy distribution and minimize wastage. Smart streetlights with motion sensors and adaptive brightness controls not only improved public safety but also contributed to energy efficiency by dimming lights during periods of low activity. These initiatives not only reduced operational costs but also positioned MetroTech City as a pioneer in sustainable urban development.

In the domain of public safety, MetroTech City leveraged IoT devices to enhance situational awareness and emergency response capabilities. Surveillance cameras equipped with advanced analytics and facial recognition capabilities were strategically deployed in public spaces, aiding law enforcement in crime prevention and investigation. IoT-enabled sensors in critical infrastructure, such as bridges and tunnels, monitored structural integrity in real-time, ensuring early detection of potential issues and minimizing safety risks. Furthermore, connected emergency response systems enabled rapid communication and coordination among first responders, improving the city's resilience in the face of unforeseen events.

Citizen services underwent a transformative evolution in MetroTech City with the integration of IoT devices to enhance urban living experiences. Smart waste management systems, equipped with sensors, optimized garbage collection routes based on fill levels, reducing operational costs and environmental impact. IoT-enabled kiosks and mobile applications provided residents with real-time information on public services, events, and civic engagement opportunities. Smart parks, equipped with environmental sensors and interactive installations, not only promoted sustainable green spaces but also fostered community engagement.

Water management emerged as a critical focus area for MetroTech City, where IoT devices played a pivotal role in optimizing usage and conservation. Smart irrigation systems, responsive to weather conditions and soil moisture levels, ensured efficient watering of public green spaces. IoT-enabled water quality sensors monitored the health of rivers and reservoirs, enabling prompt response to potential pollution incidents. Additionally, smart water meters provided residents with real-time insights into their water consumption, encouraging conservation efforts and contributing to the city's overall sustainability goals.

The seamless integration and management of such a diverse array of IoT devices in MetroTech City were made possible through a comprehensive governance framework. The city established clear policies and standards for IoT device deployment, ensuring adherence to privacy regulations, data security protocols, and ethical considerations. Collaboration with technology vendors, research institutions, and regulatory bodies facilitated the development of industry best practices, contributing to the city's reputation as a leader in responsible and transparent smart city governance.

MetroTech City's success in IoT integration was not without its challenges, and cybersecurity emerged as a paramount concern. Recognizing the potential vulnerabilities associated with a vast network of interconnected devices, the city implemented robust cybersecurity measures. These included end-to-end encryption for data transmission, continuous monitoring of network traffic for anomalies, and regular penetration testing to identify and address potential vulnerabilities. Collaboration with cybersecurity experts and the establishment of a dedicated cybersecurity task force ensured that the city stayed ahead of emerging threats, safeguarding both critical infrastructure and sensitive citizen data.

The city's commitment to inclusivity was exemplified by its efforts to bridge the digital divide and ensure equitable access to IoT-enabled services. Initiatives such as community outreach programs, digital literacy campaigns, and subsidized access to smart devices aimed to empower all residents, regardless of socioeconomic status, to benefit from the opportunities presented by the smart city ecosystem. This commitment to inclusivity not only enhanced the overall quality of life for residents but also contributed to the city's social cohesion and resilience.

The scalability of MetroTech City's IoT infrastructure was a key factor in its success. The city designed its IoT ecosystem with future expansion in mind, anticipating the integration of emerging technologies and additional devices. This scalability was achieved through the use of open standards and modular architectures, allowing for the seamless integration of new IoT devices and technologies as they became available. The city's proactive approach to scalability ensured that its smart city infrastructure remained agile and adaptable to evolving urban challenges and technological advancements.

MetroTech City's success in IoT integration and management was not only a technological triumph but also a testament to effective collaboration among stakeholders. The city actively engaged with citizens, businesses, academia, and technology innovators through forums, hackathons, and collaborative projects. Open channels of communication facilitated continuous feedback loops, enabling the city to respond to the evolving needs and expectations of its residents. This collaborative approach not only enhanced the effectiveness of the IoT ecosystem but also cultivated a sense of ownership and pride among the community.

In conclusion, MetroTech City's journey stands as a beacon of success in the integration and management of a diverse range of IoT devices within the context of a smart city. The city's strategic approach, encompassing transportation, energy, public safety, citizen services, water management, and cybersecurity, reflects a holistic vision for urban development. By leveraging IoT technologies, MetroTech City not only optimized operational efficiency and resource usage but also prioritized citizen well-being and environmental sustainability. As other cities seek to embark on their smart city transformations, the lessons learned from MetroTech City provide valuable insights into the intricacies of IoT integration, governance, and collaborative urban development.

Discuss the scalability and interoperability challenges overcome in the implementation.

The successful implementation of MetroTech City's comprehensive IoT ecosystem was not devoid of challenges, and two crucial hurdles were scalability and interoperability. Overcoming these challenges required a strategic and forward-thinking approach that addressed the city's current needs while anticipating future advancements and expansions in the IoT landscape. Scalability, the ability of the system to grow and adapt to increasing demands, was a central consideration in MetroTech City's planning. The city's leaders foresaw the rapid evolution of IoT technologies and the influx of new devices; hence, they adopted a modular and flexible architecture that allowed for seamless integration of additional devices and services. By embracing open standards, MetroTech City created an infrastructure that could easily accommodate the scaling requirements of a growing smart city, ensuring that the IoT ecosystem could expand in tandem with the city's development.

Interoperability, the ability of diverse IoT devices and systems to work together cohesively, presented a unique set of challenges due to the sheer diversity of devices deployed across MetroTech City. The city's IoT landscape encompassed an extensive array of devices, each with its own specifications, communication protocols, and data formats. Overcoming this interoperability challenge demanded a concerted effort to establish common standards and protocols that could facilitate seamless communication and data exchange among disparate devices. MetroTech City adopted a collaborative approach, engaging with device manufacturers, technology vendors, and standards organizations to define and implement interoperability standards. This collaborative effort aimed to create a unified language for IoT devices, ensuring that different devices could communicate effectively and contribute to the overall smart city ecosystem.

One of the primary scalability challenges MetroTech City faced was the sheer volume and diversity of IoT devices integrated into its urban infrastructure. With devices ranging from smart traffic lights and environmental sensors to connected public transportation systems and smart energy grids, the city needed an architecture that could accommodate not only the current deployment but also the anticipated growth of IoT applications. The city's strategic decision to adopt a modular and scalable architecture proved instrumental in overcoming this challenge. By structuring the IoT ecosystem in a modular fashion, MetroTech City created a framework where new devices and services could be seamlessly integrated without disrupting the existing infrastructure. This modular design allowed the city to scale its IoT deployment incrementally, ensuring that each new addition contributed to the overall efficiency of the smart city.

The diversity of applications within MetroTech City's IoT ecosystem necessitated a scalable infrastructure capable of handling varying workloads and data streams. The city's transportation sector, for instance, relied on real-time data from smart traffic lights, connected vehicles, and public transportation systems. Simultaneously, the public safety sector processed data from surveillance cameras, emergency response systems, and environmental sensors. Recognizing the need for differentiated scalability based on the specific requirements of each sector, MetroTech City implemented dynamic scaling mechanisms. This approach allowed resources to be allocated based on demand, ensuring optimal performance for critical applications during peak times while conserving resources during periods of lower activity. Through dynamic scaling, MetroTech City effectively managed the diverse workloads generated by its multifaceted IoT applications.

Another facet of scalability lay in the city's ability to future-proof its IoT infrastructure. MetroTech City foresaw the rapid evolution of IoT technologies and the introduction of novel devices that would contribute to the city's smart initiatives. To address this, the city adopted an anticipatory approach to scalability, ensuring that its IoT architecture could seamlessly incorporate emerging technologies. By adhering to open standards and promoting interoperability, MetroTech City created a foundation that could accommodate future innovations without necessitating major overhauls. This forward-thinking scalability strategy positioned the city to adapt to technological advancements, ensuring the longevity and relevance of its smart city initiatives.

Interoperability challenges in MetroTech City were multifaceted, stemming from the diverse nature of IoT devices deployed across different sectors. A critical consideration was the need for these devices to communicate effectively and share data cohesively. In addressing this challenge, the city prioritized the establishment of common standards and protocols that could serve as the lingua franca for its IoT ecosystem. MetroTech City engaged in collaborative partnerships with device manufacturers, industry consortia, and standards organizations to define and implement interoperability standards. The goal was to create a unified framework that transcended device-specific communication protocols, allowing diverse devices to seamlessly exchange information. By championing interoperability, MetroTech City eliminated silos in its IoT ecosystem, fostering a cohesive and synergistic environment where devices could work in concert to enhance the overall functionality of the smart city.

The transportation sector presented a poignant example of interoperability challenges, with various IoT devices contributing to the efficiency of urban mobility. Connected traffic lights, smart parking meters, and public transportation systems needed to communicate seamlessly to optimize traffic flow and enhance the overall transportation experience. MetroTech City tackled this interoperability challenge through the adoption of standardized communication protocols and open interfaces. By mandating that all transportation-related IoT devices adhere to common data exchange formats and communication standards, the city ensured that information flowed seamlessly between devices. This interoperable foundation enabled the transportation ecosystem to function as an integrated and intelligent network, mitigating congestion, and improving the overall efficiency of urban mobility.

The energy management sector within MetroTech City faced unique interoperability challenges due to the diverse array of devices contributing to smart grid optimization, energy conservation, and efficient resource utilization. Smart meters, environmental sensors, and adaptive street lighting systems needed to share data cohesively to enable real-time decision-making in energy distribution. MetroTech City addressed these challenges by fostering collaboration between device manufacturers and utility companies. By promoting adherence to common communication standards and data formats, the city established a unified energy management framework. This interoperable foundation allowed disparate devices to communicate seamlessly, optimizing energy consumption, reducing wastage, and contributing to the city's sustainability goals.

Public safety, a critical aspect of smart city initiatives, relied on the interoperability of diverse IoT devices such as surveillance cameras, emergency response systems, and environmental sensors. MetroTech City recognized that effective public safety hinged on the ability of these devices to communicate and share data in real-time. The city implemented standardized interfaces and communication protocols, ensuring that all public safety-related IoT devices adhered to a common framework. This interoperable foundation empowered law enforcement and emergency response teams with comprehensive situational awareness, facilitating quicker response times and more effective crisis management.

Citizen services in MetroTech City were enriched by the interoperability of diverse IoT applications, ranging from smart waste management systems to interactive public kiosks. Ensuring a seamless flow of information between these applications required the establishment of common standards for data exchange. MetroTech City implemented open APIs and standardized data formats to enable interoperability among various citizen service-related devices. This approach facilitated a unified and user-friendly experience for residents, who could access real-time information on public services, events, and community engagement initiatives through interconnected IoT applications.

Water management, a crucial facet of urban sustainability, faced interoperability challenges as IoT devices such as smart irrigation systems and water quality sensors needed to collaborate for efficient water usage. MetroTech City approached this challenge by fostering collaboration between environmental agencies, device manufacturers, and water utility companies. By defining common data exchange protocols and communication standards, the city established an interoperable water management ecosystem. This interoperability allowed real-time coordination between devices, optimizing irrigation schedules based on environmental conditions and ensuring prompt response to water quality concerns.

Addressing scalability and interoperability challenges in cybersecurity was paramount for MetroTech City, considering the increased attack surface presented by a growing and interconnected IoT ecosystem. The city implemented scalable security measures that could adapt to the evolving threat landscape. Dynamic scaling of cybersecurity resources ensured that the city could allocate additional security measures in response to increased workloads or emerging threats. Simultaneously, the city prioritized interoperable security protocols, ensuring that diverse cybersecurity solutions could work cohesively to protect against a spectrum of potential threats. This approach facilitated the integration of advanced threat detection, encryption, and access control measures, creating a unified cybersecurity framework that could scale with the growth of the smart city.

A significant aspect of overcoming scalability and interoperability challenges in MetroTech City was the establishment of a comprehensive governance framework. The city recognized the need for clear policies, standards, and guidelines to govern the deployment, integration, and management of IoT devices. The governance framework facilitated collaboration among different sectors, ensuring that scalability considerations were aligned with interoperability standards. Regular audits and assessments were conducted to evaluate the adherence of devices to established standards, fostering a culture of accountability among device manufacturers and service providers. This governance approach not only streamlined the deployment of IoT devices but also provided a foundation for ongoing scalability and interoperability considerations.

In conclusion, the successful implementation of MetroTech City's diverse IoT ecosystem hinged on its strategic approach to scalability and interoperability challenges. The city's forward-thinking adoption of a modular and flexible architecture, open standards, and collaborative partnerships allowed for the seamless integration of diverse devices and applications. By addressing these challenges comprehensively, MetroTech City not only optimized its current smart city initiatives but also positioned itself to adapt to future technological advancements and expansions. The lessons learned from MetroTech City's experience offer valuable insights for other cities seeking to navigate the complexities of scalable and interoperable smart city deployments.

Investigate a case study in the financial sector where real-time performance was crucial for success.

In the fast-paced realm of the financial sector, where split-second decisions can have profound implications, the case of Quantum Finance stands out as a compelling example of the critical importance of real-time performance for success. Quantum Finance, a global investment firm, found itself navigating the complexities of modern financial markets where volatility, competition, and the sheer volume of data necessitated an unprecedented level of agility and speed. Realizing that timely and accurate information could be the differentiator between profit and loss, Quantum Finance embarked on a transformative journey to overhaul its systems, placing real-time performance at the core of its operations.

Quantum Finance's commitment to real-time performance was underscored by the evolving nature of financial markets, where opportunities and risks emerged and dissipated with remarkable speed. The firm recognized that traditional batch processing systems, which operated on delayed data, were no longer sufficient to meet the demands of contemporary trading environments. In a landscape where milliseconds could determine market outcomes, Quantum Finance sought to build a technology infrastructure that would enable it to access, process, and act upon market data in real time.

The first challenge Quantum Finance confronted was the sheer volume and velocity of data generated by financial markets. With millions of transactions occurring every second across various asset classes, the firm needed a robust real-time data processing system that could handle the influx of market data with low latency. To address this challenge, Quantum Finance invested in cutting-edge data streaming technologies and high-frequency data processing engines. These technologies allowed the firm to ingest, analyze, and act upon market data in real time, ensuring that its trading algorithms were always operating on the latest information.

In the context of algorithmic trading, where automated systems execute trades based on predefined rules and market signals, real-time performance is paramount. Quantum Finance recognized that even the slightest delay in data processing could result in missed opportunities or unfavorable market conditions. The firm leveraged advanced algorithmic trading platforms that operated on a microsecond timescale. These platforms utilized sophisticated algorithms, machine learning models, and predictive analytics to make split-second trading decisions. By achieving real-time responsiveness, Quantum Finance could execute trades with precision, capitalize on market inefficiencies, and manage risk more effectively.

Market volatility, a constant in the financial landscape, presented another dimension to Quantum Finance's need for real-time performance. In times of market turbulence or unexpected events, the ability to receive and process real-time data became a strategic advantage. Quantum Finance implemented adaptive risk management systems that could dynamically adjust exposure and portfolio allocations based on real-time market conditions. These systems incorporated real-time market sentiment analysis, news sentiment analysis, and macroeconomic indicators to gauge and respond to changing market dynamics swiftly. This proactive risk management approach, empowered by real-time data, enabled Quantum Finance to navigate turbulent market periods more effectively, protecting its portfolios from potential downturns.

Trade execution speed became a defining factor in Quantum Finance's success, especially in markets where competition was fierce and price discrepancies were fleeting. The firm strategically collocated its trading infrastructure in proximity to major financial exchanges, leveraging direct high-speed data feeds. This proximity minimized network latency, allowing Quantum Finance to receive market data and execute trades with ultra-low latency. The firm also invested in advanced order routing algorithms that could identify and capitalize on the fastest execution paths. By prioritizing real-time execution speed, Quantum Finance positioned itself to seize time-sensitive opportunities and maintain a competitive edge in the dynamic landscape of high-frequency trading.

The emergence of alternative data sources, such as social media sentiment, satellite imagery, and unconventional economic indicators, added a layer of complexity and opportunity for Quantum Finance. Recognizing the value of real-time insights derived from these diverse datasets, the firm integrated advanced data analytics platforms into its infrastructure. These platforms employed real-time data processing and machine learning algorithms to extract actionable insights from alternative data sources. By incorporating real-time analysis of non-traditional datasets, Quantum Finance gained a more comprehensive view of market dynamics, identifying trends and opportunities that may not be immediately apparent through conventional financial data sources.

In the realm of real-time risk management, Quantum Finance implemented sophisticated systems that continuously monitored and evaluated its portfolio exposures. Market conditions could change rapidly, and the firm needed to ensure that its risk models were recalibrated in real time to reflect the latest market information. Quantum Finance integrated real-time scenario analysis tools that simulated potential market scenarios and their impact on portfolio risk. This dynamic risk modeling approach allowed the firm to adapt its risk management strategies swiftly in response to evolving market conditions, minimizing exposure to unforeseen risks and enhancing overall portfolio resilience.

The importance of real-time performance extended beyond trading operations for Quantum Finance; it permeated into client interactions and reporting. The firm recognized that in an era of instant information access, clients demanded real-time visibility into their portfolios, performance metrics, and market insights. Quantum Finance implemented client portals and reporting systems that provided clients with up-to-the-minute information on their investments, trade executions, and portfolio performance. This real-time transparency not only fostered trust and satisfaction among clients but also positioned Quantum Finance as a forward-thinking and client-centric financial institution.

Ensuring the security and integrity of real-time financial data became a paramount concern for Quantum Finance. The firm implemented advanced cybersecurity measures to protect its infrastructure from potential threats and attacks. Encryption protocols, multi-factor authentication, and real-time anomaly detection systems were integrated to safeguard against unauthorized access and data breaches. Quantum Finance also engaged in continuous monitoring of its network and systems, with real-time alerts and automated responses to potential security incidents. This proactive cybersecurity stance ensured that the firm's real-time financial data remained confidential, accurate, and immune to compromise.

Regulatory compliance, a cornerstone of the financial industry, added an additional layer of complexity to Quantum Finance's pursuit of real-time performance. The firm recognized the need to adhere to stringent regulatory reporting requirements and ensure that its real-time systems complied with evolving financial regulations. Quantum Finance invested in compliance management platforms that integrated regulatory reporting tools and real-time compliance monitoring. This approach allowed the firm to generate and submit regulatory reports in real time, reducing the risk of compliance breaches and ensuring alignment with industry standards.

The integration of real-time artificial intelligence (AI) and machine learning (ML) into Quantum Finance's operations marked a transformative shift in its analytical capabilities. The firm utilized real-time AI algorithms to analyze market trends, detect anomalies, and predict potential market movements. Machine learning models were trained on vast datasets of historical and real-time market data, enabling the firm to identify patterns and make data-driven predictions with remarkable accuracy. This real-time predictive analytics capability empowered Quantum Finance to anticipate market trends, optimize trading strategies, and make informed investment decisions in a landscape where timing was of the essence.

The lessons learned from Quantum Finance's emphasis on real-time performance transcend the confines of its specific case and offer broader insights into the evolving dynamics of the financial sector. The case underscores the fundamental shift in the industry towards real-time data processing, where competitive advantages are gained not only through sophisticated trading algorithms but also through the ability to harness and act upon information in the shortest time-frames. As financial markets continue to evolve, the imperative for real-time performance is likely to remain a driving force, shaping the strategies and operations of institutions seeking to thrive in this dynamic and demanding landscape.

Discuss how device management strategies contributed to high-speed data processing.

In the ever-evolving landscape of high-speed data processing, the seamless orchestration and management of devices play a pivotal role in determining the efficiency, reliability, and overall success of data-intensive operations. Device management strategies have emerged as the linchpin, providing the framework through which organizations achieve optimal performance in processing vast volumes of data in real time. One of the foundational aspects of this contribution lies in the ability of device management to ensure the synchronization and coordination of diverse devices within an ecosystem. As organizations deploy an array of devices, ranging from sensors and servers to edge computing nodes, the challenge becomes harmonizing their functions to operate in unison. Device management strategies address this challenge by providing a centralized framework that oversees device configurations, updates, and interactions, creating a cohesive environment where devices seamlessly collaborate to facilitate high-speed data processing.

Moreover, effective device management contributes to high-speed data processing by streamlining the deployment and provisioning of devices. In dynamic data processing environments, the ability to swiftly integrate new devices into the system is paramount. Device management strategies, facilitated by technologies like IoT platforms and unified endpoint management (UEM) systems, offer automated mechanisms for onboarding and configuring devices. This not only accelerates the overall deployment process but also ensures that new devices seamlessly integrate into the existing infrastructure, reducing downtime and enhancing the agility of data processing operations. The streamlined provisioning afforded by device management becomes particularly crucial in scenarios where the scalability of data processing systems is imperative, allowing organizations to rapidly adapt to evolving data requirements and scale their operations in response to growing demands.

Furthermore, the efficiency of high-speed data processing is contingent on the continuous monitoring and maintenance of devices. Device management strategies provide robust mechanisms for real-time monitoring, enabling organizations to proactively identify and address potential issues that could impede data processing speeds. Through centralized dashboards and monitoring tools, administrators gain visibility into the health, performance, and status of each device in the network. This not only facilitates early detection of anomalies or malfunctions but also allows for predictive maintenance, reducing the likelihood of device failures that could disrupt high-speed data processing workflows. The proactive nature of device management in ensuring the operational health of devices contributes directly to the overall reliability and resilience of data processing systems.

Security considerations are paramount in high-speed data processing environments, and device management strategies play a critical role in fortifying the security posture of the entire ecosystem. In the interconnected landscape of devices, each entry point becomes a potential vulnerability, and managing the security configurations of diverse devices becomes a complex challenge. Device management strategies address this challenge by enforcing security policies, ensuring that devices adhere to standardized security protocols, and facilitating the prompt deployment of security updates and patches. This not only mitigates the risk of security breaches but also safeguards the integrity of data being processed at high speeds. The comprehensive approach to security management embedded within device management strategies becomes particularly crucial in environments where sensitive or critical data is processed, ensuring compliance with regulatory requirements and instilling confidence in the robustness of the data processing infrastructure.

Interoperability is a fundamental aspect of achieving high-speed data processing, especially in heterogeneous environments where devices from various vendors and with different functionalities coexist. Device management strategies act as a unifying force, promoting interoperability by standardizing communication protocols and data formats across devices. Through the enforcement of common standards, organizations can ensure that diverse devices can seamlessly exchange information, contributing to the overall efficiency of data processing workflows. This interoperability facilitated by device management is particularly advantageous in scenarios where data processing involves the integration of data from disparate sources, such as IoT devices, edge computing nodes, and traditional servers. The ability of devices to communicate harmoniously, enabled by device management strategies, accelerates data processing by eliminating bottlenecks associated with incompatible technologies or communication barriers.

Moreover, the role of device management in enhancing the scalability of data processing systems is noteworthy. Scalability is a key consideration in environments where the volume of data fluctuates or experiences rapid growth. Device management strategies provide a framework for managing the scalability of the entire ecosystem by allowing organizations to dynamically add or remove devices based on processing needs. Through centralized control and automation, device management facilitates the seamless integration of new devices into the processing infrastructure, ensuring that the system scales efficiently to accommodate increased data loads. This adaptability is crucial in high-speed data processing scenarios where the ability to scale in real time is essential for meeting performance requirements and maintaining responsiveness to changing data dynamics.

Furthermore, device management strategies contribute to high-speed data processing by optimizing the utilization of resources across the entire device landscape. In environments where computational power, memory, and storage are distributed among different devices, effective resource management becomes critical for achieving optimal processing speeds. Device management strategies, through dynamic resource allocation and load balancing mechanisms, ensure that processing tasks are efficiently distributed across available devices. This not only maximizes the utilization of resources but also prevents bottlenecks that could hinder high-speed data processing. By orchestrating resource allocation based on real-time demand and device capabilities, device management strategies enhance the overall efficiency and throughput of data processing operations.

The advent of edge computing has introduced new dimensions to high-speed data processing, and device management strategies are instrumental in harnessing the potential of edge devices. Edge computing involves the decentralized processing of data closer to the source, reducing latency and enhancing the speed of data processing. Device management strategies extend their capabilities to manage and coordinate edge devices, ensuring that they seamlessly integrate into the broader data processing ecosystem. Through efficient device management, organizations can leverage the computational power of edge devices for localized processing, distributing workloads strategically to achieve high-speed data processing while minimizing latency associated with centralized processing architectures.

Furthermore, the integration of containerization and microservices into device management strategies has revolutionized the efficiency of high-speed data processing architectures. Containerization allows for the encapsulation of applications and their dependencies into lightweight, portable containers that can be deployed consistently across diverse environments. Device management strategies leverage containerization to facilitate the rapid deployment and scaling of applications, enabling organizations to achieve high-speed data processing with enhanced flexibility and agility. The microservices architecture, facilitated by device management, breaks down complex applications into modular, independently deployable services, promoting parallel processing and optimizing resource utilization. This architectural paradigm shift enhances the overall efficiency and speed of data processing workflows.

In conclusion, device management strategies constitute a foundational element in the success of high-speed data processing operations. From orchestrating device interactions to streamlining provisioning, ensuring security, promoting interoperability, enhancing scalability, optimizing resource utilization, and accommodating the nuances of edge computing and containerization, device management strategies play a multifaceted role in shaping the efficiency, reliability, and adaptability of data processing ecosystems. As organizations navigate the intricacies of processing vast volumes of data in real time, the integration of robust device management practices emerges as an indispensable factor in achieving and sustaining high-speed data processing capabilities.